MW00396238

FUNDAMENTALS OF

ENTERPRISE
RISK MANAGEMENT

How Top Companies Assess Risk, Manage
Exposure, and Seize Opportunity

John J. Hampton

∤AMACOM

American Management Association

New York • Atlanta • Brussels • Chicago • Mexico City • San Francisco
Shanghai • Tokyo • Toronto • Washington, D.C.

*This publication is designed to provide accurate and authoritative
information in regard to the subject matter covered. It is sold with
the understanding that the publisher is not engaged in rendering
legal, accounting, or other professional service. If legal advice or
other expert assistance is required, the services of a competent
professional person should be sought.*

Library of Congress Cataloging-in-Publication Data

Hampton, John J.
    Fundamentals of enterprise risk management : how top companies assess risk,
manage exposure, and seize opportunity / John J. Hampton.
        p.   cm.
    Includes bibliographical references and index.
    ISBN-13: 978-0-8144-1492-7
    ISBN-10: 0-8144-1492-3
    1. Corporations—Finance.   2. Risk assessment.   3. Risk management.   I. Title.

HG4026.H274   2009
658.15'5—dc22

                                                                    2009003022

Printing Number

10   9   8   7   6   5   4

To Doreen, a steady source of support through
seven versions of this book and an editor of
the final three versions.

To Alex Tango, of Freehold, New Jersey,
a rising young risk manager.

To Mary Sullivan, of Saint Peter's College,
an amazing person who understands risk firsthand
and who deals with it every time.

CONTENTS

FOREWORD

RISK QUOTE: *Keep your friends close, and your enemies closer.*
—SUN-TZU, CHINESE GENERAL
AND MILITARY STRATEGIST,
AROUND 400 B.C.

RISK QUOTE: *This was my father's study. He taught me a lot of things in this room. He taught me to keep my friends close and my enemies closer.*
—MICHAEL CORLEONE IN *THE GODFATHER* (1976)

Welcome to the world of *enterprise risk management (ERM)*, one of the most popular and misunderstood of today's important business topics. It is not very complex. It is not very expensive. It does add value. We just have to get it right. Until recently, we have been getting it wrong.

This is really a book about risk from a new perspective. The journey carries us into the heart of risk management and risk opportunity. It is mostly about how to do a better job of risk identification. If we define the problem correctly and share our findings, we can reduce surprises—not eliminate them, mind you, but get many of them under control.

ERM tells us it is a new world of risk. No longer is risk management largely the purview of the chief financial officer. The risk picture is incomplete when limited to the financial component, which actually is the scorecard, not the driver, for risk mitigation. This realization has encouraged new approaches to manage risk and seize opportunity.

Organizations have two ways to address risk. The wrong way is to assume that people can understand hundreds or even thousands of exposures. It is not possible. Risks and opportunities must be organized and accepted at various levels by risk owners. Our new paradigm will show you how to structure enterprise risks. A brief overview of the new ERM includes the following specific features:

- **Upside of Risk.** Most people discuss risk as the possibility of loss. This is totally insufficient, as risk also has an upside. A lost opportunity is just as much a financial loss as is damage to people and property. This is a key insight. Ask Sun-Tzu or Michael Corleone.

- **Alignment with the Business Model.** A business model is a framework for achieving goals. Within it, a single manager can supervise only a limited span of subordinates or subsidiaries. Similarly, one person can oversee a limited number of risks and key initiatives. ERM encourages us to align the hierarchy of risk categories with the business model.

- **Risk Owners.** As someone is accountable for revenues, profits, and efficiency, a single person should be responsible for every category of risk. When questions arise, then, we will not have to deal with a committee or multiple individuals. We will go directly to the risk owner. We will see an exception to this guideline in Part Three, where we address risks with no single risk owner.

- **Central Risk Function.** Although risks cannot be managed centrally, organizations need a central risk function. The role is to scan for changing conditions from a central vantage point and to share the findings with risk owners. In addition, some risks cross units and responsibilities, so that risk can be overlooked. In a change to traditional thinking, this book argues that such a central risk function should not, itself, have any responsibility for risk management. Risk goes with the risk owners. Risks that cross units or responsibilities are identified centrally and dealt with using customized solutions.

❧ **High-Tech ERM Knowledge Warehouse.** ERM encourages the use of new technologies to clarify risks and opportunities. This book describes in detail a cutting-edge technology platform to help understand risk mitigation efforts and the status of risk opportunities.

The book is organized into five parts, starting with the basics of a new approach to ERM:

❧ **Part One—Essentials of Enterprise Risk Management.** We first ask several important questions: What is ERM? What is not ERM? What are the key components needed to manage enterprise risk? Why do we need a central risk function and risk identification and sharing using a high-tech platform? Then, we address black swans, unexpected and unforeseen major crises or disaster that are virtually unpredictable. Where do black swans fit into the ERM picture? How could we have highly developed ERM in place in financial institutions and still have the 2008 financial crisis?

❧ **Part Two—ERM Technology.** This is big. We finally are getting the technology to visualize risk relationships and to back up the view with supporting detail. Here we cover the elements of an ultramodern technology platform that brings together risks, the factors that affect them, and the status of activities to mitigate them. We employ a tool, seamless and easy to use, which has been developed by a company called Riskonnect™. Large companies have or will soon have their own systems. Other vendors are likely to enter the market.

❧ **Part Three—Risks Without Risk Owners.** Some risks depend upon collaboration, crossing, as they do, the silos of the modern bureaucracy. With a central risk function and modern technology, we deal with such risks. We start with strategic risk. How do we monitor conflicting plans and goals? We address subculture risk, in which beliefs, assumptions, biases, and weak management practices endanger success. We recognize leadership risk, where the absence of a clear and achievable vision can be destructive. We acknowledge life cycle risk; a failure to

understand this can be devastating. Finally, we deal with horizon risk to keep everyone informed on changing external conditions.

- **Part Four—ERM Stories.** Risk management is a broad-brush
category, with the details often filled in by a focus on narrower
topics. Our stories range from avoiding business disruption to
a discussion of the future of ERM. What are different applications? How does ERM relate to Sarbanes-Oxley? Where do we
find new risk management concepts? In this part, we present
stories of ERM.

- **Part Five—The People of Risk Management.** Risk management is a people business. It takes knowledge, street smarts,
and experience to do it right. Now we get up close and personal,
introducing by name risk influencers and managers. In addition, we describe the positions and skills needed for ERM as we
listen to ideas directly from individuals who advocate ERM.

Our journey covers a mixture of concepts, tools, and stories that
add richness and depth to managing enterprise risk. ERM is both
popular and misunderstood, but, as we have said, it is not very
complex. It is not very expensive. It does add value. We just have
to get it right. Is ERM a science? An art? A mystery? Or is it plain
old common sense? In the following pages we answer these questions.

Contributors

Before we begin the journey, we wish to acknowledge the many
people who contributed to this book. Ellen Thrower, former president of the College of Insurance in New York City, showed me the
importance of risk management as a tool for dealing with hazard
risk. Chris Mandel and Susan Meltzer, former presidents of the
Risk and Insurance Management Society (RIMS), encouraged me
to understand risk from a holistic viewpoint. Felix Kloman and
Beaumont Vance were role models for creativity in risk discussions. Nathan Sambul, formerly with Marsh, and Valery Vyatkin,
my Russian partner, contributed ideas that shaped the book. Bob

Morrell, CEO of Riskonnect,™ was inspirational in his work to build technology to support a new approach to ERM. MBA candidates at Saint Peter's College in New Jersey served as test subjects for readings. Their projects and ideas contributed heavily to the evolution of my thinking as the book went through six revisions.

Thanks also to an assortment of critical thinkers and risk practitioners, including Lance Ewing, John Bayeux, George Niwa, Paul Buckley, Roger Egan, Pat Gallagher, Laurie Brooks, Ralph Russo, Anthony Terracciano, and Tom Ruggieri. Thanks also to *Business Insurance* magazine. Regis Coccia seeks the highest quality understanding of risk. Marty Ross and Paul Winston have been totally supportive of all our efforts. Finally, thanks to Bob Shuman, Mike Sivilli, Jerilyn Famighetti, and Jeremiah Birnbaum of AMACOM books. Bob understood immediately the message of the book and was a wise and steady motivator to tell it as best I can. Mike was a pleasant surprise as he guided me through the editorial/production process to completion of the book. Jerilyn did a marvelous job of smoothing out rough spots and bringing clarity to the writing during the copyediting stage.

Last but not least, my administrative assistant, Mary Sullivan, and my graduate assistants, Juan Peng (Adele) and Yu Miao (Grace), were invaluable in creating the final product. My bride, Doreen, a book author in her own right, read the final three manuscripts and contributed many suggestions to help people understand the key points.

John J. Hampton
Litchfield, Connecticut
January 2009

ESSENTIALS OF ENTERPRISE RISK MANAGEMENT

PART ONE tells the story of why organizations should create Enterprise Risk Management (ERM) programs using a new paradigm. Risks are related. One risk affects others as risks cross the often-artificial walls of day-to-day operations. People can be too close to risk or just too busy to recognize impending critical problems.

We start with how modern risk management has morphed from a narrow insurance-buying role. Stories and examples help us grasp hazard risk management as a foundation to understand ERM. What is ERM? What does it mean for an organization? What are the contributions it makes to our understanding of risk (Chapter 3)? It is an entirely new paradigm, and our presentation is different from other ERM discussions. We go to the practical heart of the value of ERM.

In Chapters 4 and 5, we take a detour. Two challenges arose in 2007 and 2008 that seem to undermine ERM. We examine Nassim Taleb's concept of the black swan and what it means for ERM. Then we look at the 2008 financial crisis and the challenge it presents to comprehensive risk management.

Part One finishes with a discussion of the implementation of the new ERM paradigm (Chapter 6). How can it be done? How should it be done? What resistance can be expected?

CHAPTER 1

MODERN RISK MANAGEMENT

RISK QUOTE: *More than at any other time in history, mankind faces a crossroads. One path leads to despair and utter hopelessness. The other to total extinction. Let us pray that we have the wisdom to choose correctly.*
—WOODY ALLEN, WRITER/ACTOR/DIRECTOR/PRODUCER

RISK QUOTE: *Better to remain silent and be thought a fool than to speak out and remove all doubt.*
—ABRAHAM LINCOLN, U.S. PRESIDENT

I n 1988, companies and managers began to discuss enterprise risk. A decision in one area can have major impact, for better or worse, on overall results, a possibility long recognized by economists, analysts, and managers. Stated differently, an optimal risk mitigation decision for a business unit may be suboptimal for the entity itself. After 1988, organizations began to take a holistic view of risk. This was a new development in companies and in the MBA programs that fed them future managers and leaders.

Prior to 1988, corporations often dealt with risk through a tactical analysis: We plan to move forward. We have some alternatives. Which one will be the best? When risk was introduced into the equation, the organization had to stretch a bit. What can derail our plans? Do we have weaknesses in our corporate culture that might imperil financial forecasts? Decision making changes when we introduce threats—financial and otherwise—that can endanger our plans.

FLORIDA INSURERS

A story can illustrate a narrow view of risk. In 1992, Hurricane Andrew caused significant losses to Allstate, State Farm, and other insurance companies because Florida insurance law did not handle flood and wind damage properly. Subsequently, insurance companies lobbied for and won changes from the Florida State Insurance Department. The changes were in place in 2004 and 2005 when hurricanes Frances, Charley, Ivan, Katrina, and Rita hit the United States. Insurers saved money as a result of the lobbying effort.

That is the good news. The bad news is that the Florida operations of the insurance companies did not share their lobbying effort. The companies did not seek changes in the laws in Georgia, Mississippi, Louisiana, or Texas. The results were big losses and bad press in 2005 in the aftermath of the hurricanes that hit those states.

Lesson Learned: A failure of one part of an organization to share risk mitigation strategies with other units is a failure of enterprise risk management.

Definitions of Risk

The term **risk** has a variety of definitions. When someone tells us to take a risk or not to take a risk, what is the message? In most cases, "risk" has one of three meanings:

1. **Possibility of Loss or Injury.** This is the most commonly recognized concept. We have something to lose, and we might lose it through an accident or misfortune.
2. **Potential for a Negative Impact.** This is the generic definition. Something could go wrong. What could go wrong? We might face a decline in the value of a brand, or competitors might penetrate our markets. The negative impact may be vague and unknown, but it would produce a negative outcome.

3. **Likelihood of an Undesirable Event.** This moves us into the world of statistics and quantitative analysis. We see a risk on the horizon. What is the likelihood it will materialize? What will be the impact if it occurs? Can we quantify the damage? What will be our best case if it occurs? Our worst case?

A broader definition is rapidly becoming the norm for businesses, nonprofit organizations, and government agencies. Enterprise risk is the likelihood that actual results will not match expected results. In this perspective, risk has two characteristics:

1. **Variability.** Expected results from operations or decisions may not match our sometimes elaborate forecasts. The organization spent considerable time on strategic planning and budgeting. Everyone had contingency plans to anticipate and respond to changing conditions. Why did we miss our forecast? What went wrong? The answer is that probably nothing did. The world is variable, and that is a characteristic of risk. This variation from expectations is fundamental in the concept of enterprise risk.

2. **Upside of Risk.** This is often not part of the calculation when one is thinking about risk. Traditional definitions deal with loss, injury, or other negative impacts, but that is not the whole story. When an enterprise engages in its activities, it accepts risk. Results may be better or worse than expected. Enterprise risk explicitly considers both possibilities, as the upside of risk is the reason for accepting exposures and opportunities.

Components of Enterprise Risk

Enterprise risk varies with the line of business, the nature of the entity, political and economic issues, and other factors. It is the aggregate risk from three components. The first of these is business risk, the possibility that an organization will not compete successfully in its operations. Exposures can erupt suddenly or develop over time. The company may fail to update a product or service. Technology may make current activities obsolete. Customer preferences may change. Markets may weaken so that products or services cannot be sold at prices sufficient to cover costs. Inefficient or obsolete operations or the inability to use current technology may endanger operations or cause inflationary rises in the cost of goods or services.

DAIMLER AND CHRYSLER

Daimler A.G. is an example of a company that suffered a business risk loss. In 1998, Daimler exchanged stock worth $38 billion to merge with Chrysler Corporation. After investing billions of dollars in Chrysler over a 10-year period, Daimler sold the bulk of the firm to Cerberus for less than $8 billion. It is likely that Daimler used a thorough acquisition analysis that considered the possibility of such a debacle. Would it succeed because of the synergies and shared technology of the two companies? Would the differences in corporate cultures prove deadly? Would external changes in consumer preferences, the price of oil, or other factors make the merger untenable? As it turned out, the synergies did not materialize, and the clash of culture proved to be disastrous. Daimler failed to merge the distinct German corporate culture with the proud but troubled executives and workers in Detroit.

Lesson Learned: Business risk can destroy the upside of risk.

The second component of enterprise risk is *financial risk,* the possibility that an entity will not have adequate funds for its operations. The problem can be caused by an inadequate initial capitalization or can result from cash flow problems in operations. Customers can fail to pay their bills, or creditors can tighten lending requirements. An organization may have excessive debt obligations relative to its asset values and cash flows. High interest costs or the aggregate level of interest may constrain expansion. The use of short-term debt to finance long-term assets may produce liquidity problems or leave insufficient cash to pay dividends.

WEBVAN

In the 1990s, two companies entered the online arena for consumer products. Amazon.com started operations in 1995, selling books via the Internet, and then diversified to sell other products. Webvan was an online food business that accepted Internet orders and delivered grocery products to customers. Amazon succeeded in its venture, becoming the largest online retailer in the world. Webvan ran out of money and filed for bankruptcy in 2001.

What accounts for the difference between Amazon and Webvan? Both looked like promising investments in the new marketplace of the Internet. An ERM analysis would have shown key differences:

- **Business Risk.** It should have been apparent that Webvan had serious problems in distribution. Amazon simply accepted orders and fulfilled them using an existing UPS distribution system. Webvan had to build its own system. Another factor was that Webvan was not aligned with its markets. It offered daytime delivery within a 30-minute window to customers who used the service because they were too busy to shop. They were not home in the daytime, so the food would spoil. Amazon could deliver its nonperishable products anytime and leave them on the doorstep.

- **Financial Risk.** Both companies needed considerable capital, but the financial risk was much greater for Webvan. One part of the exposure was of its own making. Webvan signed a billion-dollar contract with Bechtel to build warehouses, purchased a fleet of delivery trucks, and spent a large sum of money on computers and other equipment. A second part was the difference in markets for Amazon and Webvan. The expensive delivery structure squeezed the profits from the grocery business. Webvan was doomed by a combination of a tight cash flow accompanied by capital inadequacy resulting from massive up-front expenditures.

Lesson Learned: ERM recognizes the difference between business and financial risk while recognizing that they can merge to produce either good or bad results.

The third component of enterprise risk is *hazard risk,* exposures that can cause loss without the possibility of gain. These are insurable exposures with no upside. A company may suffer physical damage to assets, as when fire or explosions destroy buildings or machinery. Physical injury may occur when accidents, injuries, or disease strike employees, customers, or unrelated third parties. Lawsuits can be the outcome of contractual or liability claims.

Hazard risk is related to business and financial risk because a hazard loss can cause business and financial damage. An explosion at a refinery may be insured for replacement cost. Still, the waiting period until the refinery is repaired causes an immediate loss of sales and may cause future business and financial losses.

PHILIPS, NOKIA, AND ERICSSON

Lightning struck a Philips Electronics N.V. semiconductor fabrication plant in New Mexico in March 2000, starting a small fire that was quickly extinguished. Nobody was hurt, and damage was minor. The plant was the only source of microscopic circuits for cell phones. Forty percent of production went to Nokia and I.M. Ericsson. In addition to the trays of wafers that were destroyed in the fire, production was interrupted.

After the fire, Philips alerted 30 customers that a fire had taken place and that production had been stopped. Philips also estimated the time delay prior to restarting production, telling customers that a one-week delay was expected. The actual delay turned out to be much greater. In response to the news, Nokia behaved in accordance with the individualistic and aggressive culture of Finland. It demanded to know all details of Philips' operations so that other factories could be used to supply microchips. It put the search for microchips into a critical-risk category. The result was almost no disruption of deliveries to customers.

Ericsson was a different story. It behaved more in accordance with the consensual and laid-back culture of Sweden. Lower-level employees did not tell the head of production about the delay for several weeks. When Ericsson finally requested help from Philips and other suppliers of microchips, it learned that Nokia had locked up all spare capacity. Both cultures are proud. Does either description sound offensive?

The small fire caused significant losses. For Philips, the losses were in the range of $1 million to $3 million after $40 million in lost sales were offset by business interruption insurance. For Nokia, some additional costs were offset by a 3 percent rise in market share as it replaced Ericsson in some markets. Ericsson was the big loser, suffering a $2.3 billion loss in its mobile phone division in 2000, accompanied by a withdrawal from the market, in April 2001.

Lesson Learned: No loss is small when an organization does not understand the relationships among risks.

From Yossi Sheffi, *The Resilient Enterprise* (Cambridge, Mass.: 2005).

Levels of Enterprise Risk

ERM recognizes that some risks are serious and some are not. A *catastrophic loss* involves the destruction of a majority of assets, an unbearable financial loss, and an inability to continue operation. It produces a near-term, if not immediate, bankruptcy and a dissolution of the enterprise. A *critical* or *major* loss seriously hampers a company's ability to do business. An example is the collapse of a major operating unit or product line, followed by a substantial financial setback that could lead to bankruptcy. Lesser losses might be *significant, reducing current year earnings, or minor, hurting an operating unit but not impacting financial statements.*

Severity and Frequency

Risk is commonly measured on two scales. *Severity* refers to the intensity or magnitude of a loss or damage. A medium-high- or high-severity loss causes serious business disruption or damage to people, financial position, assets, or reputation. A medium-low- or low-severity loss causes less damage. *Frequency* refers to the likelihood of occurrence of a loss, damage, or missed opportunity. Some losses, like vehicle accidents, are fairly frequent and predictable. Some potential losses are so remote that we cannot imagine how they would happen.

WORLD TRADE CENTER

Larry Silverstein acquired the lease to operate the New York City World Trade Center two months before a terrorist attack destroyed the complex on September 11, 2001. Although the complex was damaged by a car bomb in its underground parking space in 1993, Mr. Silverstein did not foresee a high severity exposure to the WTC. Thus, he insured the twin towers for $3.6 billion, half of the replacement cost if both towers were lost in a single occurrence. Years of litigation followed the 2001 loss. Mr. Silverstein claimed that the two hijacked airliners were separate "occurrences" for insurance purposes, entitling him to collect twice on the policies.

The problem was compounded by the fact that while insurance was in force, no insurance policies had been issued as of the date of the attack. Two policy forms were under consideration. One defined occurrence. Commonly, such a policy would cover any loss within a specified time period. The other policy form did not define occurrence at all. The result was that some insurers paid for one occurrence, some for two. Mr. Silverstein did not receive full replacement cost for the property.

Lesson Learned: Frequency is not really an issue when dealing with the potential for catastrophic loss. To be protected, risk transfer should indemnify a total loss even if the possibility of its occurring is remote.

Figure 1-1 shows a graph of frequency and severity. As we move up and to the right on the graph, we increase the danger to the enterprise. Low-frequency and low-severity exposures are not of much concern. High-frequency and high-severity exposures can produce disastrous consequences.

Development of Risk Management

A growing awareness of risk led to the development of traditional risk management. This discipline includes any systematic approach to manage insurable and noninsurable hazard exposures.

FIGURE 1-1. GRAPHING RISK.

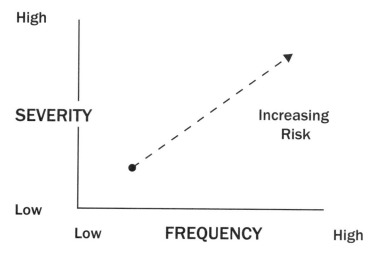

It also covers the identification of hazards and programs to avoid, mitigate, or transfer them. Traditional risk management developed over time.

- ❧ **1940s to the 1960s.** Risk management began as a formal process in North America after the Second World War and then expanded to developed countries around the world. Before the 1940s, organizations had buyers of insurance who focused almost exclusively on risk transfer. They identified exposures and bought insurance to reduce the impact of losses. This form of risk management was dominant into the 1960s.

- ❧ **1970s to the present.** Starting in the 1970s, risk management rapidly expanded into loss control, safety, and other strategies to avoid, reduce, or transfer risk. In addition to buying insurance, risk managers were expected to develop programs to reduce losses. The change in responsibility was accompanied by a shift in titles. Instead of having a director or manager of insurance, organizations had risk managers.

Hazard Risk

To be considered a hazard or insurable risk, a circumstance must meet three specific tests. First, a loss must cause a decline in monetary value. If an exposure has no financial impact, it is not an insurable risk. Second, the loss must be contingent, covering only losses not certain to happen. This is also known as a fortuitous loss. Third, no gain must be possible. Hazardous exposures by definition have only negative consequences.

Traditional risk management identifies four sources of hazard risk. *Physical risk* refers to situations where the real world creates a danger. Fire, earthquake, driving vehicles on crowded streets, and flying in hot air balloons are examples. *Moral hazard* arises from a lack of honesty or integrity. Examples are fraud, theft, tax evasion, and the sale of defective products. *Behavioral hazard,* also known as a morale hazard, derives from carelessness, as when people do not exercise a proper degree of caution driving a car, using a forklift in a factory, or cleaning a boiler. *Legal hazard* completes the list. Anybody can be sued and thus frivolous and numerous lawsuits are, by themselves, sources of hazard risk.

GLOBAL PETROLEUM HAZARD RISK MANAGEMENT

A Global Petroleum Company refined-products tanker was rounding the coast of Scotland at the height of the summer vacation season. It ran aground in a storm on rocks close to a small resort town with 300 year-round residents and one 40-room hotel. Within 24 hours, a crisis team arrived to contain the oil spill, which was growing by the hour. The team consisted of a team leader, a systems specialist, a finance specialist, a petroleum engineer, a logistics specialist, and a public relations manager. Within 12 to 36 hours after the spill, tugs from London arrived with oil containment equipment. They were joined by 150 workers who would work 12 hours on and 12 hours off for three to four weeks to clean up the spill.

The crisis team leader saw an immediate problem. Few local residents were willing to provide sleeping accommodations for workers. The hotel was booked solid with summer vacationers that the owner would not displace to make room for workers. The nearest town with hotels was 120 kilometers (75 miles) from the spill.

Searching for a solution, the team leader considered alternatives to solve the housing problem. He could negotiate with the hotel or homeowners, bring in tents or a small cruise ship, or bus workers to and from hotels in the distant town. What should he do?

In the sense of modern risk management, the company gave full authority to the team leader to mitigate risks without seeking permission. He bought the hotel and displaced the guests. Weeks later, he sold it back to the original owner at a loss that was much less than the result of indecision or inaction would likely have been.

Lesson Learned: What is the real lesson? Think about it. Do you have the authority to offer 3 million pounds sterling for a hotel? Is your organization set up with a risk management program that can transfer money on a moment's notice to a Scottish bank? This is modern risk management. Prepare for a loss. React to it with an effective mitigation strategy.

Modern Risk Management Perspective

Traditional risk management has morphed into a new concept with a broader role. Modern risk management covers four areas:

1. **Hazard Risk Management.** Risk managers follow a five-step process to assess hazard risks. First, they seek to identify exposures. Then they assess the frequency and severity of the exposures. Step three is to identify alternatives. Step four is to choose an option and implement it. The final step is to monitor the implementation and make adjustments as needed. This process sets up both preventive and crisis risk management.

2. **Internal Control.** Companies have processes, called internal controls, to provide reasonable assurance that policies are being followed. Internal control processes seek to improve effectiveness and efficiency, increase the reliability of financial reporting, and ensure conformity with laws and regulations. Elaborate systems of internal control are common in organizations, particularly in industries that are highly regulated by government agencies.

3. **Internal Audit.** Internal auditors pursue assurance that internal controls are working. This is not risk management. Rather, it focuses on the cost, efficiency, and effectiveness of processes, including risk management. From a risk management perspective, internal audit focuses specifically on whether a risk is actually being avoided, reduced, or transferred. The internal audit team examines operating activities, the consistency of procedures, and compliance with directives. Then the internal auditor prepares a report for management that identifies weaknesses and failures to follow policies.

4. **Regulatory Compliance.** This refers to efforts to ensure conformity with official requirements imposed by statutes, public agencies, or the courts. Examples are rules governing plant safety, the environment, reliable financial reporting, and compliance with social and economic mandates. Many organizations have a single compliance unit or officer who interprets directives, laws, and regulations, offers education and training, and recommends processes to conform to regulations.

Conclusion

Modern risk management builds upon a sound foundation of traditional risk management and gives organizations a number of tools to use when addressing enterprise risk. These practices continue to be essential in the areas of hazard risk, internal controls, and regulatory compliance but are finding increasing applications for dealing with the broader exposures confronting profit, nonprofit, and governmental bodies.

Russian Frozen-Chicken Case

We can gain a more in-depth understanding of modern risk management by illustrating the steps needed to pursue a risk opportunity. The following discussion shows risk management for an international project.

Expropriation Risk

A company had a project to export frozen chicken by oceangoing vessel from Virginia and North Carolina to St. Petersburg, Russia. The company planned to load 60- to 80-pound boxes on pallets for the ocean voyage. A problem arose because the port of St. Petersburg had no shoreside refrigeration to allow quick unloading of an expensive reefer vessel. The company would incur significant demurrage charges (extra costs resulting from a vessel delay) if the ship wasted time in port while it waited for containers or railroad cars. One option was to build a warehouse, but the risk manager identified an expropriation risk. She spotted an action involving the Hotel Europa in St. Petersburg, which was partly owned by European investors. In the mid-1990s, the hotel opened a foreign bank account to handle dollar transactions. Russian banking laws prohibited such accounts. When the government learned of the account, a government agency levied a heavy fine on the hotel, causing the foreigners to lose their entire investment. Effectively, the government confiscated the hotel.

The risk manager knew she could obtain insurance from an agency of the U.S. government to reimburse the company for expropriation. At the same time, was it really an expropriation? Insurance did not seem to be the answer. Thus, the company considered buying an old (and relatively inexpensive) reefer vessel and using it for storage. It could build a refrigeration facility on a barge that could be moved if the situation became sticky. Alternatively, it could find a strong Russian partner with high-level government connections and allow the partner to accept the expropriation and storage exposure. The company found such a Russian partner.

Lesson Learned: Investigate all options for risk mitigation. Do not assume that the traditional insurance approach is the answer.

Credit Risk

The company exporting frozen chicken to Russia had good news. It had a partner. This was also the bad news, as it created a credit risk. How would the U.S. company ensure payment from the Russian partner? It was not realistic to demand payment in advance or to obtain a letter of credit to guarantee a future payment. The Russian partner was not able to pay for a cargo for 30 or so days after receiving it. To deal with the credit exposure, the parties agreed that the Russian partner would have to pay for one cargo before it could receive a subsequent cargo.

How did this mitigate the exposure? The stream of profits from a series of cargos was significantly larger than the funds from a default on payment for a single cargo. If the Russian partner did not deposit funds in a Western bank account by day 45 after receipt of a cargo, the ship carrying the next cargo would be diverted from Russia to a northern European port.

Lesson Learned: Give other parties (in this case the Russian partners) incentives to help your organization mitigate risk.

Physical Security Risk

Once the Russian partner accepted the chicken in St. Petersburg, it shipped the chicken by railroad to Moscow, Yekaterinburg, and beyond. The cargo was placed in refrigerated containers that were locked and then loaded on flat railcars. On the fifth journey, one of the containers was empty when it arrived in Moscow after the three-day trip from St. Petersburg. At this point, the partner was facing a risk management problem. Two strategies were discussed. The first was to purchase insurance, an idea that was quickly eliminated. Who would insure a cargo with a high chance of loss? If a Russian insurance company agreed to provide coverage, the premiums would be prohibitively high. The second was door-to-door container placement.

The railroad company would place the containers on the flatbed railcars so the doors could not be opened if the locks were broken. This was the chosen strategy.

The story continues. Sometimes a risk mitigation solution does not actually solve the problem. Several journeys later, another container arrived empty. The partner realized that someone had a crane on a siding when the train stopped in the middle of the night. What else should be tried?

The problem was finally solved by placing a boxcar on the back of the train. The car was fitted with heaters and cots. It carried guards with Kalashnikov weapons. Whenever the train stopped, guards stepped out to protect the containers. It was a simple but effective risk management strategy.

Lesson Learned: Stay with it until a risk management strategy works. Sometimes it takes a few tries to get it right.

Upside of Risk

The story of guards on the train can be used to illustrate the upside of risk. The railroad security situation in Russia has improved significantly since the 1990s, when the story unfolded. Prior to the improvement, a business opportunity arose. Once the cargo was being protected by armed guards, the Russian partner could offer insurance services to third parties to protect their cargoes as well as the chicken. The partner would incur small costs for the guards but could be confident that the train would experience no losses. We do not know whether this opportunity was ever pursued.

Lesson Learned: Modern risk management does not end with the mitigation of an exposure. Always look for an upside.

CHAPTER 2

SCOPE OF ERM

RISK QUOTE: *When you arrive at a fork in the road, take it.*
—YOGI BERRA, BASEBALL PLAYER

RISK QUOTE: *The greatest glory in living lies not in never falling but in rising every time we fall.*
—NELSON MANDELA, SOUTH AFRICAN STATESMAN

E nterprise risk management (ERM) emerged in the late 1980s as an extension of hazard risk management. It argues that an organization should manage enterprise risks in a single, comprehensive program and coordinate ERM with hazard risk management, internal control processes, internal audit, and compliance.

Like modern risk management, ERM has existed for a sufficient period of time that we can refer to 1990 to 2006 as its traditional period. ERM raised issues about risk tolerance. How much risk are we willing to take? This goes beyond loss exposures into the arena of risk identification. What risks are we managing? ERM involved itself in risk assessment. Which risks are unbearable? Which are important? Which are unimportant?

It is difficult to deny the role and importance of enterprise risk management. The world changed dramatically after 9/11 and the corporate scandals that followed at Enron, WorldCom, and other major corporations. It became an organizational priority to identify and manage new exposures. ERM became a buzzword on the lips of CEOs, CFOs, members of boards of directors, and share-holders. Everybody understood that ERM was important. The question confronting organizations was how to get it right.

ERM Bogs Down

In the 1970s, journalists regularly referred to Brazil as "the country of the future." They would then continue, "It always has been. It always will be." The same appeared to be true for enterprise risk management in the years after Enron and 9/11; by 2005, ERM had bogged down. Still, many risk observers pushed a strong ERM agenda. They recognized the logic of coordinating the management of risk. So why did ERM implementation stall? The answer starts with definitions of ERM.

ERM Defined

Enterprise risk management is a broad and complex concept that reaches into every major area of an organization. As such, it is not surprising that many definitions of ERM have been offered. These definitions fall into three categories. A *strategic* definition focuses on results, as ERM is expressed in terms of organizational objectives. A *functional* definition describes ERM in terms of activities that reduce risk. A *process* definition focuses on actions undertaken by managers to manage risk. A consensus definition might look something like:

> *Enterprise risk management is the process of identifying major risks that confront an organization, forecasting the significance of those risks in business processes, addressing the risks in a systematic and coordinated plan, implementing the plan, and holding key individuals responsible for managing critical risks within the scope of their responsibilities.*

In addition to the consensus definition, we have many other candidates for definitions of ERM, including these:

- **Tillinghast (www.towers.com in 2002):** A rigorous approach to addressing risks from all sources that threaten strategic objectives or opportunities to exploit competitive advantage.

- **Erisk.com (www.erisk.com in 2002):** A holistic approach that fully integrates risk management into how a company conducts its business and communicates with stakeholders.

- **KPMG (www.kpmg.com in 2002):** A disciplined approach aligning strategy, processes, people, technology, and knowledge to manage uncertainties as the enterprise creates value.

- **Marsh and McLennan (www.mmc.com in 2002):** The effort to find an integrated, optimal way of managing risk by balancing financing techniques with organizational practices and processes.

- **Aon (www.aon.ars.com in 2002):** The assessment of collective risks that affect value and the implementation of a company-wide strategy to maximize that value.

The Need for ERM

The definitions of ERM set the stage for a broader discussion. Why ERM? What do we get? One answer is that it offers us survival—a better chance to identify, mitigate, avoid, and treat risks that could close us down. A second answer is that it provides stability in creating, distributing, financing, and selling products and services. Third, ERM adds to confidence that the board and CEO are meeting fiduciary, community, social, and ethical responsibilities. Finally, it helps build good relationships with regulators.

To many observers, a clear need exists for ERM. Let us not argue it. Instead, read the two stories of General Motors and JetBlue. Do we need ERM?

GENERAL MOTORS—BO ANDERSSON

As organizations reach maturity, they no longer can depend upon a rapidly growing market for goods and the continuation of the business that made them successful. They must seek new approaches to operations to increase their success managing life cycle risk. The following discussion involves Bo Andersson and his experience at General Motors Corporation. It provides a good story about modern risk management.

In 2001, Bo Andersson became the top purchasing manager at GM. When he arrived, he realized that GM was spending $85 billion on car parts each year, purchased from 3,200 suppliers. He also learned that GM had separate engineering for almost every type of vehicle it produced. Vehicles did not share common parts. Seat frames were an example of a particularly interesting subculture feature. They were expensive, partly because GM had 26 different seat frames. This compared to Toyota, which had only two.

A similar situation existed with V6 engines. Once again, GM had high costs because it had 12 V6 engines, whereas Toyota and Honda had 2 each. What about fuel pumps? GM had 12. Toyota and Nissan had 2.

Moving on, Bo Andersson addressed the rather simple topic of door hinges. He learned that they could be made out of three pieces instead of five. Making the change would save $100 million annually. He had a subculture response. Engineers and designers debated the change for more than three months. Then they reluctantly began a lengthy process of design and testing for the new door hinges.

After studying the situation to be sure he understood it, Bo Andersson identified the design and purchasing problems and brought them to the attention of the engineers who worked in manufacturing. His arguments were carefully framed. They were not well received. The different units did not support changes, arguing that a change in one component would have ripple effects throughout the entire line of automobiles. In the end, change came slowly over the period from 2001 to 2006.

"Renault-Nissan: Say Hello to Bo," *Business Week*, July 31, 2006.

Lessons Learned: GM lacked a modern risk management approach to internal manufacturing. Production efficiency lagged badly while GM failed to make desperately needed changes to be competitive. GM needed ERM. One additional note: The GM situation is also a failure of leadership risk. This is covered in Chapter 14.

JETBLUE AIRWAYS—NEED FOR ERM?

Standard and Poor's proposed a unique approach to ERM in 2008. Instead of a specific formula or checklist, S&P believes managing enterprise risk depends largely on the quality of management. Still, even a high-quality management team can stumble if it does not use ERM. An example came on February 14, 2007, when New York City's Kennedy Airport was hit by a nasty ice storm. JetBlue Airways, the largest airline at Kennedy, used the airport as the hub of its entire network. The company was not prepared for such a risk event. The result was thousands of passengers trapped in planes on runways for up to eight hours. Aircraft ran out of food. Toilets overflowed. The airline canceled more than 1,000 flights and required six days to get the backlog cleared.

Now suppose JetBlue had an ERM program constantly scanning for risk. Further assume that it had identified the possibility of such an occurrence. Let us follow this through.

- **Source of the Risk.** The risk stems from disruption of operations at Kennedy Airport at peak flying time. Examples of sources of this risk include ice storms, police action, and acts of terrorism. The upside would be to show JetBlue's high level of customer service and enhance reputation. The downside would be a negative public reaction and financial loss.
- **Risk Owners(s).** This scenario is assigned to the senior vice president of operations, who further assigns it to the Kennedy Airport Operations Center.
- **Frequency.** Ice storms hit New York City once every three winters. The likelihood is one chance in three that it will hit at a busy time. A peak-travel disruption is thus likely to happen once every nine years.
- **Severity.** The disruption could be a public relations boon if handled smoothly and a customer relations nightmare if passengers were stranded on planes for long periods of time. It could be financially beneficial if good news attracts new customers or costly if the airline has to reimburse passengers for losses or time spent.
- **Evaluation.** A disruption is a major risk opportunity.
- **Options.** First, JetBlue could arrange to have buses available for an emergency. It could unload passengers stuck in planes sitting on the tarmac when all gates are full. Second, it could provide additional personnel to solve problems, handle luggage, and mitigate discomfort. The company headquarters was a short distance from the airport. The company could train office staff on tasks needed during a crisis. Third, the company could institute rapid-response capabilities for weather or other crises.

◆ **Cost-Benefit Analysis.** Any approach you use would be good risk management compared to leaving passengers stuck on planes. Make the needed changes.

Before the incident, a *Business Week* magazine survey ranked Jet Blue Airways fourth in the United States in customer satisfaction. After the incident, the magazine pulled the ranking from its March 5, 2007, edition and reported the failure in considerable detail. Prior to this single event, JetBlue had earned many honors for customer service. It was the top choice in a national airline quality rating four years in a row. It won a reader's choice award five years in a row from *Condé Nast Traveler*. It always ranked high in J. D. Power's quality ratings. Then it stumbled.

Lesson Learned: An ERM program with constant scanning and sharing of risks might have avoided losses that exceeded $30 million. As former JetBlue customers purchase future tickets on other airlines, we will never know the true extent of the loss to JetBlue.

Towers Perrin, Moody's, and Standard and Poor's on ERM

As we move past the definitions and need for ERM, some heavy hitters have joined the discussion.

TOWERS PERRIN ON ERM

Towers Perrin, a professional services consulting firm, was an early advocate, believing that ERM is essential to achieve operating stability, build organizational resilience, and increase economic value. ERM is important for reasons other than the wish to win a high score from rating agencies. It is a value-added business initiative that should be pursued for its own value.

As shown in Figure 2-1, Towers Perrin has developed a six-stage ERM Road Map to create a customized ERM program. The first four stages cover planning. The last two involve implementation. The road map can be useful to understand ERM implementation, a topic covered in Chapter 6.

FIGURE 2-1. TOWERS PERRIN ERM ROAD MAP.

- **Stage 1.** Establish the current state of ERM capability.
- **Stage 2.** Contrast the current state to ERM best practices and produce a gap analysis highlighting areas that need improvement.
- **Stage 3.** Define a target goal for ERM based on organizational strategy and risk profile.
- **Stage 4.** Prepare a formal action plan for implementation. Seek quick wins as well as longer-term ERM objectives.
- **Stage 5.** Implement the ERM vision using timelines, milestones and assigned responsibilities.
- **Stage 6.** Establish a formal monitoring process with continuous evaluation and reporting and follow-up initiatives.

Moody's on ERM

Moody's was also an early advocate of ERM. In the 1990s, it used the tool to assess banks. In 2004, the company deployed Risk Management Assessments (RMA) to help it understand exposures facing nonfinancial companies. Moody's was particularly interested in significant economic exposure to financial, commodity, or energy risk.

An RMA is built upon four pillars, as shown in Figure 2-2.

FIGURE 2-2. MOODY'S PILLARS OF RISK MANAGEMENT ASSESSMENT.

- **Risk Governance.** Are board members engaged in defining and reviewing the company's risk philosophy and appetite? Does the reporting structure, including budgeting and capital allocation, contain risk considerations?
- **Risk Management.** Does the company have risk control processes with unit- and operating-level reporting lines and risk discipline? Does the company understand its risk appetite and have controls to set limits in portfolio diversification and business decision-making processes? Does the company use risk mitigation, risk control, and risk financing processes and technologies?

➤ **Risk Analysis and Quantification.** Does the business quantify the level of risk that is acceptable? Does it have effective risk monitoring and reporting?

➤ **Risk Infrastructure and Intelligence.** Does the company have a risk infrastructure and supporting systems? Is risk intelligence developed with valid risk models and accurate and timely data?

STANDARD AND POOR'S AND ERM

In 2008, Standard and Poor's (S&P) announced that it would use ERM in rating financial securities for nonfinancial companies. S&P acknowledged that a company's management's overall capabilities, quality of strategies, and adaptability to changing conditions are the strongest influences on its credit rating. At the same time, management judgment cannot be benchmarked by quantitative models assessing likely cash flows, capital adequacy, and earnings capacity. S&P sought a new framework to evaluate management. It chose ERM, arguing that companies with superior ERM should have greater stability of earnings and a high likelihood of repaying debt obligations.

When the final guidelines were announced, in 2008, S&P declined to require companies to comply with standards promulgated by the Committee of Sponsoring Organizations of the Treadway Commission (COSO) and the joint Australian/New Zealand Committee. Meeting any particular single set of standards would be neither a prerequisite for nor adequate evidence of effective risk management. S&P would benchmark a company's ERM efforts, comparing them to best practices in peer companies. Then, S&P would render a judgment on the effectiveness of the company's risk management processes.

S&P also decided that, while it would be "open-minded" about the risk management structure, it would begin with certain expectations. The company should be attending to all risks. Management should understand risk expectations of the board and shareholders. The company should have safeguards to avoid losses outside its risk appetite. It should shift from cost-benefit decision making to a risk and reward approach to business activities. Finally, management should be able to explain the company's efforts to maintain a manageable risk profile.

Interestingly, S&P spelled out behaviors that were not part of

ERM. It did not see ERM as a method to eliminate all risks or as a guarantee that a company will avoid losses. ERM is not a collection of "longstanding and disparate" practices, nor is it a rigid set of rules to be followed under all circumstances; it is not limited in scope to compliance and disclosure requirements and does not replace internal controls. It does not have to be exactly the same for all businesses in all sectors, nor does it have to be the same from year to year. Clearly and explicitly, S&P did not see ERM as a passing fad.

MEETING S&P AND MOODY'S EXPECTATIONS

A 2008 Deloitte survey, titled *Perspectives on ERM and the Risk Intelligent Enterprise™: Enterprise Risk Management Benchmark Survey,* shows how companies were doing in meeting the S&P and Moody's guidelines. The survey received responses from 151 internal auditors, risk managers, risk owners, and other professionals involved with ERM in Europe, North America, and South America. Most of the companies represented had annual revenues between $1 billion and $20 billion.

To meet the standards of rating agencies, one has to know what is happening after risks are accepted. The Deloitte survey answers on risk appetite and risk tolerances indicated that much work was still needed to reach that point. Figure 2-3 shows that only 18 percent of respondents had fully implemented a risk dashboard or reporting process. Deloitte observed, "An enterprise risk dashboard or reporting process is a key component of a risk intelligent organization. It will be much more difficult to make risk-informed decisions without this kind of intelligence."

FIGURE 2-3. STATUS OF ERM RISK REPORTING OR DASHBOARDS (DELOITTE).

Status	Percentage Responding
Fully Implemented Risk Reporting or Dashboard	18%
Early Stages of Implementation	14%
Completed Plan or Design	9%
Plan Under Consideration	22%
No Plan to Implement Reporting or Dashboard	6%

The Deloitte survey also addressed inherent risk and residual risk. *Inherent* risk is the exposure before management intervention. *Residual* risk is exposure after management intervention. Has the company used ERM to reduce the original exposure? Figure 2-4 shows techniques to assess risk and forecast loss. Figure 2-5 shows the level of confidence in the assessments and forecasts. It is not a good sign that 81 percent forecast the probability of occurrence but only 18 percent had high or very high confidence in the assessment.

FIGURE 2-4. RISK EVALUATION TECHNIQUES IN USE (DELOITTE).

Criteria to Assess Risk	Percentage Responding
Speed of Onset of Risk	16%
Probability of Occurrence	81%
Inherent Risk	68%
Residual Risk	66%
Other	14%

FIGURE 2-5. LEVEL OF CONFIDENCE IN PREDICTIONS (DELOITTE).

Confidence Level	Percentage Responding
Very High	3%
High	15%
Medium	57%
Low	9%
Very Low	5%
Do Not Know	12%

As organizations realize the value of ERM, we can expect changes in risk management practices. Many inputs will be sought, including quantitative models, the views of experienced risk managers, and the intuition of senior executives. Figure 2-6 shows that respondents in the 2008 Deloitte survey believed that this integration process was already under way in many organizations.

FIGURE 2-6. RISK ASSESSMENT TOOLS CURRENTLY IN USE (DELOITTE).

Tool	Percentage of Respondents
Self-Assessment of Performance and Value of Measurement Tools	41%
Economic Metrics, such as Value or Earnings at Risk and Economic Value Added	33%
Scenario Analysis	33%
Industry Benchmarks	26%
Key Risk Indicators	25%
Probability Assessments	25%
Third-Party Assessments	19%
Stress Tests	15%
Failure Mode and Effects Analysis	14%

Some of the lack of confidence in the evaluation of risk would surely be overcome by the use of new and more powerful technology. Visual risk cluster technology is examined in Part Two of this book. Such technology was not being widely used in 2008, when the Deloitte survey discovered that only 27 percent of respondents were using high-tech tools in efforts to understand and mitigate risk. Deloitte asked two questions: Are you using technology or software tools to monitor and manage risk on an integrated enterprise-wide basis? Of the companies surveyed, 27 percent said yes, and 67 percent said no. When asked whether these tools were integrated into the company's performance management system, 9 percent said yes, 10 percent said partly, and 32 percent said no.

Conclusion

The scope of ERM is broad. Therefore, it is important to simplify risk and get it right in a complex world. Thought leaders have offered many contributions, but the S&P evaluation of ERM may be the most useful. No single standard works for everyone; the key is to use ERM to improve the quality of management. These will be our lessons as we move forward from this point in the book.

CHAPTER 3

CONTRIBUTIONS OF ERM

RISK QUOTE: *Not only do I not know what's going on, I wouldn't know what to do about it if I did.*

—GEORGE CARLIN, COMEDIAN

RISK QUOTE: *What I know for sure is that behind every catastrophe, there are great lessons to be learned. Among the many that we as a country need to get is that as long as we play the "us and them" game, we don't evolve as people, as a nation, as a planet.*

—OPRAH WINFREY, BUSINESSWOMAN AND TV PERSONALITY

N ow we move into new territory. In this chapter, we identify the seven contributions of ERM. More than that, we develop a new paradigm for enterprise risk management. Having discussed the definitions and the importance of ERM, we get closer to the operational level—the place where risk comes alive and risk owners deal with it on a day-to-day basis. We distinguish between the central risk function, with its specific role, and risk owners who carry the mitigation burden. We know that ERM advocates a coordinated effort to manage enterprise exposures; now we build the structure to do exactly that by examining the seven contributions of ERM. After we build the structure of seven contributions, we provide a case study that applies them to Home Depot in the time period when Robert Nardelli was CEO.

The Seven Contributions of ERM

1. **Recognize the Upside of Risk.** As already explained, the first contribution of ERM occurs when "risk opportunity" is incorporated into the definition of "risk." This is a major conceptual advance. The semantic difference acknowledges the interaction among risks. An exposure does not occur in isolation. One risk affects other risks. This differs from traditional risk management, in which only a loss is possible. ERM adds business and strategic risk. A missed opportunity is usually more of a risk than business disruption.

2. **Identify Risk Owners.** The second contribution of ERM is to assign a risk owner for every category of risk. This is a single individual responsible for an identified risk. In an ERM structure, every risk opportunity has an "owner" with the knowledge, experience, and ability to establish real ownership of a risk. This is an important part of making sure a key person is accountable for managing the exposure. As we will see in Part Three, some risks cannot be addressed with risk owners. We will deal with these separately.

FORD MOTOR—IDENTIFY RISK OWNER

In the 1990s, Ford Motor Corp., recognized an exposure to price fluctuations in the rare metal palladium, an important component in catalytic converters. To reduce the risk, the purchasing department hedged the exposure by signing long-term contracts to purchase palladium at stable prices. While this appears to be a commodities risk mitigation strategy, it turned out to be exactly the opposite. Ford's Research and Development department recognized the same risk, and redesigned catalytic converters requiring minimal palladium. In 2001, the price per ounce of palladium dropped from $1,500 to $400, causing Ford to suffer a loss of $1 billion.

Lesson Learned: This is an example of the failure to identify a risk owner to coordinate all efforts to mitigate a specific exposure.

3. **Align Risk Accountability.** A third contribution of ERM recognizes the importance of aligning responsibility and accountability for risk management with the business model of the enterprise. This produces the least disruption of current successful practices while adding a new perspective on and capacity to understand business risk. This contribution recognizes that a business model is the strategy for a specific company's success. Alignment occurs when risks are grouped together so that they can be managed by a single owner.

A business model includes several items. The first is a value to be created for customers or clients. Second is the architecture of the organization, which creates a hierarchy, partnerships, and other structures to deliver the value. Next is the network of employee, partnerships, and other relationships that create and deliver value. Finally, there are resources aligned with the structure that provide capital, assets, and people needed to generate sustainable profits and cash flows.

ERM can be fitted to the various units and levels of the business model, ERM is enhanced when key risks have risk owners while internal controls take care of "all" risks. Then, we can use a structure of subrisks to drill down risk ownership into the entity.

Who are risk owners in a business model? Functional staff, such as managers of production, marketing, and finance, supports the business model. Business units, including relatively autonomous regions and operations, are obvious risk owners. Finally, and not to be omitted, there are key initiatives—major activities reflecting highly visible goals. These efforts can cross unit lines, provide entrepreneurial opportunities, solve major problems, or pursue other goals. As an example, a company seeking to grow through acquisitions should have a risk owner for the effort.

The final step is to match risk categories with risk owners. This enhances the chance that the risk alignment will work smoothly. Each risk owner is focused on his or her important risks—a limited list of perhaps five to eight exposures created at each level. Risks handled by organizational practices and internal controls are not part of the structure and are included only as exceptions if an internal control process breaks down.

4. **Create a Central Risk Function.** A fourth contribution of ERM is the recommendation to create a central risk function. This is an individual or unit responsible for coordination of risk discussions across the entity. It should occupy a high position in the hierarchy and have access to senior executives. Its goal should be to facilitate efforts by risk owners to manage risk. As it plays a support role across the entity, it should not manage risk itself. Managing risk is the role and responsibility of risk owners and co-owners.

    A central risk function enhances an ERM program. It can identify risks that might otherwise be missed by C-suite, business unit, or key initiative executives. By facilitating the sharing of risks and strategies, it can manage and vet information. By influencing risk discussions, it can reduce the tendency for "silos" to refuse to share information and hide negative conditions.

    In some formulations of ERM, a central risk function takes on the perceived role of managing risk. It may even be responsible for insurance buying or loss control. This is not a good model, as risk identification and risk sharing are fundamentally different from risk transfer or mitigation. Somebody other than the central risk function should buy insurance and ensure workplace safety. Organizations need a central activity that seeks out factors that are changing the business landscape. What is happening with markets, regulators, politics, competitors, and other sources of risk? What is happening inside the organization itself with cultural, management, leadership, human resources, and unit life cycle exposures? These are important issues. They deserve full attention.

5. **Create an ERM Knowledge Warehouse.** A fifth contribution of ERM is the recommendation to create an ERM knowledge warehouse, a risk management decision support system specifically designed to help understand risks. It is a tool to share identified risks and recognize the scope of each exposure. It provides a repository to show how a risk owner is evaluating each risk and the relationships among exposures. Moreover, it allows sharing alternatives, recommendations, and actions to mitigate risks. Last, it facilitates communications as managers

see and support or oppose the events that are taking place. In Part Two, we will recommend features of such a high-tech platform, including these:

- ❧ **Visual Risk Clusters.** Risk categories should be built so that risk relationships can be understood quickly and without clutter. A visual risk cluster is a grouping of related risks so that an analyst can see the interaction of exposures. As an example, a fire causes the loss of property, but it also has an impact on future business, earnings, and cash flows.

- ❧ **Risk Mitigation Details and Activities.** The individual exposures should be linked to the activities to move from inherent risks to managed risks. An inherent risk exists when no mitigation takes place. A risk owner can take actions to reduce the danger. The high-tech warehouse allows authorized parties to see details and make suggestions.

6. **Involve the Board of Directors.** A sixth contribution of ERM is the idea that the board must be concerned about the management of enterprise risk if it is properly performing its fiduciary role. The board understands the importance of complying with Sarbanes-Oxley (covered in Chapter 19). It usually requires periodic reports from internal audit. How can it not also have independent reporting on enterprise risk?

    The board has numerous options as it decides how to obtain enterprise risk progress reports. Figure 3-1 shows a structure where the central risk function is reporting directly to the chief executive officer but also has a communications line directly to a committee of board members who oversee risk identification for other board members.

    Figure 3-2 presents a different structure. The board has charged a single board member with responsibility to report on risk identification. This board member has a direct communications link with the central risk function.

7. **Employ a Standard Risk Evaluation Process.** The seventh contribution of ERM is to encourage the use of a viable evaluation process to assess risk. It is essentially a problem-solving process used widely in planning and budgeting and modified to sys-

FIGURE 3-1. ERM AND THE BOARD #1.

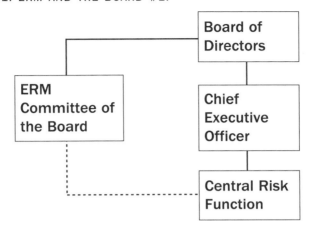

FIGURE 3-2. ERM AND THE BOARD #2.

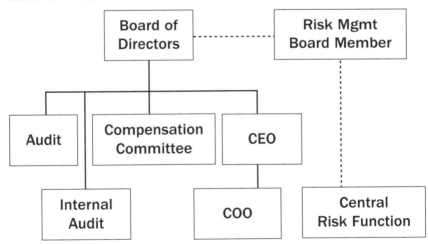

tematically approach decisions to retain, transfer, reduce, or avoid exposures. This is one version:

- **Identify the risk.** External risks are largely uncontrollable, as they arise from the competitive environment, economic factors, acts of regulatory bodies, and other outside sources. Internal risks reflect the culture, value structure, management and leadership styles, subcultures, and relationships among employees, suppliers, customers, and others. Exposures exist from faulty business processes, internal controls, and weaknesses among workers and departments.

GROCERY CHAIN ACQUISITION—RISK IDENTIFICATION

A grocery chain had an aggressive risk manager who pushed into new areas in an effort to be a strategic player. After meeting resistance, she finally was allowed to participate in major business decisions. The chain was negotiating an acquisition of a run-down group of grocery stores where extensive refitting would upgrade them to profitability. The CEO asked the risk manager to take a look at the proposal. On a visit to one of the stores, she discovered asbestos was used in the insulation. Subsequently, she confirmed many stores were in the same situation. She knew asbestos could be left alone when it was in walls but also knew the law required expensive asbestos removal when a building was being renovated. The discovery changed the economics of the transaction and resulted in a lower acquisition price.

Lesson Learned: Risk managers can make broad contributions when they are included in risk identification.

- **Assign an owner or owners.** Establish clear accountability by matching every important risk with a functional area, business unit, or key initiative. Delegate accountability down a chain of command to co-owners in a direct reporting line with the risk owner.

- **Assess the impact.** What is the expected frequency of each risk? Is the chance of loss remote or likely? What are the levels of damage severity under different assumptions? Support assessments with both quantitative analysis and qualitative considerations.

- **Evaluate mitigation options.** What choices are available? Can the risk be retained, avoided, reduced, or transferred? Recognize the trade-off between the cost of mitigating the risk and the benefits gained by accepting it.

❧ **Implement, monitor, and revise.** Pick an option, and implement it. Monitor the results so that adjustments can be made as needed. Ensure flexibility if conditions change or new information becomes available.

Conclusion

You don't need be a rocket scientist to understand the importance of modern enterprise risk management. For the fifth time, you just have to get it right. Figure 3-3 displays the seven contributions that point the way to designing an effective ERM program. In future chapters, we examine situations so that the richness of ERM comes alive. This begins with the Home Depot case study that follows.

FIGURE 3-3. SEVEN ERM CONTRIBUTIONS.

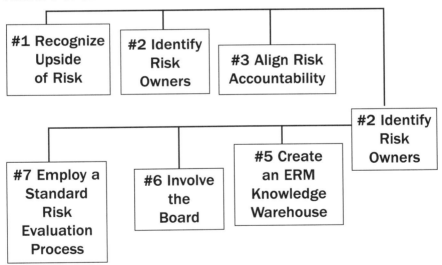

Home Depot Case

Home Depot was founded in 1978 and grew to $40 billion in revenues in 20 years. By 1999, however, growth and profits had stalled. The board of directors brought in Bob Nardelli as chief executive officer. Bob had had a successful career, rising to the top echelon of General Electric. He knew the upside of risk and was credited with taking chances and getting results. When he failed to win the position of CEO after Jack Welch retired, he left GE and started at Home Depot in December 2000.

Consider the Upside of Risk

At Home Depot, Mr. Nardelli changed the culture. To get the company moving again, he implemented a military-style management model. Thirteen percent of the company's employees had military experience (compared to 4 percent at Wal-Mart). More than 500 of the 1,100 employees hired into management between 2002 and 2006 had previously been junior military officers. By 2006, more than 100 of these were store managers. Bob knew how to respond to risk. A person who has faced a shooting enemy will be calm when dealing with a tough customer.

The military-style management was consistent with Mr. Nardelli's philosophy. Home Depot was following George Stalk's principles described in *Hardball: Are You Playing to Play or Playing to Win?* Examples of the philosophy include (1) maneuvering competitors into positions and markets where they are forced to invest heavily to stay competitive, and (2) engaging weaker rivals in a war of attrition, eventually forcing them out of business.

Lesson Learned: Mr. Nardelli aggressively pursued the upside of risk. This could be good.

Identify Risk Owners

As a result of the change in leadership, the culture at Home Depot changed dramatically. Prior to 2000, store managers had enormous authority. They were the risk owners on the front line of the business. They used their knowledge of local conditions and, in many cases, their instincts, rather than data and analytics, to run their operations. Beginning in 2000, most major decisions came from the top. Headquarters measured performance, made decisions, and set goals, using analytics such as margins of profit on products and the number of customers greeted at the door.

The new system was producing results. Between 2000 and 2005, sales at Home Depot rose 75 percent, and profits doubled. By 2006, the company was the world's third largest retailer, and its success was attracting attention. In March 2006, *Fortune* magazine identified Home Depot as the most admired specialty retailer for that year and named it the fifteenth most admired global corporation.

Lesson Learned: Risk ownership shifted from store managers to central staff that made major decisions and to corporate committees with no direct accountability for results. Home Depot moved away from identifying risk owners with accountability for risks. This might not be good.

Align Risk with the Business Model

At exactly the same time (March and April 2006) that the public press was taking favorable notice Home Depot, Saint Peter's College ran its first course ever on enterprise risk management. The class noticed a failure at Home Depot to align risk responsibility with the business model. Committees and central staff were making decisions that were not aligned with store management, including the new military-trained managers. Four teams of MBA candidates undertook an ERM analysis of Home Depot. Would it confirm the positive picture?

The first symptom of a problem was the performance of the company's stock. It dropped 7 percent between 2001 and 2006. In contrast, Lowe's, a major competitor half the size of Home Depot, saw its stock rise 210 percent over the same period.

The students looked inside the company itself. Inventory was sluggish at Home Depot. Headquarters focused store managers on a single metric—inventory turnover. To increase the ratio, a store could either sell more goods or reduce its inventory. In a number of cases, store managers stopped ordering inventory, and shelves were often empty of goods to sell. Here was a complete failure to align risk management with the business model. Store owners should be responsible for achieving goals, not managing ratios dictated by headquarters staff personnel.

A second failure to align risk with the business model involved directives to cut costs of staffing. The CEO ordered a reduction in the ratio of full-time to part-time from 70 percent to 50 percent of total staffing. A savings would result by holding back from employees health care benefits and retirement contributions. This was a disaster for morale, a hard-to-quantify but real variable in risk management. **Lesson Learned:** Aligning risk categories with the business model provides accountability not available when directives come from staff officers or committees. Who would be accountable, other than the CEO, if Home Depot were to stumble?

Establish a Central Risk Function

The Saint Peter's MBA teams were effectively acting as a central risk function for Home Depot. They found deteriorating conditions in the military-style atmosphere, accompanied by pressure to perform and a failure of the company to make a real commitment to the workforce. All four teams identified a culture of fear. It was accompanied by a whole new language that became part of employee discussions, including these terms:

◆ **"Aprons":** Store workers themselves, described by their orange aprons. An apron is useful but does not have to think.

◆ **"Bob's Army":** A reference to individuals in the store leadership program, where half of new hires were former military personnel. What happened to individuals who were not former military personnel? Not good for morale.

◆ **"Bobaganda":** A term describing company programming on televisions in employee break rooms. The TVs continuously displayed tips to help staff sell more merchandise, gave warnings on proper and improper behavior, and shared messages from senior managers and executives. The MBA teams imagined a rather stressful time when employees tried to relax for a little while.

◆ **"Home Despot":** The ultimate sign of cultural problems. This became the undercover name of the company itself to disgruntled employees.

The teams scanned outside the company for data. As a final nail in the coffin, the class discovered a University of Michigan Annual Customer Satisfaction Survey. In the 2001 survey, Home Depot and

Lowe's each scored a 75. In the 2006 survey, Home Depot dropped to 67, while Lowe's rose to 78. In spite of accolades in the media, Home Depot was not a hit with customers. Its score put it in last place in the department store and discount store category.

Lesson Learned: Without a central risk function or other scanning mechanism, signs of future danger can easily be missed.

Create an ERM Knowledge Warehouse

Home Depot did not have a central risk function operating an ERM knowledge warehouse. From all indications, the organization did not understand the relationships among customer dissatisfaction, employee low morale, and a centralized system of decision making that separated risk owners from business decisions and strategies.

Lesson Learned: In a situation like this, things can go wrong.

Involve the Board

By all indications, the board of Home Depot was highly concerned with corporate responsibility and a high degree of fiduciary responsibility. In April 2006, the *Harvard Business Review* ran a lengthy article describing Home Depot as a model of corporate governance. The article claimed that the company was committed to living values and recognized an ethical obligation to shareholders, employees, customers, suppliers, and the communities where it operates. The company claimed to follow strong corporate governance practices, compliance procedures, and transparent financial reporting practices. It had a disclosure committee that pursued accurate and complete financial reporting, a corporate compliance council that regularly monitored internal controls, and allowed only independent directors to serve on key board committees.

Lesson Learned: A board can have the best of intentions, but it can still miss important exposures if it does not have an effective program of risk identification and sharing.

Standard Evaluation Process

Four teams of Saint Peter's MBA candidates performed an ERM evaluation of Home Depot in April 2006. Every single team was negative about the future of Home Depot under the leadership of Mr. Nardelli. It turned out that the ERM analysis was right on target. Within months, the *Wall Street Journal* and other publications picked up the story. On January 2, 2007, only 10 months after the *Fortune* magazine most-admired article, Home Depot and Robert Nardelli mutually agreed on Nardelli's resignation as CEO after a six-year tenure. Nardelli resigned amid complaints over his heavy-handed management style.

Lesson Learned: Even when all seems to be going well, a strong central risk scanning activity accompanied by a standard evaluation process can help organizations identify problems.

Home Depot—Aftermath

The story of Mr. Nardelli did not end when he left Home Depot. He rebounded in August 2007 when Cerberus appointed him as the CEO of Chrysler LLC. In the fall of 2007, Saint Peter's MBA candidates applied an ERM analysis to Chrysler. They concluded that Cerberus recognized the upside of risk when it hired Mr. Nardelli. One team observed that the Cerberus decision reflects the Chinese character for risk. It is made up of two other characters—danger and opportunity. Enterprise risk management strongly endorses the duality of risk. Things were not looking good in late 2008 as the company faced possible bankruptcy, although not necessarily because of any actions attributable to Mr. Nardelli. By the time this book is published, we may know the outcome of the financial crisis. Whatever it is, the failure to take a risk is a risk itself. Mr. Nardelli may succeed or fail. The outcome for Chrysler may or may not be his fault. Those are not the issues. Cerberus evaluated options and made a bold decision. That is often the essence of ERM.

CHAPTER 4

CHALLENGE OF THE BLACK SWAN

RISK QUOTE: *The world is getting to be such a dangerous place, a man is lucky to get out of it alive.*

—W.C. FIELDS, COMEDIAN AND MOVIE STAR

RISK QUOTE: *A lie can run around the world six times while the truth is still trying to put on its pants.*

—MARK TWAIN, HUMORIST AND WRITER

Nassim Taleb, in his book *The Black Swan* (Random House, 2007), identifies a "black swan" as an event that meets three conditions. It is an outlier risk, a potential loss found outside the realm of normal expectations based on people's understanding of the world. It has an extreme impact, presenting the possibility of great danger or change in its consequences to individuals, organizations, or societies. It is not predictable in advance but can be explained and then understood only after it occurs. It is a surprise that can be a disaster.

Nassim Taleb's term "black swan" is based on the early and unassailable belief among Europeans and others that all swans were white. For millennia, that belief prevailed. What changed people's view? The discovery of Australia by James Cook in 1770, or perhaps an earlier discovery going back to 1606. That continent has black swans.

In earlier chapters, we set up the rationale for enterprise risk management. Before going further, we need to deal with Mr. Taleb's creative and quite accurate position on risk. He does not believe that anyone can predict the largest disasters that will befall us. They are black swans. He also sees fallacies in how we view risk. His challenge to the concept of ERM is massive. In this chapter, we fit ERM into a risky world with black swans.

What Is a Black Swan?

Examples of black swans can be seen throughout the course of history. Fairly recent ones include the following:

- The Rise of Hitler
- World War II
- The Demise of the Soviet Bloc
- The Rise of the Internet
- The 9/11 Terrorist Attacks
- The Financial Crisis of 2008

In 1918, no one foresaw the rise of Nazi Germany, the role of Hitler, and the launching of another world war 21 years after the devastating trench warfare of the first world war. By 1935, German activities were no longer a black swan. The financial crisis of 2008 was an example of a financial "bubble." In 2001, it was a black swan. By 2003, we had a lengthy letter to shareholders written by Warren Buffett and quoted widely. Arguably the best investor of his time, Warren Buffett shared the possibility of a black swan almost five years before the crisis.

WARREN BUFFETT IN 2003—BLACK SWAN?

"Charlie Munger [Buffett's partner at Berkshire Hathaway] and I are of one mind in how we feel about derivatives and the trading activities that go with them. . . . We try to be alert to any sort of mega-catastrophe risk, and that posture may make us unduly apprehensive about the burgeoning quantities of long-term derivatives contracts and the massive amount of uncollateralized receivables that are growing alongside. . . . In our view, however, derivatives are **financial weapons of mass destruction**, carrying dangers that, while now latent, are potentially lethal.''

Another question. Which of the following are not examples of black swans even though they are big in importance?

- The Development of Nuclear Weapons
- The Vietnam War
- The Enron Collapse
- Terrorist Attacks After 9/11
- Hurricane Katrina
- Global Warming
- AIDS Pandemic
- An Earthquake in San Francisco in the Twenty-First Century

None of these are examples of black swans. Scientists thought they could split the atom. Colonial wars were common. Companies collapse. Once we have a terrorist attack, we can conceive of a repeat. For years, we waited for a hurricane to hit New Orleans. We predicted global warming and the occurrence of a pandemic. We just did nothing to prevent them. And, sometime in the future, San Francisco will experience a devastating earthquake. Tokyo will be ready for its next earthquake, but California is likely to be unprepared.

A TRUE BLACK SWAN

There is controversy over exactly what should be labeled a black swan and when the description no longer fits. We will not resolve the issue. We can, however, point out an event that everyone agrees is a black swan. It occurs in the United States on the last Thursday in November. For a turkey, which has been pampered and fed generously for all its life, Thanksgiving is a black swan.

Aside from whether we agree on the timing of black swans, it may be argued that we are not engaging in risk management if we use tools or measurements that exclude the possibility of a black swan. How do we handle them? The answer depends on whether the event really comes without warning. Sometimes, as with 9/11, the event happens before it is on anyone's radar screen. We must adjust to its occurrence because we were unable or refused to predict it in advance. Other times, as with the 2008 financial crisis, we see the clouds forming on the horizon. We may not be able to predict the magnitude of the final disaster, but we can use warning signs to prepare to deal with it. We can, if we have the will, try to predict the damage in advance and take steps to mitigate the consequences.

The role of ERM in dealing with black swans is to try to identify exposures whenever possible and to include the exposure in risk management discussions. This is a critical rationale for a central risk function.

Control Over Our Destiny

Taleb believes that free markets improve the quality of life. They do not work because people are good at spotting risks and risk opportunities. Rather, free markets work because they allow people to be lucky. We study risk and opportunity at great lengths in modern organizations. We seek to learn how things work so that we can predict events. Taleb sees a problem with this formulation because our minds do not identify the things that we do not know. He believes that we see only white swans. To him the evidence is overwhelming. We cannot imagine black swans. We cannot predict black swans. Once again, the timing of clues that a black swan is emerging tempers this view.

Taleb expands on his view of luck. He discusses the relationship between talent and success, claiming that talent comes from success, rather than the other way around. The world is full of talented people who go unrecognized. The lucky few are recognized and courted. Talent does not create success in risk management. Luck creates success, and success allows the media, our bosses, and others to recognize our talent. He might acknowledge that success in risk management might be related to creativity and energy. Here, too, things do not look good. He believes banks specifically, and other bureaucratic institutions more generally, hire dull people and train them to be duller. If he is correct, it is not a good sign.

ACCURACY OF ESTIMATES

In an MBA class at Saint Peter's College, five teams of students were given five minutes to complete a task. They were told that homeowner insurance policies covered property damage and personal injury from animals. Then, they were asked to estimate the number of animals in U.S. homes in the categories of cats, dogs, reptiles, primates, and big cats. Five individuals, one from each team, moved to the front of the classroom where they were asked to reveal the team estimate of cats. All answers were in millions, specifically 200, 14, 12, 8, and 2. Then each individual was asked, "How confident was your team that you were close to the right answer?" Four teams were highly confident. One team stated that it had no clue. The actual number of cats was 65 million.

Lesson Learned: It is human nature to be highly confident of forecasts, even in the absence of evidence. After the students were told the actual number of cats, they resisted revealing the team estimates of the number of dogs. They reassessed the estimate in light of new evidence, and all five individuals gave answers between 55 and 80 million. The actual number was 78 million. Learning can take place as we reflect upon our confidence in estimates.

Risk Prevention

A major rationale for ERM is that it is better to deal with risk in terms of prevention than in terms of recovery. The ERM goal is to develop information systems that identify risk and share the findings. Then, the entity can seek to provide structural incentives for individuals who are ahead of their time to mitigate exposures not seen by others. Taleb says we cannot give rewards for prevention. A legislator who advocated bulletproof, locked cockpit doors prior to 9/11 would die unknown, not to mention being despised by the airlines. Statements prior to crises by Neville Chamberlain and

Martin Sullivan give Taleb considerable evidence to support a view that we do not see risk in advance and thus are not really able to prevent black swans.

TWO MISSED RISKS: NEVILLE CHAMBERLAIN AND AIG

A classic moment occurred in 1938 as Hitler was widely recognized as a threat to humanity. British prime minister Neville Chamberlain stood outside 10 Downing Street and said, "My good friends . . . there has come back from Germany to Downing Street peace with honor. I believe it is peace for our time."

A more recent example of missing a major risk occurred just before the 2008 financial crisis. On May 9, 2008, Martin Sullivan, CEO of AIG, the giant insurance company, did not see what was about to happen and thus rejected an auditor's recommendation that the company show a $19.3 billion financial loss, saying, "Excluding these external market issues, the underlying fundamentals of our core businesses remain solid." The real loss was much higher. In April 2008, AIG stock traded above $40 a share. On September 16, 2008, it sold for $1.25 a share.

Lesson Learned: Can we see black swans?

Risk Experts

Taleb discusses people who make predictions as though they truly were experts on risk. According to Taleb, only some areas are suitable for "experts." A science is an organized body of knowledge that reveals the nature and basic principles of an area of study. An art is an applied skill that makes something happen. Is risk management an art or a science? Taleb says it is an art because execution is involved. We can replicate scientific efforts. Risk management varies with each challenge, situation, and time period. Experts do not exist when behavior is an art.

People who think they are experts on risk are people who suffer from a delusion. They do not know what they do not know. When an expert is right, he believes it is the result of depth of understanding. When he is wrong, he blames the events, claiming they are random or outside our control.

EXPERTS IN RISK MANAGEMENT?

Who of the following will be most successful at risk management? Political leaders. Professors. Scientists. Cabdrivers. Taleb would not distinguish among these. None are experts. Some problems with each:

- **Political Leaders:** They have agendas that discourage prevention and outside forces that encourage expediency and dishonesty.
- **Professors:** They have not faced true decision making under uncertainty and do not realize what is important.
- **Scientists:** They are not informed until results are in from an event that already has happened and can help only when the risk is identical to a replicable activity.
- **Cabdrivers:** They think they know everything and are happy to give advice. That, too, is an impediment.

Taleb accepts some risk managers as being experts where replication is possible. This group includes astronomers, test pilots, chess masters, physicists, mathematicians, accountants, and grain inspectors. He rejects as experts stockbrokers, psychiatrists, college admissions officers, psychologists, judges, counselors, and personnel selectors.

Understanding Risk

Taleb takes strong positions on the frequent failure of individuals and organizations to understand risk. He starts with ideas, stories, the truth, and imagination as they affect one's understanding of risk. These are his views:

- **Ideas.** They are not very potent. They come and go. Some are fanciful. Some are just wrong.
- **Stories.** They are potent. They stay. People can relate to them. They can change minds. They can cause mistakes in judgment about risk.
- **Truth.** What is it? Maybe fiction reveals truth and nonfiction is used to hide the liar.
- **Imagination.** This is not of much help. We lack imagination and suppress it in others.

STEVEN LEVITT ON EXPERTS

Steven Levitt, best known for his book *Freakonomics,* is cited a number of times in this book. His opinion of experts:

The typical expert is prone to sound exceedingly sure of himself. An expert doesn't so much argue the various sides of an issue. That's because an expert whose argument reeks of restraint or nuance often doesn't get much attention. An expert must be bold if he hopes to alchemize his homespun theory into conventional wisdom.

Lesson Learned: Apparently Levitt agrees with Taleb.

Taleb introduces the concept of a triplet of opacity. The term *opacity* refers to the quality or state of a body that does not allow the entry or passage of rays of light. In people, it describes those who are mentally obtuse, dull, or dense and unable to understand what is happening. Taleb identifies three problems when managers and organizations deal with risk:

1. *Illusion of Understanding.* All people believe they know what is happening in a complex and random risk environment. People create order out of chaos when no order exists.

AIG STOCK PRICE

A group of MBA candidates in an ERM course at Saint Peter's College were given the following data for a public company:

Year	Net Income Price	Earning per Share	December 31 Stock
2003			$72
2004	$ 9.9 billion	$3.73	$64
2005	$10.5 billion	$3.99	$67
2006	$14.0 billion	$5.36	$70

They were asked to estimate the likely, high, and low ending stock price for 2007 and 2008. Answers varied from $40 to $80. They were largely confident that the estimates were good. The company was AIG, whose year-end stock price was $47 in 2007 and $1.30 in 2008.

Lesson Learned: When estimating risk, the past is not useful if we are not scanning for black swans.

2. *Retrospective Distortion.* People can assess risk accurately only after it has materialized. People look in a rearview mirror and think they see the road ahead.

3. *Overvaluation of Factual Information.* If we have data, we must use them. They must have the answer. If we have access to the views of experts, they are likely to be right. Experts are particularly valued if they have advanced degrees and untested theories.

ROLE OF EXPERTS

Taleb discusses Yevgenia Krasnova, a famous Russian writer, who could not find a publisher. She posted her book on the Web. A small publisher picked it up, and the book sold millions of copies. Encouraged by her publisher and fans, Yevgenia worked for eight years on a second book. When it was released, it flopped, selling few copies in spite of all the expectations. Yevgenia Krasnova experienced two black swans. First, no one expected her book to become a bestseller. After all, she was an unknown author rejected by "expert" publishers. Second, since her first book was a smashing success, who could imagine the total failure of her next book?

Scalability

Scalability is the degree to which something can be easily expanded on demand. Taleb believes that scalability is often ignored. True risk does not come from bad accounting because it is not scalable. It comes from the black swan. The box office performance of the movie *Titanic* is an example of scalability. Once the film is finished, it can sell few tickets or a massive number of tickets. The stock of Microsoft and Google can soar or can fall. A book by the author J. K. Rowling can go unnoticed or become a sensation before anyone has read it.

Logic and Risk

Taleb believes that a danger to identifying risk is the failure to get it right. Taleb uses examples of the need to use clear thinking and logic:

❧ **Terrorism.** Which statement is more correct: Almost all terrorists are Muslims or almost all Muslims are terrorists. The first is correct. If we know that the statement that almost all terrorists are Muslims is correct, why do many risk management solutions seem to believe that almost all Muslims are terrorists?

❧ **Data Quality.** In a region, half of children born are male and half are female. The region has two hospitals. One is large, the other small. In a given year, boys accounted for 60 percent of births at one of the hospitals. Which hospital is it likely to be? The smaller hospital, as deviations from the expected are likely to occur with a small number of observations. We must understand the database if we are to understand risk.

❧ **Evidence, Accomplishments, and Failures.** Taleb believes that the logic of risk is not always clear. He faults our use of evidence, believing that we take past events that corroborate our theories and treat them as evidence. He also faults our view of our accomplishments. We use them to advance our arguments. A better choice would be to understand our failures and use them to deal with risk.

❧ **Empiricism.** This is the practice of relying on observation to understand risk. Taleb believes we get closer to the truth by negative empiricism. I see 100 white swans. Are all swans white? I see one black swan. Are all swans white? I do not see a man kill another man. Is he a killer? I see a man kill another man. Is he a killer? Taleb essentially argues that we know what is wrong with a lot more confidence than we know what is right. He recommends formulating a bold conjecture and looking for an observation to prove it wrong.

TECHNOLOGY

Taleb believes the major problem of using information to give us probabilities lies in the fact that information is costly to (1) obtain; (2) store; (3) manipulate; and (4) retrieve.

We do not know when he reached this conclusion. It is no longer true. The problem is actually the volume and complexity of data and the difficulty of interpreting them. We can now collect, store, and access massive, interconnected databases. The technology exists. Now we need to learn how to use it, much as we began to use artificial intelligence in the 1990s.

Lesson Learned: What once was true is not necessarily still true. Even great minds need to scan the horizon.

Perceived Level of Risk

Abstract statistical information does not cause fear. The perception of risk rises when we learn of a single murder in the park, an accident on a motorcycle, or a death caused by the administration of the wrong medication in a hospital. Risk is a combination of possibility and fear. The more we can imagine something, particularly if is sensational, the greater the risk.

In developing a strong approach to risk management, Taleb realized that stories can skew our estimates of danger if they contain frightening details. He gives some examples of statements that create different levels of fear of a risk. When tested with respondents, a statement with specific frightening details created a higher perception that the risk was likely to occur than did less detailed accounts.

TALEB STATEMENTS ON RISK

For each item, which statement led respondents to perceive a higher likelihood of an occurrence and thus a greater risk?

Natural Disaster

1. A massive flood occurring somewhere in America caused 1,000 people to die.
2. An earthquake in California produced massive flooding and caused 1,000 people to die.
   The second was perceived as a higher risk.

Health Risk

1. What is your estimate of the percentage of Mexicans who will contract lung cancer in their lifetimes?

2. What is your estimate of the percentage of Mexicans who will contract lung cancer in their lifetimes as a result of smoking cigarettes?

   Once again, the second statement elicited a higher estimate of risk.

Social Risk

1. John Saunders seems happily married. What are the odds that he will kill his wife?

2. John Saunders seems happily married. What are the odds that he will kill his wife to get her inheritance?

   The second statement, with greater detail, again elicited a higher estimate of risk.

Physical Danger

1. The New York Police Commissioner issued a warning about a possible bombing on the subway. Should a person avoid taking the subway?

2. A terrorist can do major damage with a bombing on the subway. Should a person avoid taking the subway?

   Again, the first statement, which contains more detail, elicited a higher estimate of risk.

Silent Evidence

Taleb observes that people tend to impute evidence to situations, affecting their perception of risk. Some examples:

- **Unknown Silent Evidence.** The evening news showed 10 survivors of a plane crash in which 70 people lost their lives. As the plane was dropping, they joined in prayer. Did the prayer save their lives? Taleb asks the obvious question: Did any of the dead also pray? Without the silent evidence, people would assume that prayer works. Maybe it does, and maybe it does not.

- **Known Silent Evidence.** A drug saves 10,000 people a year, but side effects kill 10 others. Will a doctor prescribe the drug? Drugs and other risky products and services are banned all the time when the risks are statistically insignificant.

🎯 **Wrong Silent Evidence.** Taleb cites a casino he visited that had highly sensitive security and risk management programs in place. Yet, after his visit, Taleb identified the four biggest risks that the casino had actually faced in recent years. None was covered in the casino risk management plan:

- A tiger had injured Roy, of the magician team Siegfried and Roy, an important act that attracted gamblers to the casino. The operation suffered a $100 million loss.

- A disgruntled contractor had a dispute with the hotel. He returned with dynamite to blow up the casino. Fortunately, his plan was discovered, and he was stopped.

- The IRS requires casinos to file forms showing large winnings at casinos. An employee failed to file the IRS forms for years. The casino almost lost its license and wound up paying a significant fine.

- The casino owner's daughter was kidnapped. The owner violated gambling laws to obtain money to pay a ransom. His misappropriation of casino funds was a serious violation of the law.

Taleb argues that risks outside the risk management models are the most dangerous to organizations. His view reinforces the importance of an ERM central scanning function.

SILENT EVIDENCE AT THE O. J. TRIAL

A man was on trial for murdering his wife. The prosecution introduced evidence that the man was an inveterate wife abuser. The defendant's lawyer introduced statistics that 4 million women are battered every year by their male partners, yet only one in 2,500 is ultimately murdered by her partner. Does this evidence statistically support the likelihood that the man did not commit the murder?

The answer is no. The statistic was introduced at the O. J. Simpson trial. However, Nicole Brown Simpson was already dead. The relevant question was what percentage of all battered women who are murdered are killed by their abusers. The answer was 90 percent, but it did not come up in the trial.

Leonard Mlodinow, *The Drunkard's Walk: How Randomness Rules Our Lives* (New York: Pantheon Books, 2008).

Optimism and Pessimism

Taleb describes estimation error as a problem when forecasting risk likelihood. Two groups of students estimated the time needed to complete a project. The "optimists" estimated 26 days. The "pessimists" estimated 47 days. The actual average time to completion was 56 days.

In this example, Taleb identified our need to think we have reduced uncertainty when we are dealing with risk. We may not be able to reduce it in the real world, but we certainly can reduce it in our own minds. One of the most common techniques is to make a forecast using three scenarios: (1) likely, (2) best case, and (3) worst case. Let us test the idea of reducing uncertainty when estimating value at risk, a widely used measure of exposure and opportunity.

Suppose a company wants to minimize its exposure to fluctuations in the value of the dollar at a time when it has $60 million in receivables. As it normally collects 90 percent of the receivables ($54 million), it borrows $50 million to reduce its currency fluctuation exposure to $4 million (54 vs. 50). If it is confident that the dollar exchange rate will not fluctuate more than 20 percent in the next period, the worst case for value at risk is 20 percent of $4 million, or $800,000.

Now suppose economic conditions change, causing customers to default on their obligations. The company would not collect the receivables, yet it would owe $50 million. If 50 percent of customers default, the company collects only $30 million. The calculation quickly changes to $50 million minus $30 million, or $20 million of exposure. Now assume the fluctuation in currencies is 50 percent instead of 20 percent. The value at risk becomes 50 percent times $20 million, or $10 million. The worst case for value at risk is much greater than the overconfident estimate.

An ERM program can fail if it relies too heavily on quantitative techniques. We are trained to look at data, and estimate likely outcomes in normal times. We understand probability and the normal probability distribution curve where 95 percent of the possibilities are approximately two standard deviations from a likely outcome. The statistical analysis can create an unwarranted confidence that causes us to stop watching for changes that might move us into the 2.5 percent extremes.

Malcolm Gladwell, in *Blink: The Power of Thinking Without Thinking,* is highly critical of analytical tools even within the 95 percent confidence intervals. He claims a person's "gut" is often a better decision maker than lengthy risk analysis. It is easy to show our tendency to be overconfident when we are using numbers. Earlier this year, a group of MBA candidates in an ERM course at St. Peter's College were given the following data for a public company.

Year	Net Income	Earnings per Share	Share Price
2003			$72
2004	$ 9.9 billion	$3.73	$64
2005	$10,5 billion	$3.99	$67
2006	$14.0 billion	$5.36	$70

In the pursuit of value at risk, the candidates were asked to estimate the likely, high-, and low-ending stock price for 2007 and 2008. Answers varied from $40 to $80. Even though the financial crisis was in full bloom, most individuals were confident that their estimates were solid. The company was AIG whose year-end stock price was $47 in 2007 and $1.30 in 2008.

We can even show a tendency toward undue confidence when no statistical data supports numbers. Once somebody makes an estimate, confidence tends to rise. In a different MBA class, five teams of students were given five minutes to complete a task. They were told that homeowner insurance policies covered property damage and personal injuries that your pets cause to third parties. Then they were asked to estimate the number of animals in U.S. homes in the categories of cats, dogs, reptiles, primates, and big cats. Five individuals, one from each team, moved to the front of the classroom where they were asked to reveal the team estimate of the number of cats. The answers were 200 million, 14 million, 12 million, 8 million, and 2 million. Then each individual was asked, "How confident was your team that you were close to the right answer?" Despite the wide range and obvious situation that most estimates had to be wrong, four teams were highly confident. One team stated that it had no clue. The actual number of cats was 65 million.

It is human nature to believe that we can make reasonable estimates, even in the absence of evidence. After the team representatives were told the actual number of cats, they resisted revealing the team estimates for dogs. They reassessed the estimate in light of new evidence, and all five individuals gave answers between 55 and 80 million. The actual number was 78 million.

Let us conclude by recognizing that we can be too optimistic in an uncertain world. Taleb is right. In the area of 2.5 percent at each tail of the distribution, we often find the greatest opportunities and the most dangerous exposures. Figure 4-1 graphically shows an improved ERM approach to assessing risk. We need to be looking for a future Google or Apple at one end of the distribution and an AIG or Lehman Brothers at the other. We seek an early warning for risks and opportunities that might otherwise be missed in the 95 percent range of "normal" times. Once exposures or opportunities are identified in the 2.5 percent areas, the central risk function can shares its findings, thus opening channels for collaboration to pursue opportunities and mitigate exposures.

What are some of the 2.5 percent risks and opportunities? We can start searching areas such as technology, the financial system,

FIGURE 4-1. THE NEW MATH OF VALUE AT RISK.

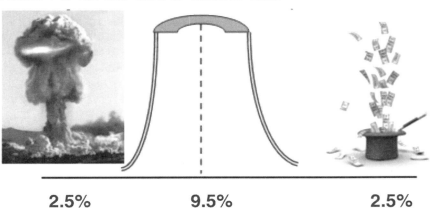

2.5%   **9.5%**   **2.5%**

pandemics, fossil fuel shortages, pollution, environmental change, earthquakes in California, and disruption in supply lines. Thanks to thinkers like Nassim Taleb, the issue of excessive optimism is at the cutting edge of enterprise risk management in 2009.

Conclusion

Taleb raises a number of issues that deserve serious attention in any program of enterprise risk management. Clearly, black swans do exist. The only role ERM can play in minimizing the damage they inflict is to serve as an early observer of emerging dangers or opportunities. In 2009, we should be watching developing countries (such as China, India, and other second-world countries), technology, financially interlocking risks, changing markets, fossil fuel infrastructures, global warming directly, shortages of clean water, and the environment indirectly. We may see the early stages of a black swan. Some people argue that we are seeing them already as any of these situations or conditions could have massive but unexpected risk consequences.

Taleb does not challenge the more structured role of ERM. If we cannot observe black swans, surely we can observe a company's many exposures to them. Further, fiduciary responsibility demands that boards and senior officers pay attention to potential exposures and opportunities and address them in a systematic and logical way. We incorporate black swans by incorporating flexibility and responsiveness, as was done by Nokia and was not done by Ericsson (see Chapter 1). We address other important risks by pursuing early identification and sharing important information.

CHAPTER 5

CHALLENGE OF THE 2008 FINANCIAL CRISIS

RISK QUOTE: *The greatest lesson in life is to know that even fools are right sometimes.*

—WINSTON CHURCHILL, BRITISH STATESMAN

RISK QUOTE: *Never pick a fight with an ugly person. They've got nothing to lose.*

—ROBIN WILLIAMS, COMEDIAN

I f the prospect of black swans brings a challenge to ERM, so does the 2008 global financial crisis. Before discussing the challenge, let us review the history of the crisis.

History of the Crisis

The crisis can be traced back to the dot-com frenzy of the late 1990s. The Internet, and the doors it opened, created opportunities to launch businesses that took advantage of new technologies. Changes were envisioned in consumer behavior, marketing, advertising, and communications. People believed that exciting investment opportunities were available to those who moved first and fastest. Venture capitalists and general investors adjusted their investment strategies as they pursued startup companies. They encouraged the companies to sustain a negative cash flow in a frantic effort to ensure future dominance of a technology or market. Record-setting rises in stock valuations became the name of the game as many early investors became extremely wealthy.

The bubble burst. We can see the outcome in the Nasdaq composite index, where most high-tech companies traded. Consider the level of the Nasdaq in the years between 1995 and 2002:

Year	Index
1995	800
1999	1,800
2000	5,100
2002	1,100

AOL AND TIME WARNER—SPECULATIVE FRENZY

In 1991, Stephen Case founded America Online (AOL) and led it to rapid growth. In 2000, AOL and Time Warner merged, with AOL shareholders receiving 55 percent of the stock of the new AOL Time Warner. Thus, AOL was valued more highly than Time Warner. Following the merger, AOL suffered a major decline in profitability and cash flow. As a result, AOL Time Warner reported a loss of $99 billion in 2002, the largest corporate loss ever reported up to that time. Less than 15 months after the merger, the stock price had dropped more than 50 percent. In 2003, Time Warner dropped AOL from its name and replaced Case as executive chairman. In 2005, Case resigned from the Time Warner board.

Lesson Learned: Speculative bubbles can affect companies as well as people.

Move into the Housing Market

After the crash of the Nasdaq and its high-tech companies, investors sought new places to put their money. Those who missed the early dot-com rise in stock prices had watched as others became wealthy while they lost their own savings. The search for the next opportunity soon showed that real estate values were rising rapidly. Investors who speculated in California, Florida, the Northeast, and the Southwest housing booms were making a great deal of money by 2002. They believed that prices would rise indefinitely. They were partly right. From 2002 to 2005, prices continued to rise even though construction costs were relatively level.

New Mortgages

In the middle of the frenzy, banks and investors developed new forms of mortgages: "We can do you a favor. We can approve a mortgage you cannot afford." Banks offered adjustable interest rate mortgages (ARMs) with low rates for the first few years. Homeowners could worry about the higher payments later. If the family could not pay the mortgage when rates rose, the owner could sell the house at a profit. The owner could use the proceeds from the sale to buy another house, possibly a smaller house that the owner could actually afford.

LEVITT ON SELF-INTEREST—A FACTOR IN THE CRISIS

As we try to understand the current financial crisis, many actors come to the stage. Was it greed and thievery, foolish politicians, incredibly stupid and unethical executives, dozing regulators, homebuyers who demanded something for nothing, or executive decision makers who lacked the courage to shift the tide? Steven Levitt has observations on the source of risk when it appears that no risk exists at all. He describes Paul Feldman, who delivered 8,000 bagels a week to 140 corporate offices. An honor system allowed employees to pay for the bagels as they took them. On the average, 95 percent of individuals paid for the bagels. One company had executives on one floor and sales, service, and administrative employees on other floors. There was more cheating on the executive floor than on the floor with lower-paid employees.

Lesson Learned: Maybe senior executives have a sense of entitlement, or maybe people who tend to cheat are more likely to become executives. Make sure we do not make the wrong assumptions in the absence of investigation. Gather as much information as possible when evaluating risk. It is not easy to understand the source of an exposure.

What would happen to buyers who could not afford the adjustable-rate mortgages? This, too, had a unique solution. Banks offered interest-only mortgages that had lower payments than ARMs. Like ARMs, these mortgages would adjust in a few years and require higher payments that reflected both the higher interest rate and repayment of the principal.

New Lending Capital

Part of the ensuing problems resulted from the availability of capital from banks. Did the banking regulators limit the lending? The answer is no. It is true that a bank must have adequate capital to support lending. Regulators monitor closely the relationships among mortgage assets, deposits, and bank capital. To increase the funds they had available to lend and to receive the fees that go with the origination of a mortgage, banks sold off the mortgages and thus freed capital to make new loans. Investment banks, an unregulated component of global financial markets, bought the mortgages and packaged them into new securities called collateralized debt obligations (CDOs). Investment bankers could sell these securities to eager investors who sought above-market rates of return at the perceived level of risk. Mortgage bankers facilitated the process of collecting mortgages and transferring them from banks to investment banks.

The mortgage market changed completely. Banks had a financial incentive to make as many mortgages as possible. At the same time, they faced no risk of default because the banks immediately transferred the mortgages to investment banks. Because they faced no risk, many banks dropped their credit standards and began offering so-called subprime mortgages—mortgages given to those who could not qualify for traditional fixed-rate mortgages. Banks offered "stated income loans" that required no verification of the source of the funds with which the borrower would pay interest and repay principal on the loan. When a potential borrower lacked adequate income, some banks encouraged them to inflate their stated income. Others overlooked credit card and other debt.

LEVITT ON ECONOMIC AND SOCIAL RISK— BLOOD BANK

It sounded like a good idea when the government encouraged banks to lend money to people who could not otherwise afford to own their own homes. An economic and social risk joined to cause a crisis. Steven Levitt discusses the economic incentives that face a different kind of bank. He describes a blood bank that sought to increase donations of blood. It offered a newly minted $10 bill to anyone who donated blood. The impact was a decrease in the level of donations. The first risk mitigation task in resolving this problem is to identify the cause-and-effect relationship. The second task is to consider options. What negative effects would result if the economic incentive were $1,000 instead of $10?

To answer the first question, Levitt points out that an economic incentive replaced a moral incentive. With a $10 incentive, a person received a small amount of money instead of being praised for a good act. As for the second question, Levitt speculated that donations might rise if there were a $1,000 incentive because the economic incentive is much greater. Risks arise because of the potential for misbehavior in pursuit of a large economic incentive. The blood bank may have to deal with actions such as the theft of blood, counterfeit blood (from pigs?), and fake identification cards used by dishonest or ineligible donors. In the context of economic incentives, Levitt quotes W. C. Fields: "A thing worth having is worth cheating for."

Lesson Learned: Conventional wisdom is often wrong. We reduce risk when we reconsider and maybe even challenge the basic assumptions of risk relationships. People behave in ways that achieve their goals, even though they exhibit behaviors that seem to be inconsistent. Incorrect assumptions or interpretations lead to the wrong conclusion about the source of risk and the steps needed to manage risk. This can happen in blood banks, and it can happen to an entire financial system when basic economic and social risks are ignored.

One of the worst developments was the creation of down payment assistance (DPA) mortgages. The seller would donate money to a charitable organization so that it could provide a down payment for a buyer. The buyer would purchase the seller's house at a price above the market, and the charity would make the down payment. Effectively, the buyer made no down payment. Banks made 650,000 such loans between 2000 and 2006. In 2006, the IRS barred tax exemptions for the practice.

Scanning for Exposures

The simplest ERM scanning of the horizon showed that improper lending practices had serious and easily recognized exposures for homeowners and investors. As an example, we can use a 30-year $500,000 mortgage that starts at an interest rate of 4 percent and adjusts to 7 percent in three years. If it is an adjustable rate mortgage, the monthly payment will change from $2,400 to $3,300. If it is an interest-only loan, the monthly payment will rise from $1,700 to $3,400. As the volume of these mortgages increased, the danger became substantial. One measure of exposure can be seen in San Diego, California, where, in 2004, almost half the mortgages were interest-only, and 80 percent were either interest-only or ARMs.

An ERM scan of the landscape would have posed big questions. Start with interest rates, which were dropping. Between 2000 and 2003, fixed-rate mortgages went from 8 percent to 5.5 percent. ARMs went from 7 percent to between 2 and 4 percent. In 1998, banks declined 29 percent of mortgage applications. In 2003, they declined only 14 percent. In 1995, 600,000 new single-family homes were built in the United States. In 2005, the number more than doubled, to 1.3 million. Homeowners who did not need funds to buy a house took out mortgages anyway. They used the easily obtained loans against their homes to buy personal products, take vacations, and make home improvements. Between 1996 and 2005, home equity loans rose from $100 billion to $750 billion. When these loans reset at the higher levels of payment, many homeowners could not make the payments, and their homes went into foreclosure. And the prices of homes plummeted, because of the flood of homes on the market and the decreasing pool of available buyers, leaving many homeowners owing more on their homes than the houses were worth.

Aftermath

After spotting the exposure and all the wrongdoing, politicians and others sought to place the blame on regulators, auditors, rating agencies, and even homeowners. The issue of bailouts dominated the media. Should governments around the world intervene to stop a liquidity run that would destroy the global financial system? In the United States, the government had encouraged banks to make loans to poor families, and many of these loans were later sold to Fannie Mae and Freddie Mac, former government-supported agencies. Should we blame commercial and community banks for the crisis, even though the banks did not hold the loans? Was it the fault of investment banks that sold the worst mortgages to others? Did the rating agencies fail us by giving prime ratings to investment banks that were issuing securities nobody really understood? Did AIG, the giant insurer, insure too many securities without even backing them up with reserves?

Whatever the answer to these questions, governments around the world quickly realized that drastic steps were needed immediately. They sought to stop the erosion in home values, which meant stopping the foreclosures. They provided liquidity to the credit markets and to businesses operating in a global economy. As this is being written, in early 2009, they are trying to restore confidence in the value of equity securities. U.S. regulators knew that a $2-trillion-dollar new guarantee or other commitment of the U.S. government was a $12,000 obligation to each U.S. taxpayer. They also knew that U.S. investors make up 20 percent of global equity holders. If global markets suffered a 20 percent drop in stock values, the loss would be $33,000 for every U.S. citizen.

Non-U.S. governments and regulatory agencies also recognized the magnitude of the problem. They concluded that the short-term issue was not whether governments should bail out poor decision makers and crooks. It was not about severance packages for mediocre or worse U.S. CEOs. They defined the problem correctly. The solution was to take steps to stabilize the financial system and the economy of the world.

PARALLEL WITH THE GREAT DEPRESSION

The Great Depression started with the U.S. stock market crash in October 1929 and became a worldwide economic downturn. It had a devastating economic impact on trade, economic activity, agriculture, and the morale of the people of the world. It did not end until the start of World War II.

The stock market collapse in 1929 was not the whole story. The market actually rebounded to early-1929 levels in 1930. The problem was fear. Consumers who experienced stock losses conserved their remaining capital. When bank lending became readily available, in 1930, people did not take advantage of it. As spending dropped, job losses increased, and a downward spiral ensued. Government protectionist policies that weakened trade made the situation worse. The economic decline continued until 1933, when a new administration in Washington, D.C., began programs to create jobs. In some ways, it was too little too late.

Lesson Learned: Governments need to recognize that times of economic and financial crisis may not be the time to be timid.

Visible Signs of Danger

We need only to scan externally to see what was happening. In 2004, dramatic radio commercials were telling people that they should not be paying market rates for mortgages and that maybe they should be paying only interest. How could a financial services companies, regulators, and others miss such a signal? Something was wrong.

Following up the external scan, we can easily understand the rising exposure. Housing prices had been in a steep climb for nine years, and it was likely that many people could not afford the homes they sought. We can surmise that buyers had watched their neighbors get rich by purchasing and flipping second homes and condos. Las Vegas and Florida were particularly hot, and mortgages were huge. It did not take an economist to figure out that a downturn in housing prices would be bad news for many people.

Enterprise risk management can help us understand the failure. Banks were the originators of loans, but they did not hold them. They took no risk churning their mortgage portfolios. As security markets searched for higher yields, investment banks helped. They sold off packages of housing loans and earned a return far greater than that on their invested capital. For a time, everybody gained on mortgages that carried low initial interest rates, and then jumped dramatically after a few years. The temptation to relax credit standards or to eliminate them entirely was real. And it led to disaster when the bubble broke.

AIG, Merrill Lynch, and other financial companies have bright leaders and managers. How could they not have seen their exposure? One answer is that they had internal auditors, compliance officers, and quantitative models to manage risk. The training of these professionals and their tools they use focus entities inward and lull them into believing that they can predict the future and limit the impact of exposures. This may be true for risks subject to internal audit. It is not the point of ERM. We gain little value from central management of hundreds or thousands of business risks. Such a program can be nothing more than a description of internal controls. We need something different.

Impact of the Crisis on ERM

As of mid-2008, only two industry sectors had embraced ERM in any meaningful way—energy companies and financial service institutions. After the collapse of Bear Sterns and Lehman Brothers and the near-collapse of Merrill Lynch and AIG, we could draw the conclusion that ERM had failed the shareholders and employees of financial firms. We could recognize a failure to understand ERM.

The Committee of Sponsoring Organizations (www.coso.org) developed the ERM framework most commonly discussed in the years leading up to the 2008 crisis. According to COSO, ERM is a process, used by boards of directors and management and applied across the enterprise, whose goal is to identify risk events, manage risks within a risk appetite, and provide a reasonable assurance of achievement of objectives. Pursuing ERM, one global corporation identified 2,900 business risks and sought to manage them in an integrated process. Most companies do not see the value of such an effort.

The subprime debacle shows us that the COSO approach to ERM is a failure. We definitely need a central risk function, but its job is not to manage risk. It should identify critical risks and share its concerns. It should scan the horizon for changing conditions and the organization itself for weaknesses in leadership, culture, and management. Then it should share its findings.

CHAPTER 6

IMPLEMENTING ERM

RISK QUOTE: *The secret of life is honesty and fair dealing. if you can fake that, you've got it made.*

— GROUCHO MARX, COMEDIAN AND MOVIE STAR

RISK QUOTE: *I wake up every morning at nine and grab for the morning paper. Then I look at the obituary page. If my name is not on it, I get up.*

— BENJAMIN FRANKLIN, SCIENTIST, PUBLISHER, AND DIPLOMAT

As organizations evaluate the implementation of an ERM program, the discussion can quickly bog down. Should the entity form a central risk committee, hire a chief risk officer, or bring in outside consultants to set up a program? What should be the reporting structure? In this chapter, we look at research on the status of ERM implementation and conclude with a checklist of questions that can be completed prior to attempting to create an ERM process.

Governance Driver of ERM

The board of directors is often a driving force for ERM and a central risk function. The board needs direct knowledge of how risks are addressed throughout the organization. This should justify a central risk function all by itself. The board should communicate its appetite for risk including opportunities and exposures to be accepted. It should insist that the CEO align the risk framework with the business model so that the entity coordinates goals, values, and risk appetite.

Deloitte Survey on ERM Drivers

The Deloitte 2008 survey offers evidence that boards of directors are the primary drivers of ERM. Deloitte asked, "Who is primarily driving the interest in enterprise risk management in your organization?" As Figure 6-1 shows, the board, including its audit committee, was the primary champion for ERM. Add the category of "all of the above" and the board's role rises to 52 percent.

FIGURE 6-1. DELOITTE FINDINGS ON PRIMARY ADVOCATES OF ERM.

Primary Advocate	
Internal Auditor	21%
Senior Management	18%
Board of Directors	16%
Audit Committee of the Board of Directors	15%
Other	9%
All of the Above	21%

LEVITT DRIVERS OF RISK—ELECTION SPENDING

Steven Levitt, in his book *Freakonomics*, describes two candidates who ran for public office. Candidate X spent $2 million for campaign funding. Y spent $400,000. X won with 56 percent of the vote. Levitt's conclusion was that campaign spending barely affected the number of votes. His research compared spending in different races and time periods. He determined that a winning candidate can cut spending by 50 percent and still suffer a loss of only 1 percent of the vote. A losing candidate can double spending and gain only 1 percent more votes. Levitt's conclusion is that no correlation exists between campaign spending and changes in the number of votes won. He recommends that campaign managers seek statistical relationships other than advertising and changes in vote totals. As an example, the campaign organization might find a correlation between candidates' attractiveness and voting results. If this is the case, as is logical, political parties can spend less money and win more elections if they carefully select candidates.

Lesson Learned: The board has to understand the relationships between management actions and success. ERM can help identify the source of risk and opportunities, and then the board can evaluate whether management is properly dealing with both the downside (loss of the election) and the upside (winning the election). Levitt's conclusion is consistent with ERM.

In addition to those listed in Figure 6-1, we have other drivers of ERM. Regulators are imposing new requirements on private businesses and nonprofits. Corporate scandals and misbehaviors, prior to and during the 2008 financial crisis, have created pressure for reliable financial statements and monitoring of rogue behavior. In the United States, the Securities and Exchange Commission requires public companies to file 10-K reports discussing risk in plain English. Basel II requires banks to have adequate capital matched against risks. The Sarbanes-Oxley Act of 2002, passed in the wake of the Enron and Worldcom scandals, tightens accounting requirements for public companies and requires CEOs and CFOs of public companies to verify internal controls and the reliability of financial statements. Securities exchanges around the world have tighter requirements for risk reporting. The New York Stock Exchange and others require listed companies to discuss risk assessment and risk management. Rating agencies evaluate risk management programs, including ERM specifically, as part of their decisions on whether to award favorable ratings to debt issues.

Benefits of ERM

Understanding the rationale for ERM is an early implementation step. The Deloitte 2008 survey asked respondents to identify the benefits from ERM. Figure 6-2 shows respondents' assessment of benefits already experienced. The most frequent response is the creation of a risk-aware culture, an idea that is reinforced in the other responses.

FIGURE 6-2. ERM BENEFITS EXPERIENCED BY DELOITTE RESPONDENTS.

Benefit	Percentage
ERM created a risk-aware culture.	34%
We can now identify and manage cross-enterprise risks.	29%
ERM provided integrated management reporting.	26%
ERM enabled a focus on the most important risks.	26%
ERM reduced vulnerability to adverse events	25%
ERM enhanced risk response decisions.	25%

Figure 6-3 shows the benefits respondents expect to achieve in the future. These, too, all support the importance of creating a risk-aware culture.

FIGURE 6-3. DELOITTE SURVEY RESPONSE ON FUTURE ERM BENEFITS.

Benefit	Percentage
Ability to link growth, risk, and return.	49%
Ability to align risk appetite and strategy.	44%
Ability to provide integrated responses to multiple risks.	44%
Help to minimize operational surprises and losses.	42%
Help to seize opportunities.	39%

ZERO PERCENT FINANCING—RISK-AWARE CULTURE

In late 2001, U.S. automakers offered zero percent financing on new car purchases. Such an action effectively reduces average profit per car while selling more cars in the current year. In theory, the strategy should produce higher profits.

Were the interrelationships among risks fully considered? The increase in sales and profits was offset by other factors. Two impacts occurred as a result of zero percent financing:

- **Lost Sales Next Year.** People bought earlier, so companies lost the sale of cars that would have been purchased in 2002. Such a loss can be substantial.

- **Reduced Residual Value on Leased Cars.** The companies had leases expiring on cars they had financed for buyers. The lower price of new cars lowered the residual value of the leased cars when they were eventually sold.

  Thus, a risk-return analysis that is limited to the silo of new automobile sales can affect the silos of a loss of future sales at higher profit margins and losses in the leasing unit.

Lesson Learned: If the board and management want to understand risk in business decisions, they need to grasp risk relationships. Failing to take a broad view means that an organization does not really have a risk-aware culture. Having said this, we understand that companies often follow competitors' actions to avoid even greater losses when a competitor makes a poor decision.

The Deloitte findings on benefits encourage companies to align ERM with risk responsibility, particularly the business model. What are the goals? How does the company pursue them? We develop risk categories and create clusters of subrisks below each category.

An important step in implementation is to define the role of a central risk function. As we already discussed, this function will not manage risk itself, as its primary roles are risk identification and sharing. Figure 6-4 gives an overview of the process.

LEVITT CRIME RATES—RISK IDENTIFICATION

Steven Levitt understands the importance of risk identification. In the mid-1990s, murder rates were high in the United States. Sociologists and criminologists were predicting spiraling increases in the rate of homicide. Instead, the rate dropped dramatically between 1995 and 2003. The same was true for rates of assault, automobile thefts, and other crimes. As an example, the number of murders in New York City dropped from 2,200 a year in the early 1990s to 600 in 2003. Levitt investigated the causes of the declines.

FIGURE 6-4. IMPLEMENTING A CENTRAL RISK FUNCTION.

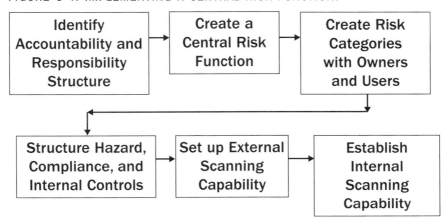

According to Levitt, the decline came from the 1973 decision of the U.S. Supreme Court in *Roe vs. Wade* that allowed legal abortions. He cited studies showing that children born into adverse family environments are statistically more likely to become criminals. He used statistical techniques to control factors such as gun control laws, rising economy, and police activity.

Lesson Learned: When implementing ERM, we should be careful of assumptions and opinions. People think they know the source of risk even though they have inadequate information to make a correct decision to mitigate it.

ERM Knowledge Warehouse

We previously described an ERM knowledge warehouse as a decision support system. Now let us look at it in more detail to show how ERM is enhanced by a high-technology platform that can be queried by remote parties in a system controlled by passwords and authorizations.

The central risk function ensures the integrity of activities, keeps out unwanted visitors and messages, makes queries easily searchable by key words, and creates user-friendly structures and formats. As with the central risk function, we can visualize our effort. Figure 6-5 shows the process.

Answering Questions

A major ERM issue occurs when myriad questions pour forth from affected parties and units. In the Deloitte survey, 47 percent of respondents believed that it would be a moderate or significant challenge to measure and assess risk and to justify the time and cost of an ERM program. Almost as many saw the same challenge arising because people lack an understanding of the benefits of integrated risk management. Thirty-five percent saw obstacles from a lack of support among management, largely as a result of the difficulty of proving the business case.

The Deloitte study makes an insightful observation regarding what is effectively a catch-22 of ERM. Organizations must implement ERM to prove its value, but management often expects the value to be proven prior to implementation. This is a generic problem with any effort to prepare for the future or to prevent a loss before it happens. Organizations are often reactive. They see more value in prevention after a loss has occurred. If a program is implemented, particularly if it is costly or time consuming, and nothing happens, criticism will be immediate. Why did we waste that

FIGURE 6-5. IMPLEMENTING ERM.

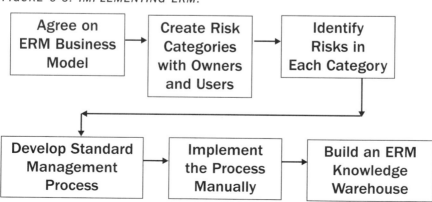

money? This cultural norm could be a major deterrent to ERM implementation.

LEVITT INCENTIVES—DAY CARE

Skepticism about ERM often arises because we do not create the right incentives to support the implementation. As an example of a wrong incentive, Steven Levitt describes a day care center that required parents to pick up children by 4:00 P.M. Ten percent of parents were late by 10 to 20 minutes. The day care center imposed a fine of $3 a day on late pickups. After using the fine system for a few months, the day care center ended it. Parents no longer paid a financial penalty for lateness. Did lateness grow, decline, or stay the same after each action? Levitt cited a study in Israel that showed that the percentage of parents who arrived late went up from 10 percent to 25 percent when the center imposed the fine. When the fine was eliminated, lateness stayed at 25 percent.

What happened? A financial incentive replaced a moral incentive. At $3, the fine was too small. Sixty dollars a month was relatively unimportant, a minor addition to the already high cost of day care. The small fine also showed that lateness was not very painful to the day care center. By imposing a fine, the center in effect told parents that they could pay the center to keep the child a little longer in school. Parents did not think they were doing any harm. If the day care center employees were being hurt, the original fine would have been larger.

Lesson Learned: Understanding incentives is critical when implementing ERM. Should an economic incentive—financial reward or penalty—encourage participation? Will a social incentive—recognition or avoiding disapproval—work better? How about a moral incentive so that individuals feel good about avoiding risks that harm others? Levitt reminds us of the importance of incentives in ERM implementation.

The skepticism about ERM does not come from a belief that all is well. The Deloitte study shows that half of all respondents believe that their companies are only somewhat prepared to manage mission critical risks. Sixty-four percent have a medium or low level of confidence in their company's preparedness for managing risks. We see that respondents believe they should do something to improve their positions with contingent risks and opportunities.

What is the answer to deal with skepticism and create incentives? One proposal is to recognize an *ERM premise*, an assumption or belief that shapes people's view of risk. We think we know what will work, what will not work, what should be done, and what should be avoided. As a start to implementation, we can share views of ERM premises. Figure 6-6 contains a checklist of questions to ask to see whether key players agree or disagree with several ERM premises or have mixed views on key issues. Resolving conflicting viewpoints early in the process greatly increases the chance for a successful implementation.

FIGURE 6-6. CHECKLIST OF ERM PREMISES.

- **Premise 1.** The chance for a successful enterprise risk management (ERM) implementation rises if we align our risk categories with our business model. If we disagree, how should we view risk categories?

- **Premise 2.** Coordinating risk in an ERM framework means creating a central risk function that shares information across the entity. If we disagree, do we have a need to share? If we agree, what mechanisms do we currently use, or which ones should be used in the future?

- **Premise 3.** An effective ERM program requires a risk knowledge warehouse. If we disagree, do we need to share the status of identified risks and risk mitigation? If we agree, how do we share our views today? How should it be done in the future?

- **Premise 4.** Subcategories of risk should be created in a hierarchical structure and shared in the risk knowledge warehouse or through another mechanism. If we disagree, do we have other ideas for creating a structure of risk categories? Do we need such a structure?

- **Premise 5.** A central risk committee should occasionally share its thoughts on risk. Do we need such a committee? If not, do we need any other sharing mechanism?

- **Premise 6.** The central risk function should have a defined relationship to the board of directors. Do we need a central risk function? If not, what should the board know, and how does it currently obtain that knowledge, and how should it do so in the future?

 ◆ **Premise 7.** Different management levels play different roles in risk management. Do we have an accountability structure at present? If not, what
 structure would work? Is such a structure even needed?

 ◆ **Premise 8.** All risk events should be evaluated using the same process.
 All risk managers should be trained in the process. If we disagree, are
 current processes adequate for addressing those disagreements? Do
 we need training on how to assess risk?

LEVITT REAL ESTATE—MOTIVATION FOR ERM

In the area of incentives, Steven Levitt addresses one hidden motivation
of a real estate agent who agrees to sell the home of another person.
Suppose a house has a market value ranging from $400,000 to
$450,000. The low number is achievable in 30 days, while the higher
number is possible if the house remains on the market for 180 days. The
agent's commission is 6 percent, which will be divided into four parts
(25% each) among the two real estate companies representing the
buyer and seller and the two individual agents. Levitt searched for an
understanding of the economic incentive for the owner and the agent.

  Levitt believes the owner has an incentive to wait. The agent has an
incentive to sell quickly and move on.

	Price	Commission	Agent Share
In 1 month	400,000	24,000	6,000
In 6 months	450,000	27,000	6,750

The agent loses $750 on a one-month sale but can use the next five
months to make sales that can net $6,000 a month. The owner loses
$47,000, the $50,000 of the higher price minus the $3,000 increase in
the commission.

Lesson Learned: Self-serving behavior drives actions. Risk mitigation
strategies work only if individuals see them as achieving their goals.
Remember this concept when implementing ERM.

Conclusion

The discussion in this chapter shows that ERM promises a number
of contributions to the company's ability to manage risk, but the

implementation process must be tailored to specific organizations and must fit within their cultures. ERM implementation starts with an examination of certain premises and considers whether most people are on the same page. If they are, the program can be introduced and vetted by comparing its benefits to the time and cost it requires. The organization can expect skepticism and resistance. With or without ERM, organizations need a central risk function and accountability by risk owners. Further, they should share risk information on a high-tech platform with a visual approach to understanding risk. This will be the focus of upcoming chapters.

Part Two

ERM TECHNOLOGY

IN APRIL 2007, Bob Morrell came up to the author at a reception during the annual conference of the Risk and Insurance Management Society (RIMS). He had been reading the "Emerging Risk Strategies" column in *Business Insurance* magazine and was interested in the new paradigm for ERM that was unfolding. He asked the author if we could build the ERM knowledge warehouse that was so prominent in the discussions of a new ERM framework.

For the next year, we worked together—Bob and his people had incredible computer and Internet skills accompanied by a keen understanding of risk. My role was to represent the risk manager—the user of the system who wants to understand risk as well as to document mitigation strategies. Forming a company called Riskonnect™, Bob brought the concept of visual risk clusters to life. For the first time, we could see and manipulate risk relationships. We could also see the backup information that showed previous and current risk mitigation attempts and plans for dealing with interrelated risks in the future. The tool was a significant advance on spreadsheets and earlier approaches to understanding risk and risk relationships.

In Part Two, we present the Riskonnect™ visual risk cluster tool, which illustrates five different risk evaluations. First, we have a generic view (Chapter 7), using no technology but setting up the subsequent discussions. Then, using Riskonnect™, with permission, we structure a variety of risk categories, showing risk owners, risk relationships, and how an ERM warehouse helps us understand complex exposures. Chapter 8 shows the value of visual risk clusters using an energy company as an example. Chapter 9 uses a similar company to illustrate tagging visual risks. Chapter 10 broadens the use of technology using an application with the Airbus A380 project. Chapter 11 completes the technology illustrations switching the focus to the launch of a new product. The ERM knowledge warehouse and visual risk cluster technology is a cutting-edge and innovative technology. This part should present an interesting journey for the reader.

CHAPTER 7

VISUAL RISK CLUSTERS

A cluster is a number of similar things that occur together. An integral part of our approach to ERM is to encourage visual risk clustering. We align risks with the business model, bring them together into clusters at each level of a hierarchy, assign risk owners, and limit the number of categories assigned to each owner. We support the effort with technology, which we describe starting in Chapter 8.

Visual Risk Structure

A number of benefits accrue from a carefully designed risk cluster structure. For one thing, we limit the risk vision at each level. An owner can focus on critical risks and break them up into subrisks for lower-level owners. Second, we achieve accountability. Because the structure is linked to risk owners, the organization knows who is responsible for managing each risk. Third, risk owners can create visual representations to see the interaction among risks. Finally, we can provide documentation for the status of risk mitigation because risks are backed up by detailed strategies, assessments, activities, and risk history.

A sophisticated risk-mapping program can now be a component of ERM. It can display a dashboard with colors indicating the mitigation status. Red can identify critical risks with deficient mitigation. Other colors can show risks that need significant or minor improvement, risks that are fully under control, and risks that are under review and that have not yet been evaluated.

We can start risk clustering at any level in an organization. The starting point becomes the highest level of exposure. After identifying a limited number of subrisks, we align them with the business model and assign risk owners. Risks and risk relationships can be visualized at different levels. Figure 7-1 shows the generic format for a risk cluster. Red has the most impact, while green has the least.

The technology allows visual relationships to be supported by quantitative and qualitative documentation. This includes mathematical data, narrative descriptions, qualitative assessments, likely impact, and alternative strategies. It shows the history of risk mitigation, information on prior or similar risks, and comments by risk owners and others.

FIGURE 7-1. CLUSTER TOOL.

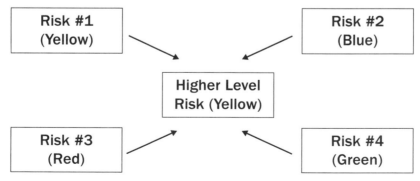

Visual Cluster Versus Spreadsheets

Many ERM programs have been built using an electronic spread-sheet. Figure 7-2 shows an alphabetic listing of risks from an electronic spreadsheet used by a company with an ERM program. The weaknesses of unclustered risks are immediately visible. They include impact (What risks are important?), relationships (How do risks interact?), and accountability (Who is responsible for mitigation and documentation? Where are the details, so that managers at different levels and with varying responsibilities can contribute to risk strategies?).

FIGURE 7-2. SPREADSHEET RISK LIST.

- Administration Risk
- Business support Risk
- Capital budgeting Risk
- Capital structure Risk
- Communications Risk
- Compliance Risk
- Credit Risk
- Design Risk
- Distribution Risk
- Efficiency Risk
- Financial Reporting Risk
- Finance Risk
- Information Systems Risk
- Key Initiative Risk
- Marketing Risk
- Needs Risk
- Performance Risk
- Portfolio Risk
- Pricing Risk
- Process Risk
- Production Risk

- Records management Risk
- Supply Risk
- Technology Risk
- Valuation Risk
- Volume Risk

Generic Visual Risk Cluster

To overcome the weakness of unclustered risks, we build visual risk clusters. As an example, suppose senior executives are interested in critical risks in Asian and European operations, production, marketing, finance, and in key initiatives. Figure 7-3 shows a possible visual risk cluster.

The CFO, the risk owner for the financial cluster, has identified subcategories in Figure 7-4. One of them is a missed revenue target, a failure to achieve budgeted revenues. The corporate controller is the risk owner for the revenue target. Figure 7-5 shows subrisks that can cause the company to miss its revenue target, including a disruption of the supply chain. Notice that we have now added color to identify the impact of each risk.

Continuing down the chain, Figure 7-6 shows that the controller has assigned the purchasing manager to act as risk owner for supply chain disruption. A subrisk is supplier concentration, a

FIGURE 7-3. LEVEL 1 RISK CATEGORIES.

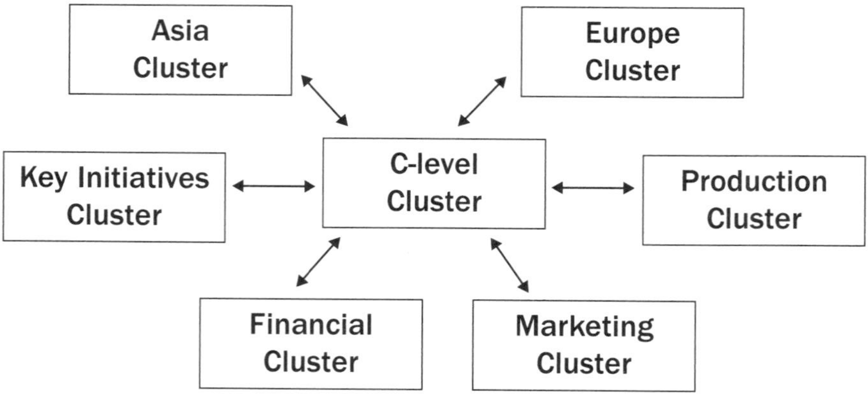

FIGURE 7-4. FINANCIAL RISK CLUSTER.

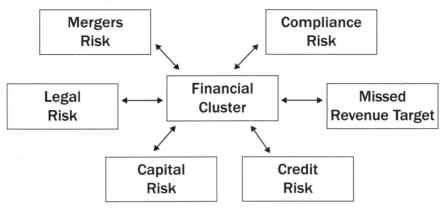

FIGURE 7-5. MISSED-REVENUE RISK CLUSTER.

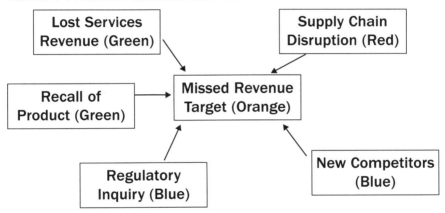

situation in which a limited number of suppliers provide a large percentage of a key component. In discussions with production managers, the purchasing manager learns that an interruption to the supply of three key components will have a major impact on production. As shown in Figure 7-7, these components are memory chips, controller boards, and packaging materials. The purchasing manager also learns that many components are produced in China. Even though no single component is critical, a shutdown of supplies from China would be a serious business disruption.

FIGURE 7-6. SUPPLY CHAIN DISRUPTION RISK CLUSTER.

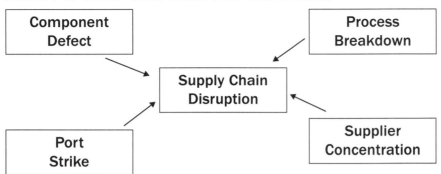

FIGURE 7-7. SUPPLIER CONCENTRATION RISK CLUSTER.

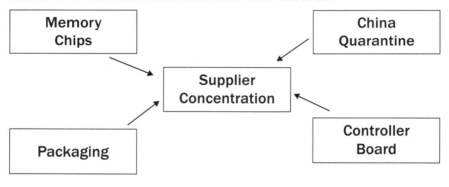

Even though production is now involved in the discussion, the purchasing manager is still the risk owner. Investigating the situation with controller boards, the purchasing manager discovers that Samsung, Lenovo, and Cisco are the main suppliers, as shown in Figure 7-8. Is this an excessive concentration?

The purchasing manager keeps digging and learns that 40 percent of controller boards are provided by Cisco. This raises a red flag that will carry all the way up to supply chain disruption. As the risk owner, the purchasing manager alerts the organization of the exposure and works with others to develop and implement a mitigation strategy.

After arranging the hierarchy, we can now develop composite

FIGURE 7-8. CONTROLLER-BOARD-DISRUPTION RISK CLUSTER.

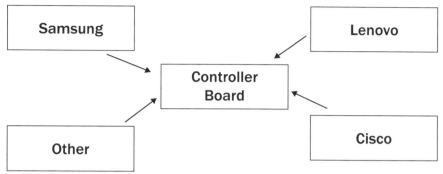

views that show other linkages or reveal multiple impacts on a single exposure and use other risk-mapping techniques to understand exposures. Figure 7-9 shows a tagging of risks that enables an analyst to see details of supply chain disruption. It also reveals how that exposure affects other risks of failing to achieve a revenue target. Figure 7-10 shows a second example of tagging, focusing on the concentration of suppliers, and, more specifically, the controller board concentration.

FIGURE 7-9. TAGGING MISSED REVENUE RISKS.

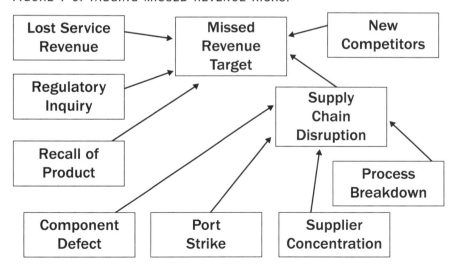

FIGURE 7-10. SUPPLIER CONCENTRATION AND CONTROLLER BOARD RISK CLUSTERS.

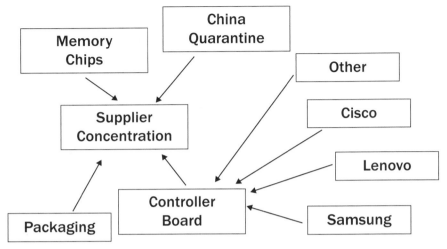

Conclusion

Comparing the list of exposures at the start of this discussion with the visual risk cluster tool, we recognize that a graphic presentation of risk in a hierarchical structure significantly enhances our understanding of enterprise risks and their relationships.

AIG Visual Risk Cluster Case

A different view of the role of visual risk clusters comes from the American International Group (AIG), which faced a full-blown liquidity crisis on September 15, 2008. Was this an ERM failure? Let us examine the situation.

Historically, AIG had a business model with three major components:

1. **Sale of Insurance Policies.** As an insurer, AIG reimbursed organizations and individuals that suffered financial losses. It provided significant levels of liability coverage and defended policyholders when they were sued.

2. **Asset Management.** AIG borrowed money and used it to purchase assets needed by clients to conduct their business. As an example, it borrowed money to purchase a plane and showed the asset and debt on its balance sheet. Then, it leased the plane to an airline that did not want to show the debt on its own balance sheet.

3. **Smoothing of Earnings.** AIG used its financial strength to reduce the volatility of net income for clients. It used increasingly complex alternative risk transfer mechanisms, such as credit derivatives.

Under the leadership of former chairman and chief executive Maurice Greenberg, the model worked well for many years. AIG aggressively evaluated and accepted risks that other financial institutions considered to be too risky. The company used its financial muscle to develop risk transfer products beyond the capabilities of smaller or weaker institutions. AIG executives developed creative and profitable solutions for clients, thus creating a successful culture that rewarded success and punished failure.

The Start of Problems

To understand AIG and its liquidity struggles, which moved steadily over a few months in 2008 from a cash shortfall of $80 billion to above $150 billion, we start with conservative insurance accounting. Underwriters recommend insurance products and standards by which to evaluate risks. Insurers forecast the likely level of losses from insured risks. Regulators allow only the most safe and liquid assets to be shown on balance sheets. New business, profits, and growth are restricted by a highly conservative calculation of capital.

The next problem arose because insurers and reinsurers lacked sufficient capital to handle large insured losses, such as Hurricane Katrina ($60 billion); Hurricane Andrew ($23 billion); the September 11, 2001, terrorist attacks ($70 billion); and the Northridge, California, earthquake ($18 billion). These figures, compiled by the Insurance Information Institute, represent 2007 dollars.

The assets of insurance companies, commonly expressed as reserves and capital, make up a small percentage of the exposures. The solution to catastrophic risk was to partner with global capital markets, with more than $50 trillion in capital in 2008. The number was fairly large even when compared with U.S. housing market values of $30 trillion. AIG got into the game, adding to its business model the sale and guarantee of derivatives—securities whose value derives from another security or asset. Also called alternative risk transfer (ART) and risk securitization, these transfer underwriting risks from the insurance company to the capital markets, in the following ways:

- ❦ **Financial Securities.** These can be sold in pieces, or tranches, to many investors. In normal times, they are relatively liquid.

- ❦ **Contingencies.** Investors agree to waive principal repayment if a contingent loss occurs.

- ❦ **Interest Rates.** The securities offer relatively high returns to holders of the portions of the security. This is the case because the principal is exposed to loss if the contingency occurs.

- ❦ **Principal Repayment.** Investors receive a return of the principal, either periodically or at maturity, if no contingency occurs.

An example of ART is the catastrophe bond. Assume that an insurer faces a $500 million loss if a hurricane damages insured property in Texas. The insurer creates a two-year catastrophe bond, slices it up into parts, called tranches, and sells the tranches to investors. The insurer places the cash received in a safe investment yielding 6 percent while paying investors 13 percent. How can that make sense?

The answer is that the insurance company augments its own earnings by charging premiums to policyholders in Texas who purchase hurricane protection insurance. Now the insurer is not at risk for the $500 million of coverage it provides. Investors agree to forfeit their investment if a hurricane causes insured losses in Texas. For two years, investors collect interest even as they hope no hurricane hits Texas. If no loss occurs, they receive $500 million at maturity. If a hurricane causes a $300 million insured loss, they receive only $200 million. The balance is used by the insurer to pay claims.

Two things occur with catastrophe bonds and similar insurance securities. First, security holders earn profits by protecting insurers against a natural or other disaster. Second, the security is actually a form of insurance. The money is held in escrow and is available to pay losses if they occur. AIG and others were not likely to get into trouble with cat bonds and other insurance derivatives.

The risk level changes dramatically when insurers move into noninsurance securitization. These securities are attractive to investors because they offer above-market returns and have a low correlation to other investments that move in tandem with interest rates, inflation, and economic optimism. The combination of high return and low correlation diversifies a financial portfolio—at least in theory.

Three specific noninsurance securities offered by AIG can help us understand what happened:

1. **Guaranteed Investment Contracts (GICs).** Suppose a municipality approves a project to build a new school and issues a bond to finance construction. It sells the bond to investors and deposits the proceeds in a low-rate interest account. It buys a GIC from an investment bank that ensures the return of principal when needed. The investment bank profits by investing the cash elsewhere at a higher rate of interest.

2. **Collateralized Debt Obligations.** Suppose an investor has a goal to diversify a financial portfolio. It purchases from an investment bank a security with 1,000 mortgages as collateral. An investment bank could have created the CDOs from nonmortgage assets, but subprime mortgages were the source of the financial crisis. The investor collects monthly mortgage payments and receives the remaining principal as homeowners repay the mortgages.

3. **Credit Default Swaps.** The CDOs that were just described play a large role in AIG's troubles. The investor who buys a CDO is concerned about the risk of default of the underlying loans. This would occur if homeowners were to default on their mort-

gages. To reduce the risk, the investment bank guarantees the monthly mortgage payments and the eventual repayment of principal. The investor pays the bank a fee for the guarantee, called a credit default swap.

AIG got into investment banking when it decided to offer non-insurance securitization. The derivatives offered high returns, growth, and no government regulation. The company did not have to maintain reserves or otherwise comply with statutory restrictions.

As the credit markets went into freefall in 2008, AIG was trapped in a liquidity squeeze. Municipalities, concerned about home mortgages, demanded funds immediately. Homeowners defaulted on mortgage payments, causing banks to foreclose on houses. Holders of AIG credit default swaps demanded their money. It was only after these events that AIG began to understand the full impact of its exposure, and sought a massive federal bailout.

Fortunately, governments around the world moved to stop foreclosures, provide liquidity, and offer guarantees to avoid collapse of the financial system. At the time of this writing, we do not know whether governments will succeed at restoring normalcy in the capital market. If it fails, AIG will still be in danger of collapse.

Role of Modern ERM

Let us move now to the linkage between AIG and ERM. No linkage existed previously. Early in 2008, Martin Sullivan, the CEO of AIG, assured investors and others that AIG had no exposure in a declining market for home mortgages. If AIG had an ERM knowledge warehouse, Mr. Sullivan could have seen the exposure, as shown in Figure 7-11. He would have been able to look right down the hierarchy, see the United Kingdom unit offering the swaps, and view the exposure and mitigation efforts. If he had had the view in 2005, the world might have avoided the 2008 financial crisis.

Lesson Learned: Risk can get complex, and we can fail to understand our exposure. A visual story supported by mitigation strategies and actions might help us identify an exposure before it becomes a crisis.

FIGURE 7-11. AIG VIEW IF IT HAD AN ERM KNOWLEDGE WAREHOUSE.

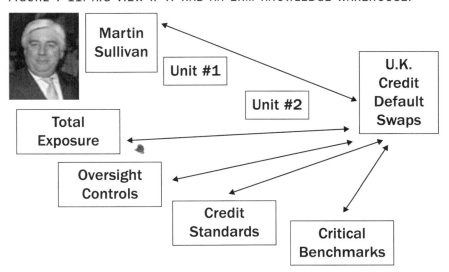

CHAPTER 8

VISUAL RISK— A HYPOTHETICAL CASE

RISK QUOTE: *A life spent making mistakes is not only more honorable but more useful than a life spent in doing nothing.*

—GEORGE BERNARD SHAW, IRISH PLAYWRIGHT

RISK QUOTE: *In the end, you're measured not by how much you undertake but by what you finally accomplish.*

—DONALD TRUMP, BUSINESSMAN

I n the previous chapters, we set up a hierarchical approach to ERM with risk owners, accountability, a high-tech platform, and visual risk clusters. Now we use the Riskonnect™ tool with Central Power and Light (CP&L), a thinly disguised major unregulated independent electricity producer. It is based on an energy company that has an extensive ERM program.

CP&L wants to be sure it is scanning externally for changing conditions and risk factors that might affect future production, sales, and technology. It wants to examine internal cultural and life cycle risks and structural weaknesses. It has decided to implement an ERM program to identify risks that impede sustainable competitive advantage. CP&L has provided certain directives for the initial

ERM implementation. The program should have a focus far broader than internal controls and compliance, should not involve elaborate quantitative models nor require the interviewing of a large number of employees, customers, or suppliers. It should identify broad risk categories, align them with the existing business model, assign risk owners, create subrisks, and bring the picture together visually, using the Riskonnect™ Visual Risk Cluster Tool.

CP&L Business Model

CP&L has three main subsidiaries. Central Fossil generates electricity for a wide range of commercial and residential customers, operating natural gas, coal, and oil-fired electricity-generating units. Central Nuclear also creates electricity, but the source of power is two nuclear generating stations. Central Energy Trading is a fast-moving and fast-response unit that buys and sells oil, coal, gas, and other commodities and trades in environmental credits. The unit connects electronically to the world, trades 24 hours a day, and seeks a reliable supply of oil, gas, and other commodities at market prices and in compliance with environmental regulations.

Although the structure has three operating units, CP&L does not see the organizational hierarchy as its business model. Essentially, the company conducts business by focusing on reliable, affordable, and uninterruptible electricity generation. These goals are affected by broad risks that make up the company's level 2 risk categories. These risks are concentrated in these areas:

- **Electricity Generation.** Risks from a mixture of oil, gas, coal, and nuclear capabilities. Prices and availability of commodities and fluctuating levels of production and consumption must be carefully managed.
- **Nuclear Future.** The company believes the United States will need greater nuclear capability in the future. CP&L wants close scrutiny of risks that will block it from adding new nuclear generating facilities or extending the life of current nuclear power plants.
- **Regulatory.** Public utilities are regulated, and the level of regulation is increasing. An apparently minor piece of legislation or

a directive from a government agency can cause serious problems for the conduct of business.

- **Financial.** The company is capital intensive. It must concern itself with long-term adequacy of capitalization of facilities and operations. It must monitor cash flow, both from the viewpoint of its obligations to its suppliers and with respect to collections from its customers.

- **Technology.** The rapid march of technology changes everything from electricity generation and alternative energy sources to modifications in telecommunications, data mining, analytical tools, and the Internet. Technology is a stand-alone category that presents exposures and opportunities in electricity generation, marketing, and commodity trading.

- **Business Disruption.** Many things can disrupt the supply of electricity, including local storms that affect facilities, distant events that disrupt suppliers or partners, and unexpected developments in various areas of the world. The company wants full attention to the adequacy of backup systems, desired redundancy, and contingency planning.

ERM Project

CP&L brought in a consulting firm to undertake a pilot ERM project. The firm interviewed the C-suite officers and made a list of their concerns (30 days). It scanned for external risk factors that might affect production, marketing, finance, and technology (60 days). It identified cultural, product life cycle, structural, and other internal concerns (60 days). Working with the consulting firm, management identified the critical risks, shown in Figure 8-1. CP&L corporate is level 1, and level 2 has the risks aligned with the business model. The risk categories are color-coded from red (most in need of mitigation) to green (relatively under control).

BACKUP INFORMATION

CP&L recognizes the importance of backing up visual risks with details, mitigation strategies, and expected outcomes. The backup support can be manual, real-time, or any combination of information that shows details about a risk. Figures 8-2 and 8-3 shows

FIGURE 8-1. CP&L LEVELS 1 AND 2 RISK CATEGORIES.

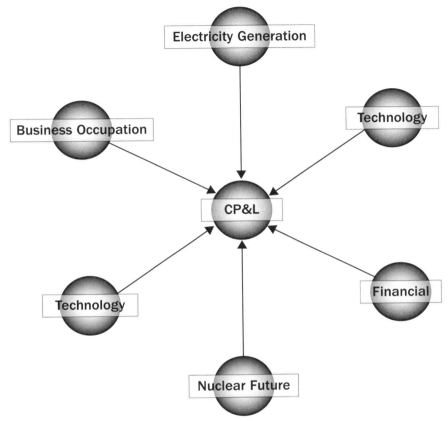

the backup provided by Riskonnect™. The tool is automated and integrated so that visual risks are linked to documentation of their status and are supported by notes, attachments, open activities, and history.

CP&L can take the next step to identify subrisks at level 3. Figure 8-4 shows business disruption, technology, financial, regulatory, electricity generation, and the future of nuclear power.

BROADENING THE RISK PICTURE

A high-tech tool can be designed to allow restrictive views of risk relationships or expansive views. Figure 8-5 shows levels 1, 2 and 3 risks in a single view.

FIGURE 8-2. RISK DETAIL, METRICS, RISK MITIGATION, AND OUTCOMES FOR CP&L.

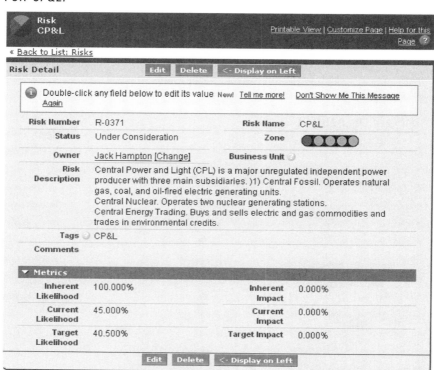

ALTERNATIVE VIEW

Figure 8-6 shows a *risk profile,* a graphic representation of a risk, displayed against X- and Y-axes. The axes can represent different variables. Frequency and impact are the most common set of axes, so the Riskonnect™ tool uses frequency and impact with an adjustable log rhythmic scale.

Alternatively, risk and return could be the axes. Risk, as the

FIGURE 8-3. BACKUP INFORMATION.

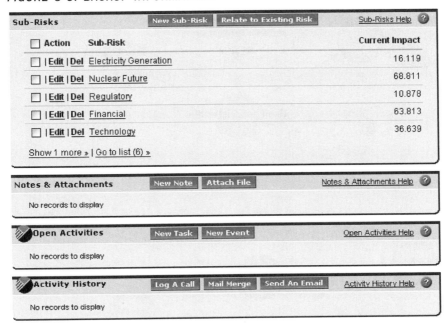

independent variable, would be on the X-axis, with likely or required return on the Y-axis. Finally, control and impact might be used. The level of mitigation could be displayed on the X-axis, with unmitigated impact plotted on the Y-axis.

NEXT STEPS

After an ERM system is installed and supported by a high-tech platform, an organization can spread the program across the entity. Features that can be incorporated into a growing and maturing system include:

- **Expansion.** This is the migration of risk categories to units and initiatives not included in the original implementation. The organization adds subrisks of sister entities or lower units.

- **Filtering and Tagging.** The system can add the capability to restrict visual representations of related risks and the number of risk linkages on the screen in a single view.

FIGURE 8-4. LEVELS 2 AND 3 SUBRISK CATEGORIES.

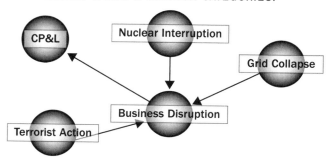

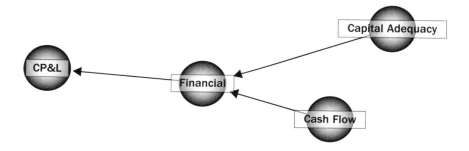

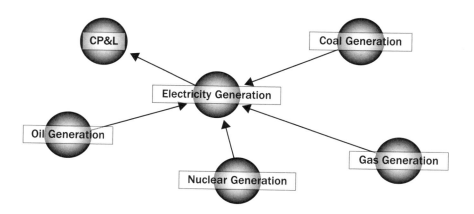

FIGURE 8-4. (CONTINUED)

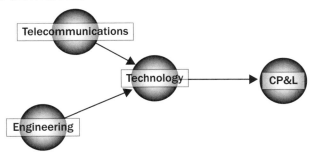

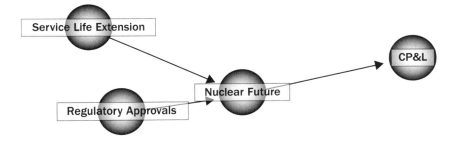

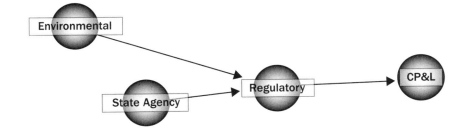

- **Supporting Documentation.** The organization can attach documents, integrated systems, and other data to provide details and clarity of risk mitigation activities.

- **Report Writers.** The central risk function can work with units to create standard and customized risk management reports.

FIGURE 8-5. LEVELS 1, 2, AND 3 RISK CATEGORIES.

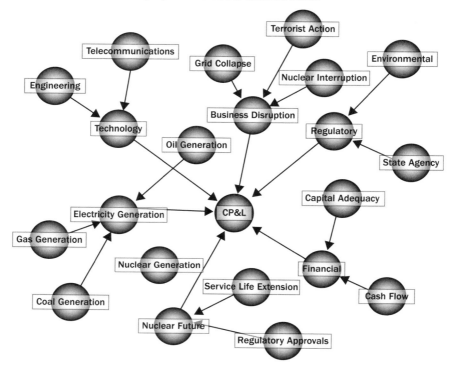

- ◈ **Collaboration.** The system can create periodic communications that share risk strategies and the status of mitigation efforts.
- ◈ **Presentations.** The central risk function can create PowerPoint and other visual graphics for risk management presentations to senior management, the board of directors, rating agencies, investors, and others.

As the organization grows in maturity with its ERM program and the technology to support it, it can provide information not previously available to key managers. This is the essence of successful ERM, as it provides both consistency and flexibility in the acceptance of enterprise risk and pursuit of opportunity.

FIGURE 8-6. RISK PROFILE PLOTTED ON TWO AXES.

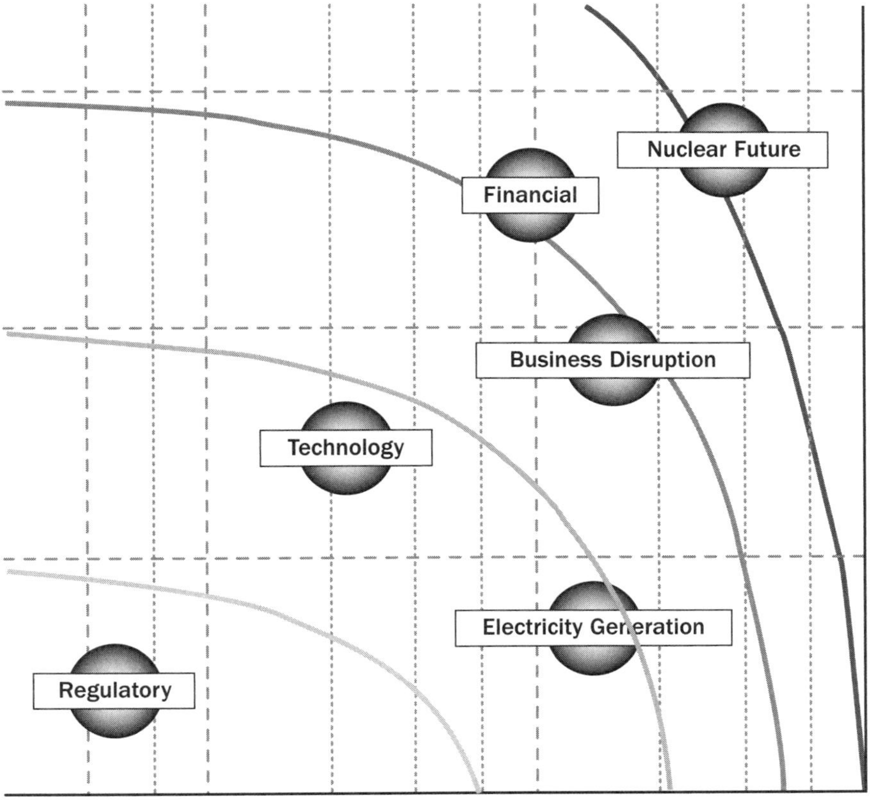

CHAPTER 9

TAGGING RISK—AN EXAMPLE

RISK QUOTE: *The safety lecture continues. "In the unlikely event of a water landing . . ." Well, what exactly is a water landing? Am I mistaken, or does this sound somewhat similar to CRASHING INTO THE OCEAN?*

—GEORGE CARLIN, COMEDIAN

RISK QUOTE: *Nothing can stop the man with the right mental attitude from achieving his goal; nothing on earth can help the man with the wrong mental attitude.*

—THOMAS JEFFERSON, U.S. PRESIDENT

In the previous chapter, we saw the basics of a high-tech platform. In this chapter, we show how the system is enhanced if it allows us to tag risks. *Tagging* is a process of identifying a series of interrelated risks and looking only at the "tagged" risks. Tagging removes the clutter of multiple levels of exposure. It is the technique used in the discussion of AIG and credit default swaps in Chapter 7. Now let us take a look at tagging using the Riskonnect™ technology.

Our example is CP&L once again, but let us change the name to avoid confusion. We are working with an environmental project. As shown in Figure 9-1, our company, now called Public Power and Light (PP&L), has the same top business units as CP&L.

Instead of looking through the business units, we focus on a

FIGURE 9-1. PP&E TOP-LEVEL STRUCTURE.

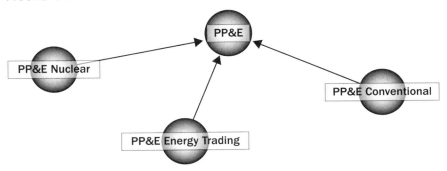

key initiative critical to the future of electricity generation. PP&E wants to build a new nuclear power plant, one with possible wetlands impact. Pollution problems could derail nuclear approvals and even interrupt other aspects of energy trading. Although it presents a critical risk, the key initiative is far down the hierarchical structure. At the same time, the pollution issue is important to top management. The CEO and others want to see details on the status of the initiative.

The project is assigned to Energy Trading, and the head of the unit is identified as the risk owner. Accountability is delegated to subrisk owners in a hierarchical structure as follows:

- **Energy Trading.** This unit retains top-level responsibility for identifying risks that the company will not be allowed to operate existing conventional or nuclear facilities or have a breakdown in government relations when seeking to build new nuclear generating facilities. It oversees relationships with government agencies.

- **Federal and State Agency Liaison.** This unit has day-to-day responsibility for managing often-conflicting federal agency environmental regulations or interpreting existing regulations.

- **EPA Liaison.** This unit handles relationships with the federal Environmental Protection Agency.

- **Water, Air, and Ground Pollution Departments.** These three units work specifically on compliance with EPA environmental regulations in the areas of cooling, water usage, discharge into the air, wetlands, porous surfaces, and related exposures. One manager is responsible for each area of water, air, and ground pollution.

Every one of these levels has a risk owner responsible for identifying exposures, sharing them with authorized parties, and mitigating water, air, and ground pollution risks that would endanger the ability of PP&E to produce electricity. In addition to the risk owners, other line and staff managers have interests in EPA environmental risks. They include the CEO and CFO, who seek transparency and accountability under Sarbanes-Oxley requirements. Rating agencies require risk programs to achieve favorable ratings on debt issues. The internal auditor is responsible for monitoring compliance with company policies and directives. The risk manager must present the wetlands exposure to insurance companies as part the purchase of liability coverage.

All interested parties can become part of the ERM structure with EPA risks, but their interests are specific. When checking the status of the key initiative, the CEO does not want to see other projects. Figure 9-2 shows a visual risk cluster from the CEO down

FIGURE 9-2. RISKS FROM THE TOP TO EPA.

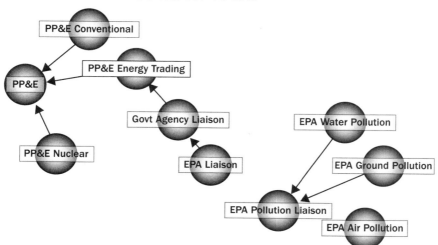

to the three departments handling pollution. It is tagged so that the subrisks at the levels of government and EPA liaison are suppressed. The CEO can go directly to documentation at the EPA pollution level.

The common question to all parties is "What is happening to mitigate risk? What are the plans, activities, and timetable?" Figure 9-3 shows the ground pollution mitigation, which includes two University of Michigan studies, an environmental compliance study, and a scheduled meeting. Over time, a complete history of risk activities and mitigation will be created and stored in one place, where it will be accessible to authorized users who can open and read supporting documentation. Figure 9-4 is the entry into the University of Michigan impact study.

Lesson Learned: The story of Public Power and Light shows the power of ERM when it focuses on important risks or opportunities and makes them visible to interested parties. New technology can facilitate collaboration and provide new tools for understanding and managing risk.

FIGURE 9-3. GROUND POLLUTION MITIGATION BACKUP.

Notes & Attachments			New Note	Attach File	View All	Notes & Atta
Action	**Type**	**Title**			**Last Modified**	
Edit | Del | View	Attachment	Univ of Michigan Impact Study.doc			5/30/2008 9:49 AM	
Edit | Del | View	Attachment	Univ of Mich Impact Study Data.xls			5/30/2008 9:48 AM	
Edit | Del	Note	Environmental Compliance Study (December 2006)			5/30/2008 9:45 AM	

Open Activities			New Task	New Event		Open
Action	**Subject**	**Name**	**Task**	**Due Date**	**Status**	**Priority**
Edit | Del	Meeting	John Hampton		7/24/2008 All Day		

FIGURE 9-4. REACHING DOWN INTO IMPACT STUDY.

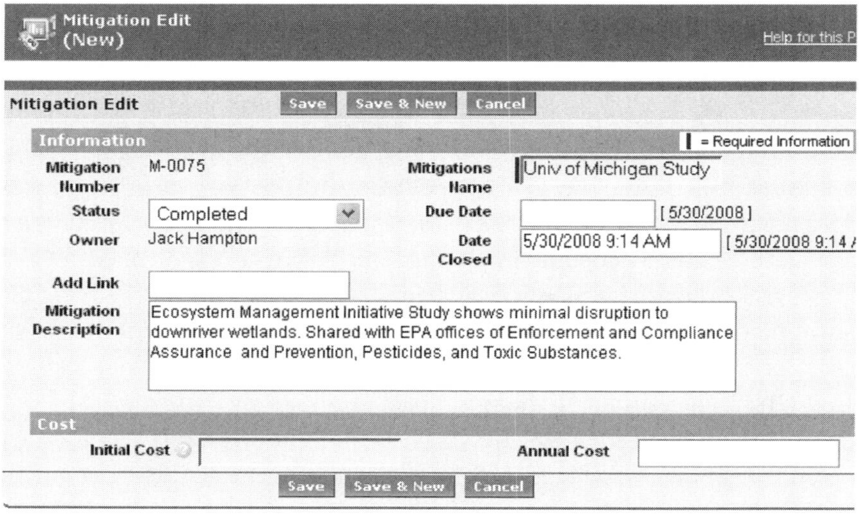

Mitigation Edit (New)	Help for this P

Mitigation Edit   [Save] [Save & New] [Cancel]

Information   ▌ = Required Information

Mitigation Number	M-0075	Mitigations Name	Univ of Michigan Study
Status	Completed ⌄	Due Date	[5/30/2008]
Owner	Jack Hampton	Date Closed	5/30/2008 9:14 AM [5/30/2008 9:14 A
Add Link			
Mitigation Description	Ecosystem Management Initiative Study shows minimal disruption to downriver wetlands. Shared with EPA offices of Enforcement and Compliance Assurance and Prevention, Pesticides, and Toxic Substances.		

Cost

| Initial Cost ◌ | | Annual Cost | |

[Save] [Save & New] [Cancel]

CHAPTER 10

AIRBUS A380 JUMBO JET

RISK QUOTE: *Don't worry about your heart; it will last you as long as you live.*

—W. C. FIELDS, COMEDIAN AND MOVIE STAR

RISK QUOTE: *They that are on their guard and appear ready to receive their adversaries are in much less danger of being attacked than the supine, secure and negligent.*

—BENJAMIN FRANKLIN, SCIENTIST, PUBLISHER, AND DIPLOMAT

EADS Levels 1 and 2

In our discussion in this chapter, we provide still another example of the power of an ERM high-tech platform. The Airbus A380 is the project under consideration, and the time is 2006. Airbus was concerned about exposures to completion of development and launch of the A380 jumbo jet. The company had implemented a key risk management initiative, known as the Power8 program. Figure 10-1 shows EADS, the parent company of Airbus, as level 1, along with four other operating units that managed their own risks.

FIGURE 10-1. EADS TOP VIEW OF RISK CATEGORIES.

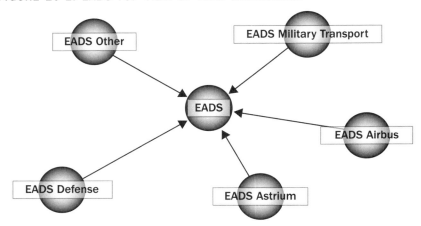

Airbus View, Levels 2 and 3

All by itself, the A380 jumbo jet key initiative was a major exposure to Airbus in terms of development, marketing, and operations. Figure 10-2 shows four Airbus subrisk categories aligned with the Airbus business model. It also shows the A380 key initiative, which structurally could report to Airbus Aircraft but which, because of its importance, was moved up in the business model.

A380 View, Levels 3, 4, and 5

Airbus implemented a Power8 risk management program to deal with rising problems of development and sale of the A380. Figure 10-3 shows subrisks identified in the Power8 structure. Aircraft structure covers risks of setting up efficient aircraft production, integrating the complex supply chain, and improving and stream-lining assembly of the giant plane once mass production begins. Financial operations involves risks such as handling cash and managing cash flow, shortening the development time to full production, and solving problems in manufacturing and operations.

The figure shows something else, namely the intervention of ERM by teams of MBA candidates at Saint Peter's College. In 2006, they studied the Power8 program and observed that it was omit-

FIGURE 10-2. AIRBUS RISK CATEGORIES.

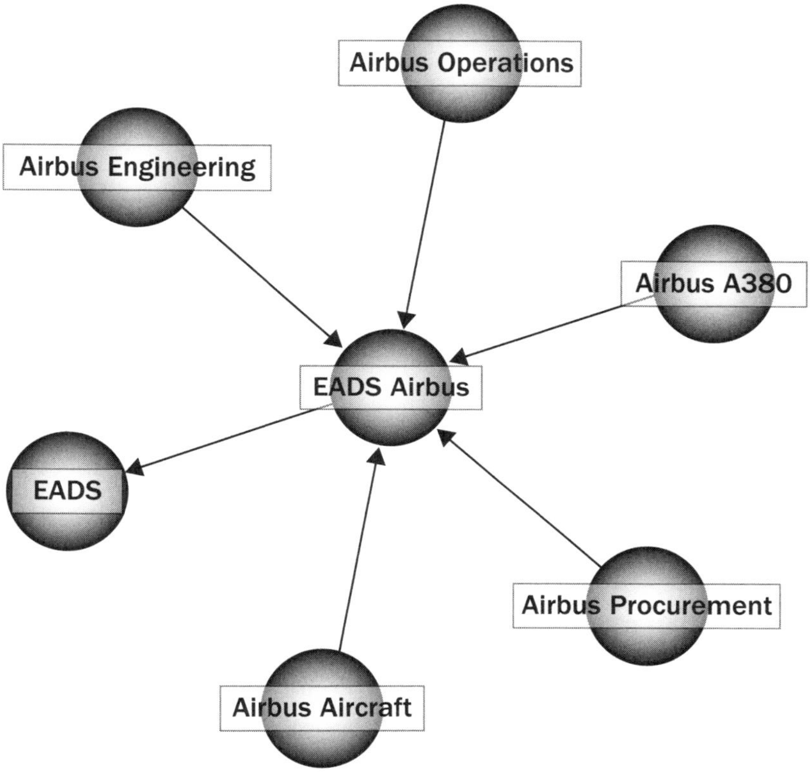

ting a risk category that should have been visible at the level of A380 subrisks. In formal presentations in class, they made the argument that a key success factor in the sale of the jumbo jet would be the existence of a large number of airports capable of efficiently handling the plane. This exposure needed greater visibility at EADS and Airbus. Thus, Power8 should add an airport risk category to the first level of visibility, as has been done in Figure 10-3.

Airport Risk, Levels 4 and 5

The Saint Peter's teams went further, developing their own view of subrisks in the newly created airport category. They identified four subrisks, shown in Figure 10-4. Emergencies are an obvious

FIGURE 10-3. A380 POWER8 RISK CATEGORIES, REVISED.

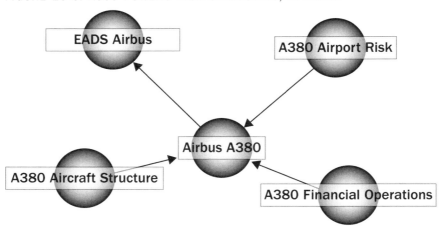

FIGURE 10-4. AIRPORT RISKS.

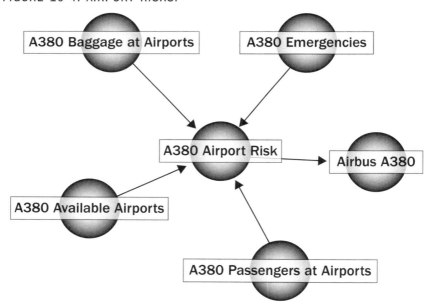

risk. Airlines and airports that accept the A380 would need new procedures to deal with unexpected or dangerous situations because of the large number and concentration of passengers in the terminal or loaded on a single plane. Baggage and passenger handling are two other exposures. Most airports lacked the capability to move efficiently a large volume of baggage between the terminal and a single passenger plane. Since the A380 has double-decker doors, airports might have to modify physical facilities to load and unload passengers efficiently. A final problem was the availability of an adequate network of airports to handle the plane. In 2006, only eight airports in the world proclaimed themselves ready to handle the large aircraft. The absence of many alternative sites at which to take off and land would reduce the flexibility of aircraft operations and limit the ability of the plane to fly alternative routes in response to market conditions This situation could encourage airlines to delay orders for the plane until more airports created the capability to handle it.

Available Airports, Levels 5 & 6

One team extended the analysis to two subrisks under the number of available airports. Two risk owners were needed. One needed to negotiate with airports to encourage investments in infrastructure and upgraded systems to handle jumbo planes. The other needed to work with the airlines on efforts to convince carriers to upgrade baggage and passenger handling capabilities. Figure 10-5 completes the hierarchical structure aligned with the business model.

Levels 1 to 6 Without Tagging

We are now all the way down the structure to the airport negotiations. Figure 10-6 shows all the risk relationships and allows us see the entire picture through six levels. The good news is that we see everything. The bad news is clutter. There is too much detail.

Levels 1 to 6 with Tagging

Figure 10-7 corrects the clutter problem by showing a tagged view. We can still see the linkage from EADS through Airbus, the A380,

FIGURE 10-5. AVAILABLE AIRPORTS SUBRISK CATEGORIES.

and airport risk. We can focus on airport and airline negotiations, far down the list but critically important to success.

Supporting Visual Risks

As in our previous Riskonnect™ illustrations, we can combine clusters with backup documentation. For A380 risk, Figure 10-8 shows details on risks and subrisks, Figure 10-9 displays mitigations and outcomes, and Figure 10-10, shows access to notes, attachments, open activities, and activity history.

Lesson Learned: Even with a high complexity of risks, as reflected in the A380 project, we can use modern technology to visualize risk relationships and support decision making with documentation.

FIGURE 10-6. CLUTTERED VIEW OF SIX LEVELS OF RISK.

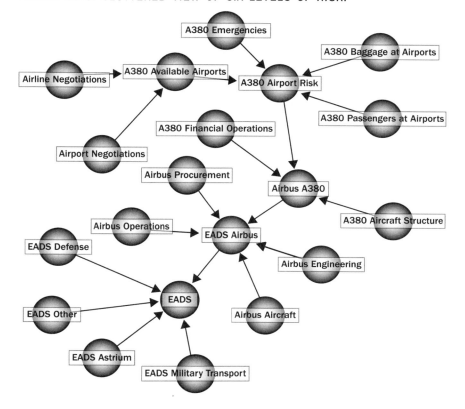

FIGURE 10-7. TAGGED VIEW OF SIX HIERARCHICAL LEVELS.

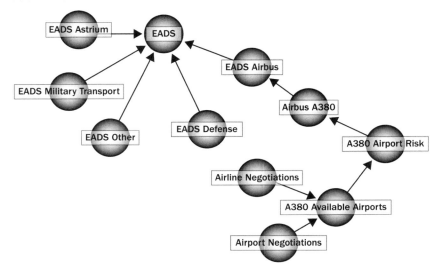

FIGURE 10-8. RISK DETAILS AND SUBRISKS.

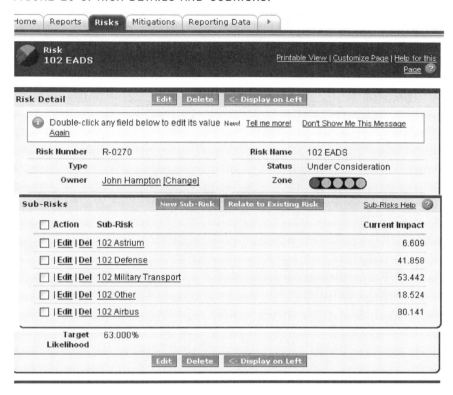

FIGURE 10-9. MITIGATIONS AND OUTCOMES.

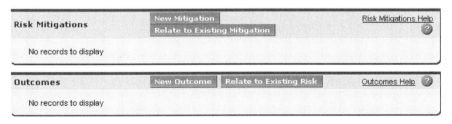

FIGURE 10-10. NOTES, ATTACHMENTS, OPEN ACTIVITIES, AND HISTORY.

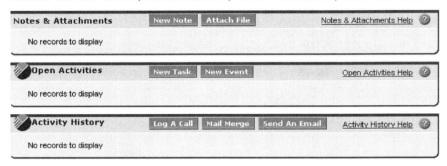

CHAPTER 11

PRODUCT LAUNCH APPLICATION

RISK QUOTE: *You got to be careful if you don't know where you're going, because you might not get there.*

— YOGI BERRA, BASEBALL PLAYER

RISK QUOTE: *I could tell that my parents hated me. My bath toys were a toaster and a radio.*

— RODNEY DANGERFIELD, COMEDIAN

Establishing a hierarchical ERM system gives us a tool to address projects using the same philosophy as we would with a key initiative. The visual risk cluster tool of Riskonnect™ shows us that ERM is quite flexible. To demonstrate such capability, in this chapter we apply ERM to a product launch evaluation. The discussion builds on a December 2007 *Harvard Business Review* article titled "Managing Risk and Reward in an Innovation Portfolio."

The launch of a new product or service can be a high-risk venture. One exposure lies in the development of the product. A second involves the identification or creation of a market. A third occurs from the capital needed to support the product until cash flow turns positive. A fourth lies in the possibility of theft of intellectual property. These separate risks can be brought together in an ERM analysis. Figure 11-1 shows them visually.

FIGURE 11-1. PRODUCT LAUNCH RISKS.

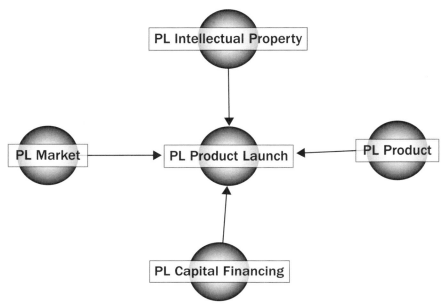

Market Risk

Figure 11-2 identifies six factors that affect market risk. Customer behavior comes first. Will customers behave like, something like, or differently from existing customers? Next, we ask whether brand recognition will be a major asset, a minor asset, or have no value at all. Sales capability is next: Should sales activities be largely identical to, similar to, or different from current efforts? Fourth, we are concerned about new competitors. Do we understand, understand to some degree, or have no knowledge of likely competitor behavior and intentions? Fifth, what is our knowledge of the market? Do we know it well, or are we entering a new arena? Finally, we assess our current customer relationships. Are our existing strengths with customers important, helpful, or of no value in the new market?

Product Risk

Figure 11-3 shows the subrisks for product risk. The first subrisk is product development. Is the product largely the same as, similar

FIGURE 11-2. MARKET SUBRISK IN A PRODUCT LAUNCH.

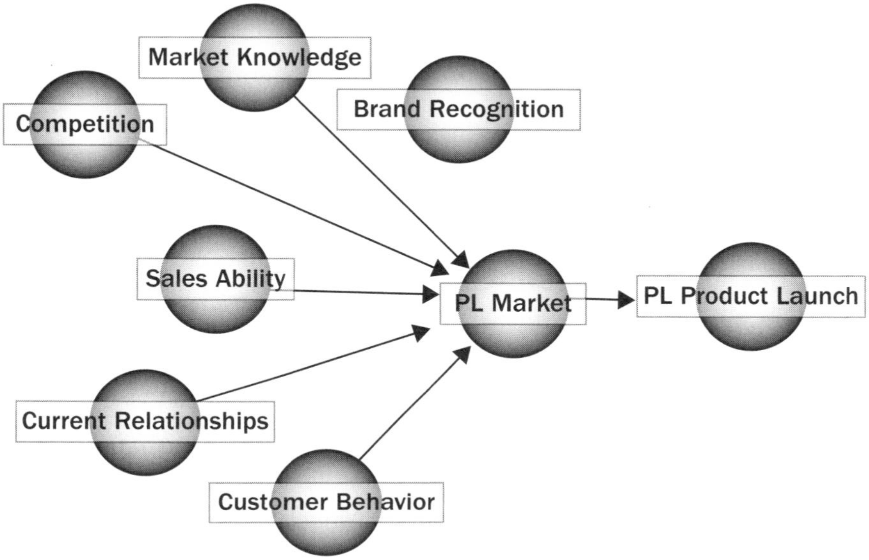

FIGURE 11-3. PRODUCT SUBRISKS IN A PRODUCT LAUNCH.

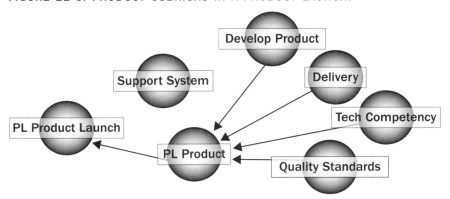

to, or completely different from our current products? Do our current development capabilities fully apply, require significant new learning, or apply not at all? The next subrisk is technical competency. Are our technological skills fully, partly, or not at all applicable to developing the product? Next is our delivery capability. Is our current distribution system suitable, partly suitable, or inap-

propriate for handling the product? Fourth is our support system.
Do we have a system currently or partly in place? If not, do we
need a totally new system to support the product? Finally, we assess quality standards. Is the level of product quality identical to,
related to, or completely different from the level of quality of our
current products?

Capital Risk

In our product launch analysis, we identified two major capital-
financing exposures, as shown in Figure 11-4. The first is burn
rate, defined as the speed at which capital is expended in a startup
venture or product launch company. It refers to the period when
the company must finance launch and overhead costs prior to the
generation of positive cash flow. In an ERM perspective, we are
asking whether we can control money spent on development and
marketing in advance of break-even. The other risk involves a second round of financing. Will an angel investor—a wealthy individual who provides capital for new business ventures—step up to
provide additional funding without totally diluting ownership of
the product or venture?

Factors Affecting Intellectual Property Risk

Figure 11-5 shows the fourth risk category, which is the danger of
a loss of intellectual property. It also has two subrisks. The first

FIGURE 11-4. CAPITAL FINANCING RISK IN A PRODUCT LAUNCH.

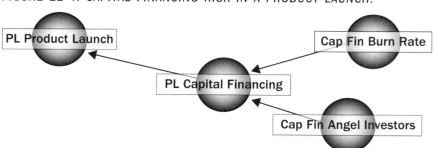

FIGURE 11-5. INTELLECTUAL PROPERTY RISK IN A PRODUCT LAUNCH.

involves patents: Will they be granted by various governments to provide legal protection in jurisdictions where they can be enforced? The second involves China. Will major Chinese competitors steal the technology and be able to hide from legal enforcement of patents?

Risk Profile

As with the model in earlier chapters, we can display the four top-level risks on two axes, from green (lowest) in the lower left area to red (highest) in the upper right. The axes can represent frequency and severity, control and impact, or other variables. Figure 11-6 displays such a profile.

Expanding the View

As we have seen, we can expand the view. Figure 11-7 displays a larger cluster that incorporates three levels of risk relationships. The view is cluttered, but we know we can tag risks and filter them to customize our view.

Lesson Learned: Once we employ visual risk clusters in an ERM framework, we can find stand-alone applications that allow us to see risk relationships and supporting documentation.

FIGURE 11-6. RISK PROFILE ON TWO AXES.

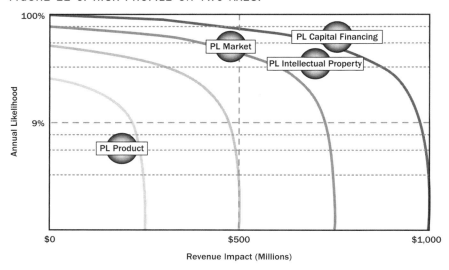

FIGURE 11-7. PRODUCT LAUNCH WITH SUBRISKS AND SUB-SUBRISKS.

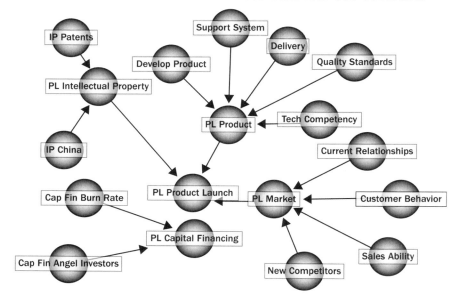

PART THREE

RISKS WITHOUT RISK OWNERS

WE HAVE NOW covered an ERM system and the technology to support it. That is not the whole story. Organizations face exposures that are all too often overlooked in discussions on risk. We have repeatedly made the point that when people think of risk, they think of loss. ERM recognizes the upside of risk and the importance of accepting danger in order to pursue opportunity.

Risk management will fail if we do not consider things that are close to us, endanger us, and are hard to see. Are we managing strategic risk? Do we understand the weaknesses in our strategies? Do we consider how subcultures can destroy our goals? What kind of leadership do we need? What kind do we have? What life cycle stages are represented by different lines of business or operating units? What problems arise from life cycle risks? Finally, what are we doing to increase our understanding of what is happening on the distant horizon?

Consider the difficulty of answering these questions. Do the people who develop strategies pay enough attention to the weaknesses of a plan? Do they become defensive when exposures are noted? Are individuals able to understand themselves and their culture? Do they see the obstacles that a subculture can pose for achieving goals? Do managers who lack leadership skills know it? Do they see the failure of leadership in others? Finally, we face life cycle risks. Do struggling business units see the world through the same risk glasses as successful units?

In Part Three we examine risks that are fundamentally different from the risk structure built in Part One. No single risk owner can manage them all, but the failure to manage them can destroy the organization. In a proactive ERM program, they can be identified by the central risk function and can be addressed by executives or managers. What are these exposures? How can we understand them? These questions are answered in chapters on strategic risk (Chapter 12), subculture risk (Chapter 13), leadership risk (Chapter 14), life cycle risk (Chapter 15), and horizon risk (Chapter 16).

STRATEGIC RISK

RISK QUOTE: *There is no reason anyone would want a computer in their home.*

—KEN OLSEN, PRESIDENT, CHAIRMAN AND FOUNDER
OF DIGITAL EQUIPMENT CORPORATION, 1977

RISK QUOTE: *100 percent of the shots you don't take don't go in.*
—WAYNE GRETZKY, PROFESSIONAL HOCKEY PLAYER

The first part of this story builds upon the article "Why the Economy Is a Lot Stronger Than You Think" by Michael Mander, which appeared in the February 13, 2006, issue of *Business Week*. Prior to the 2008 financial crisis, risk existed but somehow did not seem to be difficult to forecast; however, the crisis has given new urgency to understanding strategic risk.

Strategic Risk

Strategic risk is the positive or negative impact of risk on an organization in the following conditions:

● **Risk Identification.** The upside is opportunity to achieve a goal. The downside is the possibility of loss.

● **Problem Solving.** Defining a problem correctly allows the pursuit of an effective strategy. Failure to recognize the real problem can do significant damage.

FedEx—STRATEGIC RISK

FedEx shipped 6 million packages a day in 2006. It had 39 hubs in 180 countries, 677 airplanes and 90,000 vehicles, and employed 200,000 people. Rob Carter was the chief information officer of FedEx. He was asked the question "What business are you in?" How do you think he answered? Not the shipping business. Not the package delivery industry. He said, "FedEx engineers time." As the world shrinks and changes, FedEx offers solutions that allow customers to make things happen on time schedules that otherwise would be impossible.

FedEx spent more than $1 billion in 2005 on information technology. Customers could track any individual FedEx shipment using the Internet. It did not matter whether the customer knew the tracking number. FedEx gave customers the ability to see every inbound package. As an example, suppose a laboratory wants to know what bone-marrow shipments it will receive today to prepare for testing the samples. As a sample has a useful life span of only 24 hours, tracking every inbound shipment early in the day allows the laboratory to have enough technicians available to test all the samples that will arrive each day.

The philosophy of the U.S. Marine Corps is to "move, communicate, and shoot." It is also the strategy of FedEx: Start the package toward its destination (Move); make its position known to the addressee (Communicate); deliver it (Shoot). Intuitive decision making tells Marines whether they are winning the battlefield and tells FedEx whether it is staying ahead of the less innovative but highly competitive UPS.

Lesson Learned: When FedEx started in business, the United States Postal Service thought it just had another competitor. Instead, it had an organization that knew how to manage strategic risk.

◉ *Changing Conditions.* Successful adaptation to trends, emerging opportunities, or exposures can produce successful business operations. Failure to adjust or respond can cause damage.

❧ **Execution.** The achievement of a goal helps an organization. The failure to perform effectively hurts it.

Strategic Risk Management

Strategic risk management encompasses all activities intended to identify risks, solve problems, adapt to change, and successfully execute plans. It includes these components:

❧ **Goals and Strategies.** Does the entity have realistic goals and suitable strategies to achieve them?

❧ **Resources.** Is it identifying and allocating adequate assets, people, and other resources to solve problems or pursue opportunities?

❧ **Organizational Structure.** Does it have the right staff and line units for the tasks at hand?

❧ **Capabilities of People.** Does it understand the abilities and skills of its personnel and employ them to pursue goals where they can succeed?

❧ **Systems.** Are the entity's communication channels, operating systems, and delivery networks designed to support efficient operations?

❧ **Risk Identification.** Does the organization have an effective means for scanning for the impacts from external economic, competitive, technological, legal, regulatory, and other changing circumstances?

Strategic Risk and Knowledge

A *knowledge economy* is a local, national, regional, or global system that uses knowledge to produce economic benefits. The phrase was popularized by Peter Drucker in *The Age of Discontinuity* (1968). As barriers to trade dropped and developing countries used technology and education to raise workers' skill levels and increase interactions beyond their borders, the world morphed into a true global knowledge economy. Strategic risk management assumes that the world has become such an economy, with all the dangers and opportunities that accompany the transformation.

Corporate strategists recognize that government economic data do not reflect the factors that make a modern economy strong. A nation's economic level is not understood solely in terms of its physical assets, raw materials, and labor. Rather, an additional shadow economy exists as a result of investment in intangibles. Some expenditures consume resources, as with the burning of oil. Others strengthen an economy, as with education and research and development. This increases the level of strategic challenge and also the dangers and opportunities. In effect, strategies recognize the existence of two distinct systems:

1. **Physical Economy.** This consists of production and consumption activities that reflect the use of physical assets, consumption of raw materials, employment of labor and the workforce, and consumer and business spending on goods and services.

2. **Shadow Economy.** In both developed and developing nations, we can identify a separate economic machine that reflects individual and organizational investments in intangibles. Examples strengthen the economy rather than consume its resources.

Pursuit of Knowledge

Organizations pursue knowledge when it yields new product innovations and adds to the knowledge base of industry and the marketplace as a whole. The pursuit of knowledge is a precursor to risk management efforts that solve problems and allow adaptation to changing conditions. Three types of knowledge pursuit have been identified:

1. **Basic Research.** This category covers efforts to discover basic truths in science, technology, health care, environment, and other areas where empirical data can be observed. It has no specific end goal, although its findings are often incorporated subsequently into practical applications. It is performed largely

by universities, pharmaceutical and chemical companies, biologists, and scientists and is supported by government or non-profit foundation funding.

2. **Applied Research.** Applied researchers are seeking solutions for specific problems. Funding is provided by industry, the military, and nonprofit groups seeking a particular outcome that solves a social or other problem.

3. **Development.** These efforts create a new or revised product or application by bringing new technology, materials, or processes to improve existing products, services, or activities.

SAMSUNG—STRATEGIC RISK

By 2007, Asia had become a key player in product design. The move started with Samsung, a company whose great design catapulted it to the top ranks of global brands. In 1993, chairman Lee Kun Hee visited Los Angeles. He observed that Sony products stood out, while Samsung's were lost in the crowd. When he returned to Korea, he put less focus on cost saving and a high emphasis on developing unique products. Between 2000 and 2005, Samsung earned 100 citations at top design contests in the United States, Europe, and Asia. Samsung's revenues jumped 25 percent in 2005, and its profits doubled.

To be successful with its strategy, Samsung had to overcome the traditional respect for elders and workers' reluctance to speak out of turn. Samsung created a separate design center near the company headquarters but not in it. It had its own unique culture. There was no dress code. Some younger staffers dyed their hair green or pink. All employees were encouraged to speak up and challenge their superiors. Designers worked as equals in three- to five-person teams.

Lesson Learned: Strategic risk is the failure to respond to conditions that are harmful to success. When new strategies are needed, boldness can produce impressive results.

Historical Perspective of Strategic Risk

A number of developments led up to the present practice of strategic risk management. Sudden change destroyed entities that did not adapt to it. If we take an historical view, we can think about how many risks we would have seen coming if we had been alive at the time they occurred. We start by observing that risk management has changed as the world has moved from the agricultural age to the industrial age. Think about the eighteenth century. We had horse power, wind power, and water power. Horses could be connected in a limited number to harness the power of multiple animals pulling in the same direction. Windmills could do some things, and sailing vessels moved people and cargo. Water power was limited to the speed and volume of rivers flowing over waterwheels. The use of levers, inclined planes, and other tools multiplied to some extent the amount of power that could be created.

As we entered the completely new world of the nineteenth and then the twentieth centuries, Newcomen and Watt's steam engine was used by factories to create massive power to produce textiles, machinery, and other goods. Rotary motion allowed the steam engine to drive locomotives. Factories distributed goods widely. The combination of steel, electricity, and the elevator allowed the construction of taller buildings and a greater concentration of population in cities. Air conditioning eventually made tropical and subtropical areas new centers of major business.

What is the link between strategic risk and these developments? On the one hand, innovation brought a rising risk level. Accidents, injuries, wars, and competitors are far more prevalent in an industrial-age environment. On the other hand, we had a virtually unlimited number of opportunities. To earn a living, we did not have to figure out how to take over the businesses of shoeing horses or cutting up animals in the local village against the ingrained opposition of the long-time families of the blacksmith or butcher. Instead, the world became a stage, and, with the right strategy and a little innovation and energy, we could play on it.

What is the common thread that links productivity developments? The answer is the emergence of new risks and a need for new techniques of risk management. These developments occurred without an explicit recognition that people were dealing with risk. In the age of ERM, we deal directly with risk and opportunity.

FROM THE AGRICULTURAL AGE TO THE INDUSTRIAL AGE

Year	Event
1712	**Steam Engine.** Newcomen's invention made the Industrial Age possible. Previously, we were limited to power created by linking horses, oxen, or even elephants together, or derived from the force of rushing water moving down a slope.
1769	**Condenser.** Watt's invention did even more. It made the steam engine a practical tool to generate reliable power. It took 57 years, but now we really had something big.
1782	**Rotary Motion.** Watt also figured out how steam could turn a wheel. This had applications in factories, and it also opened a door for something that could move goods to distance places.
1829	**Locomotive.** Stephenson joined the practical steam engine with rotary motion, enabling railroads to change the quantity of goods and the number of people that could move long distances in relative comfort.
1871	**Dynamo.** This device, which converts steam to electricity, was Ben Franklin's dream a hundred years earlier. All sorts of new risks and opportunities were now on the horizon.
1856	**Steel.** Bessemer discovered something better than iron for railroad tracks and buildings. This would be big.
1852	**Elevator.** Steel may be strong, but people could climb only so high on a regular basis. Tall buildings were feasible only after Otis developed elevators. Skyscrapers would come next.
1911	**Air Conditioning.** It took 40 years or so, but comfortable homes and skyscrapers in summer were on the horizon. People could also now live and work year-round in comfort in southern climates, affecting markets and demographics.

Henry Ford's Strategic Risk Opportunity

The developments in the nineteenth century that led to the industrial age also set up an important event that occurred shortly after the start of the twentieth century. Henry Ford was manufacturing the Model T automobile in a plant near Detroit. Employees worked

10 hours a day for six days a week to earn $18 per week. Such a schedule did not leave time to drive automobiles or do much else. In 1914, Ford changed the nature of work in the United States when he began to pay workers $5 a day for five days work per week. He also shortened the workday to eight hours. As other companies followed, Ford's action changed the nature of products and markets, because they gave people time for activities other than paid work. A leisure society was being born. It became a fully developed consumer economy after the end of the Second World War.

Ford played two roles in the world of risk management. First, automobiles created a massive new kind of risk exposure. There were few deaths on roadways when horses were the primary means of transportation. Automobiles and trucks changed that. The second outcome was an early insight later incorporated into ERM: Ford saw an exposure if people were unable to buy his cars. He saw a reduction in working hours accompanied by a rise in income as a risk opportunity that would increase demand for his vehicles. How many times do we see organizations cut costs rather than increase costs as a way to achieve a positive leveraging of profits? This did not happen to Mr. Ford.

Strategic Risk and Synergy

The movement from an agricultural to an industrial age was driven by creativity in new inventions. This energy could be seen on all sides, operating nearly independently and then coming together in wonderful synergy. As an example, consider improvements in communications. People in agricultural societies knew little of the world outside a narrow territory. One estimate of the knowledge of information in a rural village in the seventeenth century is instructive. A typical villager knew as much information about the world as would be contained today in a single issue of a newspaper. What newspaper? The *New York Times*. Not the Sunday issue, mind you. A weekday issue. Modern communications changed the situation dramatically.

The expansion of commerce was accompanied by faster ways to move information and people. With the telegraph, information could move immediately. Over the next century or so, the world went from the highly important and innovative dot-dash-dot of the telegraph to the blindingly swift and often annoying advent of the Internet. Transportation was equally innovative. The steamboat was a major advance over water transport that relied on sailing and wind power, the only serious way to travel long-distances previously. The railroad represented a giant advance from travel by horse and carriage. And the freedom and speed offered by automobiles and airplanes could hardly have been imagined 100 years before they arrived.

What does this mean for strategic risk? History tells us clearly that we should not ignore the synergies outside our immediate span of vision. For organizations, this is the responsibility of a central risk function.

COMMUNICATIONS DEVELOPMENTS

Year	Event
1837	**Telegraph.** Morse developed a long-distance communication means that allowed information to move faster than people and their animals. The combination of trains and rapid access to information would allow Russia to take over distant empires and companies to react quickly to changing market conditions.
1876	**Telephone.** Bell gave us better long-distance communication. No longer did information move one letter at a time, with dots and dashes. Nor did we have to wait for feedback. Oral responses could be obtained immediately.
1920	**Radio.** Radio meant that a single message could be disseminated to many people simultaneously. It led to major developments in advertising, entertainment, propaganda, and emergency warning systems.
1923	**Television.** TV was better than radio because a visual component was added to audio messages. It took about 25 years for television to be commercially viable.
1995	**Internet.** The ultimate tool for sharing information, communicating urgent messages, sharing communications we want to share, and receiving communications we do not want to receive.

TRANSPORTATION DEVELOPMENTS

Year	Event
1807	**Steamboat.** Steamboats were faster than sailing vessels and soon would be larger.
1830s	**Railroads.** This development provided transportation that was faster than covered wagons and stagecoaches, which would both be obsolete in 40 years.
1889	**Automobile.** Cars offered more flexible land transportation than the railroads. They allowed people to spread out and made leisure travel an option.
1903	**Airplane.** Faster and more flexible than the automobile, they were also likely to change the nature of war.
1939	**Jet Plane.** These were really fast. People could be in Europe in the morning and in India in the afternoon.

Strategic Risk and Tools of Knowledge

What is the common link among the steam engine, telephone, jet plane, and other change agents? The answer is technology, arguably the most important single factor in strategic risk management. People needed a rising level of knowledge and skills to understand and use new technology. They got it from new tools in two phases. The first phase was slow and took a long time. It includes early changes in our ability to manipulate numbers and words. It took a long time to arrive at the adding machine and the calculating machine. Similarly, Gutenberg's movable type replaced handwritten documents and allowed for the creation of significant books. Centuries later, the typewriter followed, itself shoved aside by punch-card machines that sorted and prioritized information needed to understand isolated transactions.

Phase two was a seismic leap in our ability to handle numbers, words, and data. The electronic digital computer changed everything with respect to strategic risk. Starting with large machines used by governments and large companies, with miniaturization it morphed into the personal computer. Now, individuals can handle numbers, words, and data, augmented with new capabilities in graphics and communications. The Internet is the current culmination of phase two.

KNOWLEDGE DEVELOPMENTS, PHASE ONE

Year	Event
300 B.C.	**Abacus.** This is the earliest known technology for counting and performing math functions.
1450	**Movable Type.** Gutenberg made it much easier and much less expensive to print books. Learning and amusement spread widely.
1820	**Adding Machine.** A Western tool to crank numbers soon had multiple applications in commerce and accounting.
1833	**Calculating Machine.** This added multiplication and division to the easy handling of numbers.
1867	**Typewriter.** The typewriter made it much easier to put words on paper. The number of communications skyrocketed.
1889	**Punch Card Machine.** IBM gave us a tool that counted inventory and more.

KNOWLEDGE DEVELOPMENTS, PHASE TWO

Year	Event
1946	**Electronic Digital Computer.** The computer gave us a single device, however large in its first version, that could handle words, numbers, and data.
1947	**Transistor.** Replacing vacuum tubes, these made the computer faster, smaller, and more reliable.
1958	**Integrated Circuit.** This new development made the computer even faster, smaller, and more reliable as it replaced the transistor.
1976	**Personal computer.** This was a really big step forward.
1979	**Electronic Spreadsheet.** If word processing were not enough, this guarantees the business need for personal computers.
1995	**Internet.** Already mentioned for its communications role, the Internet also deserves mention as a technological development.

Strategic Risk and Opportunity Since 1980

As we closed the twentieth century, there was an acceleration in the rate of change in products and markets. Developments such as the following increased both danger and opportunity:

- **1980–1995.** Personal computers provided new tools for handling words, numbers, data, graphics, and communications.
- **1991–2005.** We created and expanded communications networks, using the Internet to link people and organizations.
- **1995–2006.** We saw the amazing rise of industry in China, accompanied by growing economic strength in other developing countries.
- **2002–2009.** Pocket computing supplemented and replaced personal computers, day planners, telephones, and televisions. People became free to take their offices and homes with them anywhere they went.

Scanning Post-2008

From this historical perspective, we know where we are or where we think we are. What comes next? What sources of strategic risk are on the horizon? Here are some nominees:

- **Emerging Nations.** China and India, with 36 percent of the global population and growing economies. need constant surveillance. We should not overlook emerging countries and regions as well, particularly Pakistan, Indonesia, and the Middle East. In 2002, everybody was investing in China. When intellectual property problems surfaced in 2004, the focus switched to India and opportunities in Mumbai, Chennai, and Bangalore. The financial crisis that began in 2008 will cause the landscape to shift again. In the fast-moving post-American world, we do not have a long-term life cycle for controlling strategic risk.
- **Technology and Knowledge.** Everything a business needs with respect to information and amusement can be carried in small portable devices. All of our strategies and proprietary secrets

can be leaked via the Internet. Today's innovative new product is tomorrow's obsolete relic. Strategic risk tells us to check constantly the validity of a budget prepared just a few months ago, a strategy that took much time to create, and an assumption that seemed quite reasonable just yesterday.

❧ **Logistics.** A company's raw materials are likely to come from 20 suppliers in 15 countries, and its components are probably fabricated in six different countries. Czechs who update massive databases and Mexican engineers who upgrade computer and telecommunications systems support the supply chain. Products designated for customers in North America are shipped at the last minute through the congested and vulnerable port of Shanghai. We must carefully manage redundancy and stability in the supply chain.

Maybe the biggest strategic risk involves our reliance on fossil fuels. Daily world oil consumption was 86 million barrels of oil a day in 2008. Globally, we had the long-term capacity to refine somewhere between 84 and 86 million barrels a day, depending on the refineries that are off-line. With only minor exceptions, oil companies and others were not making an effort to expand refining capacity.

Who consumed oil in 2008? The United States consumed 19 million barrels a day, or 22 percent of the total. The larger European Union consumed 15 million. China increased its consumption from a few million barrels daily a short time ago to seven million barrels a day in 2008. Forecasters believe that China's consumption will grow to 12 million barrels by 2014.

Finally, let us scan internally. Who provides the oil products that fuel 95 percent of the world's transportation? The answer is oil companies, OPEC, and countries outside the Middle East that have oil reserves. Governments were asking the providers to increase production and invest in refining capacity. This would, however, tie up providers' capital, lower gas prices, and reduce their profits. Why would anyone agree to do that?

A central risk function cannot predict the future, but it can alert management and boards of directors to strategic risks. It is likely that the world will need 100 million barrels of oil a day in 2014 but will have a refining capacity of only 85 to 90 million barrels per day. To any board, CEO, chief risk officer, or person on the street, an economic structure based on fossil fuels poses a strategic risk.

Case in Point—Boeing vs. Airbus

The competition between the airplane manufacturers Boeing and Airbus is instructive for what it reveals about the importance of ERM as companies make strategic decisions.

BOEING AND AIRBUS—STRATEGIC RISK

Strategic risk reaches its pinnacle on really big alternatives— when the company can go one way or another and a great deal rides on the outcome. This was the situation in the competition between Boeing and Airbus, between 1998 and 2009, to build the next-generation jet airplane.

In late 2005, Boeing and Airbus were locked in a duel to sell widebody jets to three major Asia-Pacific carriers. The carriers took different roads to reach that point:

- **Boeing's Strategy.** Boeing put its development money into the 787, a plane with a seating capacity of from 200 to 300 passengers. The 787 is attractive to airlines that fly from point to point and avoid crowded hubs. It is also fuel-efficient because it has only two engines.

- **Airbus's Strategy.** Airbus pursued a strategy based on the belief that airlines would want larger planes to operate from crowded airport hubs. It developed the A380, a jumbo jet capable of carrying from 500 to 800 passengers. The plane has four engines and is 25 percent less fuel efficient per passenger seat than the 787.

The Boeing and Airbus strategies recognized inherent risks. Development costs were extensive as new technologies were required. The success or failure of each company's strategy was dependent upon decisions by airlines and governments, which were outside their control.

Lesson Learned: Two organizations can view the same risk opportunity and draw markedly different conclusions as to the strategic risk it poses.

BOEING AND AIRBUS—CUSTOMER STRATEGIES

In making their original decisions, Boeing and Airbus had to assess the likely strategies of the airlines on route structures. Two strategic models were being considered:

1. **Hub and Spoke.** This structure exists when an airline uses one main airport as a transfer point to get passengers to their intended destination. Travelers move between airports not served by direct flights by flying to the hub and changing planes en route to their destinations. Hubs are used for both passenger and cargo flights.

2. **Point to Point.** The second structure occurs when an airline flies passengers and cargo directly between two destinations without passing through a central hub. Nonstop flights can be popular to fliers because they require less travel time.

Airlines that use hubs would be more likely to buy the A380. Airlines flying point to point would probably prefer the 787. The airlines might not decide until both planes were ready for delivery.

Boeing and Airbus also had to incorporate fuel prices into their predictions about buyers' likely strategies. If airlines expected a future rise in fuel prices, the fuel-efficient 787 would be the preferable aircraft. If they expect only minor price increases, a larger, four-engine plane would be advantageous.

Another customer issue involved the development period for the planes. Both companies had target dates, but problems always arise. Delivery of new aircraft often is delayed. If the planes were not ready to fly by the planned starting dates for deliveries, what would be the reaction of customers? Would they abandon the contracts or refuse to purchase additional aircraft?

Lesson Learned: A component of strategic risk involves assessing the strategies of related parties. A misjudgment can lead to serious future problems.

BOEING AND AIRBUS—TECHNOLOGY RISKS

When a strategy requires new inventions or untested systems, the risk level rises. Both the Boeing 787 and the Airbus A380 required aircraft technology that did not exist at the time the decision to build each plane was made. This magnified the risk.

The A380 would be larger than any prior aircraft. Its wingspan is huge, at 262 feet (80 meters). The physical size poses all sorts of problems. Can Airbus build such an aircraft within development costs that can eventually be recaptured? Would known technology about electrical, computer, and other systems on the plane translate smoothly into the machinery needed on a jumbo jet?

Boeing had different technology issues. The 787 has a one-piece carbon composite fuselage. This is a new technology and had never been used before in commercial aircraft. It allows manufacturers to build a plane that is 15 percent lighter than a plane made of aluminum sheets and rivets. Boeing's advances in carbon-fiber layering demonstrated its commitment to research and development, but that is not the point. What happens if carbon-fiber layering does not work?

Lesson Learned: Strategic risk can be big. As it turned out, both companies had technology problems that slowed the development and delivery of the planes.

Boeing and Airbus—Market Risks

The overall size of a market is a critical variable in strategic risk management. If adequate demand does not materialize, a project can fail even if all other issues are resolved. The delivery date for the Boeing and the Airbus planes was forecast to be 2005. The companies had to forecast sales from 2006 to 2025. One view of the demand for new commercial jet aircraft called for 25,700 units of 50 seats or more. The growth rates of the aircraft market were forecast at 5 percent annually for passenger traffic and 6 percent for cargo.

The size of the market depends upon two factors. The first involves load, defined as the percentage of passengers or cargo per available space on an aircraft. In 1980, load rates were 63 percent of capacity. By 2005, airlines were doing better, at a 75 percent load. An aircraft fleet can never reach 100 percent, but airlines typically seek a goal of 80 percent. The second factor is utilization, defined as the percentage of time an aircraft is in the air carrying passengers or cargo. Both factors need to be addressed in sizing up a market.

Lesson Learned: In some cases, strategic risk is managed by intuition. In other situations, we need quantitative data. An ERM analysis would encourage a wide-sweeping scan of economic and political developments around the world prior to forecasting the size of a market for these aircraft.

BOEING AND AIRBUS—ADJUSTMENTS TO STRATEGIES

Both companies ran into problems that required adjustments to their initial strategy. This intensified the competition for sales. Boeing's early sales success with the 787 encouraged Airbus to counter with the A350, a new plane designed to compete with the 787. In 2004, Airbus announced that the A350 would be close in size to the 787 and that the first planes would be delivered in 2010.

Boeing, for its part, countered the A380. Prior to the A380, the Boeing 747 was the largest plane in the sky. In 2005, Boeing announced that it would produce a new version of the 747 with a capacity of 450 passengers. It would use the same engine and cockpit as the 787 and have parts interchangeable with those for the earlier 747 models. Even though it is smaller, this plane would be in direct competition with the A380.

Lesson Learned: ERM argues that organizations must scan for changes in conditions, monitor strategies for continuing relevance, and make adjustments as situations change.

BOEING AND AIRBUS—INTERRELATED RISKS

As Boeing company developed the 787, the situation was clouded by unrelated developments. The board had to deal with a series of scandals, including the following:

❧ **Employee Misconduct.** In 1997, Kenneth Branch left Lockheed Martin, taking 25,000 pages of Lockheed's proprietary intellectual capital. He joined the Boeing subsidiary McDonnell Douglas, which used the documents to compete with Lockheed Martin. In 1999, a Boeing employee blew the whistle. The result was that Boeing lost $1 billion in government business and Lockheed Martin sued for damages.

❧ **Conflict of Interest.** In 2003, Darleen Druyun was the top procurement officer for the U.S. Air Force. She provided Boeing with preferential treatment, awarding it a large contract. Shortly thereafter, Boeing's CFO gave Druyun a high-level job at Boeing. Both parties went to jail in 2004 after being found guilty of conflict of interest.

❧ **Personal Scandal.** Boeing hired Harry Stonecipher in 2004 to clean up the company after the Air Force procurement scandal. The Boeing board of directors fired him in early 2005 after learning that he previously had a personal relationship with a female Boeing vice president. At the same time, Boeing claimed attorney-client privilege to avoid releasing information showing that male employees at Boeing earned more than females. *Lesson Learned:* Strategies can often be derailed by interrelated risk. In this situation, Boeing was fortunate. The scandals caused other problems and financial losses but did not hurt the sales of the 787.

BOEING AND AIRBUS—STRATEGIC RISK OUTCOME

After dealing with scandals, Boeing hired James McNerney as CEO in 2005. His extensive experience was in brand marketing at Procter & Gamble, consulting at McKinsey, and aircraft management at General Electric. His objectives for Boeing were to improve productivity, undertake global sourcing by purchasing components from around the world, and increase funding so that Boeing would be a global leader in research and development.

McNerney got Boeing back on track, but development problems delayed delivery. He established a new schedule, with production to start in 2009. As of the end of 2008, Boeing had 900 orders for the 787, with delivery dates ranging out to 2017. As Boeing and Airbus vied with the 787 and A380, other planes were selling well. Historically, the best year for sales of large commercial airliners was 1989, when 1,600 units were sold. In 2005, sales surpassed that number, with Airbus selling 1055 and Boeing selling 1002 aircraft.

Airbus also survived development problems and delays. The company had orders for 200 planes from 17 customers at the end of 2008. It had scheduled deliveries of 12 A380s in 2008 and 21 in 2009.

Lesson Learned: The experiences of Boeing and Airbus are amazing when viewed in an ERM framework. Both companies were close to a "bet the company" strategy with the development of totally new airplanes. As this is being written, in 2008, we do not know the outcome: who will win and who will survive. It is not clear that either company undertook an ERM evaluation prior to making high-risk decisions with the 787 and A380. From the facts, we can see a need for a thoughtful ERM analysis when a company seeks to seize a massive risk opportunity.

CONCLUSION

Strategic risk is a serious enterprise risk and opportunity that crosses operations, finance, and other units. It is not likely to have a single risk owner. To ensure attention to and vetting of strategies, ERM suggests that a central risk function be assigned the responsibility to scan for risks and opportunities and to share them with key players.

Taiwan Strategic Risk Case

In this case study, we examine the change from industrial organizations to knowledge organizations and show the impact of small and seemingly unrelated events and developments. At the heart of the story are the United States Shoe Corporation in Cincinnati, Ohio, and an imaginary Mr. Wang in Taiwan.

INDUSTRIAL-AGE ORGANIZATION

A central risk function in the 1970s would have observed large organizations with formal hierarchical structures and an industrial-age model of efficiency and, in fairness, inefficiency. Individuals had formal titles and responsibilities. U.S. Shoe had been such a structure since its founding as the Stern-Auer Shoe Company in 1879, when it opened a small factory in the heart of Cincinnati.

Industrial-age organizations resisted change, often meeting challenges with inappropriate responses. In the mid-1980s, organizations faced major changes largely driven by a convergence of technology and opportunity.

Mr. Wang, in Taiwan, wanted to seize a risk opportunity. Could he take advantage of an environmental shift to become a manufacturer of sneakers? Yes, if he took advantage of the most important technological invention of the 1970s, one that would become a key component of the transition organization in Taiwan and elsewhere in the 1980s. Even today, many people do not understand its significance in global commerce and the role it played. What was it? It was the fax machine.

The fax machine changed long-distance communication from oral, on the telephone, or tedious, on the Telex machine. Lengthy, complex written communication could move instantaneously around the world. Labor costs were low in Taiwan, and the Taiwanese government was supporting industrialization. The world had a growing consumer demand for sneakers. Mr. Wang was ready.

Mr. Wang accepted faxed orders to manufacture sneakers. When Sears in Chicago ordered 1 million pairs of sneakers, the purchasing agent sent to Taiwan a 50-page fax with sizes, design, colors, and other specifications. Mr. Wang broke up the fax and sent 5 to 10 pages to his neighbors or partners around the island. When the recipients received orders for sneakers along with detailed specifications, they started up production.

Assume that Mr. Wang's associates were producing 3 million pairs of sneakers in 1987. His revenues were $35 million. Can we estimate the total number of full-time positions in his company and the U.S. dollar value of his capital assets? Amazingly, the operation was smaller than a single staff department at U.S. Shoe. He might have 10 people—family members and friends. In terms of capital assets, he operated out of a small office with a telephone, a fax machine, and minor equipment. He did not manufacture sneakers, so he ran a lean and low-cost operation.

Figure 12-1 shows Mr. Wang's business structure. We have inserted random Chinese names into the exhibit to represent Mr. Wang's business associates who ran their own manufacturing operations. In this transition organization, independent entrepreneurs were grouped around a center or "headquarters." The center performed a few administrative functions, mostly to match high-quality products with Western buyers.

We can observe the absence of vice presidents, assistant vice presidents, supervisors, and managers—not to mention an elaborate human resources function handling time sheets, vacation days, and annual performance reviews.

In industrial organizations, a vice president represents the highest position in middle management. A defining characteristic is that such a person has a secretary. The vice president's job is to relay policies from senior executives to lower-level employees, establish goals, appraise subordinates, prepare reports, and attend meetings.

Below the vice president, middle managers do basically the

FIGURE 12-1. MR. WANG'S CIRCULAR ORGANIZATION.

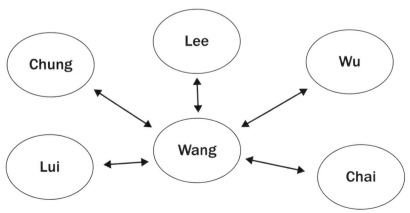

same things—perform redundant functions. Below middle managers, secretaries greet visitors, answer the telephone, type letters, file documents, and schedule appointments and meetings. Nobody performs most of these duties for Mr. Wang because he does not need any support.

Strategically, Mr. Wang had a competitive advantage over U.S. Shoe. As the low-cost provider, he could expect higher profits and long-term value. Moreover, lower costs lead to lower prices. When Mr. Wang's costs drop below the costs of competing industrial-age manufacturers, their business becomes unprofitable and eventually must be abandoned.

The real impact of Mr. Wang touched many entities beyond shoe manufacturers. He and others like him were about to change the industrial-age organization. The fax machine allowed information to cross borders by electronic means without interference. Products and services were likely to follow, causing borders to decline in importance and even disappear. The fax machine also threatened the existence of myriad languages, as English was likely to become the global tongue. If Mr. Wang or family members knew English, they could communicate with the world's dominant economic power. All other countries would line up to understand the most important language in the world. In addition, the fax machine changed productivity. Sears was no longer paying higher wages by the hour—essentially paying for time. Now Sears and Mr. Wang paid for sneakers. The fax machine was increasing efficiency and changing employment practices.

These developments had a major impact on the industrial-age hierarchy and culture. Pressure built to eliminate redundant middle management and other positions. Individuals recognized they could not spend an entire career climbing a corporate hierarchy. New organizational forms and relationships were created. Partnerships replaced business units, production might not be a line and staff function, and companies would sell products produced by partners like Mr. Wang.

Lesson Learned: The fax machine provides abundant evidence of the importance of managing strategic risk by identifying changing conditions and developing new strategies in response. So what happened to the United States Shoe Company? The company recognized that changes were occurring and altered its strategy. In 1985, it reduced its dependence upon shoes. In 2008, the company had 49,000 employees and almost $3 billion in annual revenues. You may not know its name, but perhaps you know some of its brands, which include Lens Crafters, Casual Corner, Petite Sophisticate, and August Max.

CHAPTER 13

SUBCULTURE RISK

RISK QUOTE: *Our loyalties must transcend our race, our tribe, our class, and our nation; and this means we must develop a world perspective.*

—REV. DR. MARTIN LUTHER KING, JR., CIVIL RIGHTS LEADER

RISK QUOTE: *Why do they call it rush hour when nothing moves?*

—ROBIN WILLIAMS, COMEDIAN

J ust as strategic risk is not the responsibility of a single risk owner, cultural exposures are the culmination of multiple units and activities. Subculture risk, sometimes called hierarchy risk, is inherent in a large entity. The concept dates back to the mid-1800s, when growing organizations developed a structure and techniques to manage relationships, tasks, and behavior. Elaborate sets of rules accompanied the growth, so each entity took on a life and behavior of its own—or, more accurately, lives and behaviors of different units.

First, we need to define two terms. *Organizational culture* is the shared values, attitudes, behaviors, and beliefs of individuals who work together for a common goal. A subculture has its own individual culture that may or may not be aligned with the overall values and behaviors of the entity. *Subculture risk* refers to problems that occur because unit cultures vary in terms of their ability to operate effectively within a larger structure.

Next, we need to consider two issues in managing subcultural risk. The first deals with cultural values—assumptions, convictions, and beliefs about how people should behave. Alternatively, values are principles or standards that are considered worthwhile or desirable. Values determine how individuals and groups react to the world around them. Subculture risk arises from differences in values.

CHARACTERISTICS OF VALUES

- **Formed Early.** People develop values early in life, and they are quite resistant to change. They develop from our experiences with individuals who are important to us. They arise not from what people say but rather from how others behave toward us.

- **Inherently Right or Wrong.** Values define what is right and what is wrong. A person does not need external standards or direction to tell right or wrong. Knowing what is right is intrinsic. A person knows what is "right" and resists or rejects what is "wrong."

- **Subjective in Nature.** A value itself cannot be proved correct or incorrect. It is neither valid nor invalid, neither right nor wrong. If we can prove that a statement is true or false, it cannot be a value. Values tell people how to behave whether or not any evidence exists to support the behavior.

Bureaucracy as a Structure

The bureaucracy is the dominant structure of large organizations. It has specific values independent of the values of the individuals and units that are part of the structure. Problem areas include:

- **Integrity.** The organization has a standard for doing business and ethical behavior. Some individuals agree with these standards and comply with them. Others disagree. Do they resist the entity's guidance, policies, and expectations?

- **Use of Knowledge.** One person relies on facts. Another person relies on emotion. Are individuals and units complying with internal control procedures and the use of data and feedback when making decisions?

❧ **Interpersonal Relations.** One person makes others feel comfortable. Another upsets them. How do individuals and units resolve conflicts between employees, suppliers, customers, and others?

❧ **Sharing.** One person shares information. Another guards it. Can the organization protect its intellectual capital while providing information that individuals and units need to achieve their goals?

DEALING WITH VARYING VALUES IN A BUREAUCRACY

➤ **Standard Procedures.** The organization has detailed policies that are supposed to be followed by everyone. When a problem arises, a manager checks written policies for a course of action to solve the problem. We all must follow the same rules.

➤ **Formal Division of Responsibilities.** The entity has identified positions and tasks. Responsibilities are assigned to positions, and individuals in those positions are directed to perform tasks. Employees are limited to narrow jobs, and managers check to see that they follow policies.

➤ **Chain of Command.** Every individual has a position in a formal hierarchy. Each person reports to a boss who reports to another boss. Many individuals have subordinates who may also have individuals reporting to them. Bosses enforce the rules.

➤ **Impersonal Relationships.** The entity is focused on tasks and individuals to perform them. If a person leaves, another "qualified" person is assigned to the tasks. The organization pursues new managers and other workers on the basis of their objective qualifications. Relationships are not personal. Managers do not do favors for "friends." They follow the rules.

Understanding Subculture Risk

Although the bureaucracy is the dominant structure, subcultures are shaped by many factors. To identify subculture risks, a central risk function must first understand what is happening in a unit.

One starting place is the mission, a brief statement of the role assigned to the unit. Is it routine? Is it challenging? Does it require creativity? Another factor is the boss. What is the relationship between the personal characteristics of the unit manager and the values of the entity and of the individuals doing the work? If a new boss seeks behaviors that are inconsistent with the values of the entity or of his or her subordinates, problems will quickly arise. A third factor is the behaviors of the lower-level workers. These employees have both visible and hidden values that determine whether tasks will be successfully accomplished.

One approach to understanding subculture risk addresses decision making and problem solving. An ERM system is more likely to be successful if it helps key managers, line and staff personnel, and workers interact and share information. Do general behavior patterns within the unit support or harm successful performance? How does the subculture deal with routine situations, unexpected developments, and conflicts? How does the unit learn and internalize new knowledge, skills, and behaviors? If we understand how a troublesome unit learns, we can help it to change its behavior to be more in line with the environment and the value system of the larger entity. Conversely, individuals who fail to learn the right lessons or who learn the wrong lessons can cause damage to the entity.

ERM encourages the reduction of subculture risk. The central risk function seeks to understand different subcultures. Executives encourage units and individuals to use sound and stable approaches to problem solving consistent with the business model. Effective decision making is covered in more detail in Chapter 14.

FORD-TOYOTA ROWING CONTEST

One of the marvelous things about the Internet is that all sorts of stories get posted. One story pokes fun at General Motors, showing how it would engage in a canoe race with Toyota. In another version of the story, Toyota is in the contest, but this time it is competing with Ford. Retelling the Ford story gives us insight into subculture risk.

Ford and Toyota decided to have a canoe race. Both teams practiced long and hard. On the big day, the Japanese won by a mile. The Americans, very discouraged and depressed, decided to investigate. A senior management team learned that Toyota had eight people rowing and one person steering. Ford had eight people steering and one person rowing. Ford hired a consultant who confirmed the findings.

Ford acted. It reorganized to four steering supervisors, three area steering superintendents, one steering manager, and one rower. The company implemented a "Rowing Team Quality First Program" to give the rowing person greater incentive to work harder. It included meetings, dinners, free pens, and a certificate of appreciation.

The teams met again the next year. The Japanese won by two miles. Again Ford responded. It laid off the rower for poor performance, halted development of a new canoe, and sold the paddles. It distributed the money saved and the proceeds from the sale of paddles to senior executives.

In 2007, Ford was expanding outside the United States. It is too costly for Ford to make cars in the United States. Toyota was expanding in the United States. It had or was building 12 manufacturing facilities.

Lesson Learned: We can ask how many of the differences between Ford and Toyota are explained by different cultures. The same applies to General Motors and Chrysler. Some observers believe virtually all the differences, and thus the problems of the U.S. auto industry, lie in subculture risk.

Charles Handy on Culture

ERM can use many models to observe subculture risk. Perhaps the most powerful model was developed by Charles Handy, a British management thinker. He identified four dominant subcultures in large organizations, which he described in detail in two books, *Gods of Management* and *The Age of Unreason*.

Handy recognized that the industrial age had shaped the world as we know it. As organizations grew larger, they needed a structure. A hierarchical organization called a bureaucracy became the norm. Handy observed that units in the bureaucracy contained four distinct categories of subculture, each with its own risks. We cover each in turn.

HANDY'S FOUR SUBCULTURES

➤ **Bureaucratic Culture.** It values standard procedures, divisions of responsibility, and impersonal relationships.

➤ **Team Culture.** Teams consist of a collection of individuals working together on a common goal.

➤ **Spider's Web Culture.** In this environment, all parties focus on the leader.

➤ **Individual Culture.** In this culture, each person has his or her own specialties, knowledge, and goals and has only a limited orientation to the organization itself.

BUREAUCRACY

The first organizational model is the most familiar. It is the culture of the bureaucracy itself. Its characteristics are as follows:

● **Leaders.** A bureaucratic culture has many leaders, with power diffused throughout the structure. The chief executive officer is all-powerful, but power is shared with individuals at every level. Each person has a position in the structure, and, generally, people stay within the leadership roles authorized for the position.

● **Results.** A bureaucratic culture achieves its greatest efficiencies when many people must work together to provide products or services. Large organizations tend to be bureaucracies.

● **Primary Loyalty.** Employees feel that their primary loyalty is to the organization. When someone asks what an employee does, the response is likely to identify the entity.

● **Governance.** Bureaucratic cultures are governed by rules. To learn the rules, people are told to read written policies. The mechanism to create change is simple: Management distributes new written rules and regulations.

● **Individual Goal.** The goal is to provide products and services in a consistent manner over a long period of time. The culture seeks order and predictability. Individuals are in danger if they have separate goals. Free thinking and entrepreneurial individuals are usually not welcome or tolerated.

❧ **Management Style.** The management mechanisms extend through the entire structure. People who violate company policies or procedures are punished. People who comply with the rules are rewarded.

❧ **Skills.** Bureaucrats improve skills by attending formal training programs. Management identifies the new skills that are needed. The human resources department arranges formal training to teach them.

SPIDER'S WEB

The spider's web represents a distinctly different organizational model, one that reflects a powerful leader. While it may have the hierarchy of a bureaucracy, all authority, power, and responsibility depend upon the person in charge. These are its defining characteristics:

❧ **Leader.** This person can be characterized by a number of terms. Because he or she can survive alone, the person is a jungle fighter. Because the person demands undying allegiance, he or she is the tribal leader. However, perhaps the best descriptive term is the spider. In a spider's web, the structure is not important. A person's location in the web is secondary. The key is the location of the individual relative to the head of the unit. If the head of the unit is offended, it can quickly move to any individual or location in the web and attack.

❧ **Results.** A spider's web produces its best results in a crisis. If a company has a tight timetable to develop a software product, decisive leadership may be the key to success or failure. If costs are rising quickly and bankruptcy is threatened, a spider may be able to save the organization.

❧ **Primary Loyalty.** The individual who is part of this culture develops an identity with the leader. Employees who are asked about their jobs usually identify the boss.

❧ **Governance.** This organization has a simple answer to instituting new policies and procedures. It fires the existing people who do not fit the new model and brings in new people who have the needed skills or abilities.

❧ **Individual Goal.** The spider's web organization places a high value on statements made by credible persons. Who is credible? Anyone who is close to the head of the unit.

❧ **Management Style.** How does the spider's web manage the activities of the organization? It gives responsibility and power to those individuals who are loyal to the head of the unit. If a decision needs to be made, the first question is "what would the leader do?" Then, the decision is made.

❧ **Skills.** How do people in this culture improve their knowledge and skills? The answer is by trial and error. The organization tries something. If it works, it repeats the behavior; if it does not work, it tries something else.

TEAM CULTURE

The third type of subculture focuses on individuals who work together. It is also called the task or problem-solving culture. Its characteristics are these:

❧ **Leader.** The manager is a working member of the team. He or she behaves like the coach of an athletic event. The leader works closely with the group on the playing field.

❧ **Results.** The team culture excels in situations where individuals must solve problems together. A problem may require the skills of a financial analyst, marketing specialist, or data-processing technician. The coach encourages each individual to participate in the group problem-solving process.

❧ **Primary Loyalty.** Even though a coach is clearly visible, he or she does not provide the primary identity for an individual. The identity of a soccer player is as a "goalie" or "striker." Similarly, in the team culture, individuals identify with a task or functional area.

❧ **Governance.** To manage, the team culture seeks to persuade other members of the team and obtain agreement on goals or methods. People look to each other rather than to a leader (spider) or to the rules (bureaucratic culture).

- **Individual Goal.** Team cultures have individuals who do not want to provide the same product or service year after year: This year we solve one problem; give us a new problem for next year.

- **Management Style.** Managers focus on past data or performance. If the goalie is allowing too many opposing goals and is hurting the team, the goalie will be replaced. Similarly, in this context, if the individual performs well, relatively little management will be imposed. Following the rules or demonstrating loyalty to the coach are less important.

- **Skills.** The subculture develops new skills and abilities anywhere where individuals can improve their skills. People learn during strategy sessions. They learn when they are playing the game. They learn after the game is over but is being discussed.

INDIVIDUAL CULTURE

The fourth subculture is concerned with enabling individuals to do their own thing. Its characteristics are as follows:

- **Leader.** Effective individuals in this group are not easy to find. The organization is composed of a group of craftsmen or craftswomen. In many cases, they are loners pursuing their own unique missions. For example, faculty members in a university work in the classroom, but their real goal is to pursue a research agenda. When accepting a position as a chairperson or dean, they tend be lost. Management and the achievement of organizational goals is not their thing.

- **Results.** An individual culture is at its best when a single individual can serve clients by using his or her skills. It works in a law firm where each partner has a specialized skill. Similarly, a medical doctor can build a reputation for successfully performing a particular form of complex surgery.

- **Primary Loyalty.** Individuals are loyal to their particular skill or knowledge area. It might be a discipline or a profession such as accountantcy, computer programming, or the law.

- **Governance.** To manage an individual culture, the head of the unit must gain the respect of the individuals in the unit. The managing partner in a law firm must convince the key partners of the need for change. Similarly, the dean must convince the faculty in a university that change is necessary.

- **Individual Goal.** The most important thing for individuals is the ability to achieve the goals they set for themselves. They want support from the organization but not interference. They do not want to help with other goals or to have to deal with their fellow workers.

- **Management Style.** Individual cultures allow professionals to concentrate on their main areas of interest. Organizational administrative tasks are performed by persons hired to do them. For example, hospitals, law firms, and colleges hire administrators who try not to interfere with the physicians, lawyers, and professors.

- **Skills.** In most cases, individuals in such groups do not develop new skills at the same time. Skill is built on an individual basis by total immersion in a new area. Thus, an accountant studies the new tax law; a doctor develops new surgical skills.

GOLDCORP—CULTURAL COLLABORATION

Tapscott & Williams' book Wikinomics: *How Mass Collaboration Changes Everything* (New York: Penguin Books, 2006) contains a story that illustrates how we can change a culture to seize opportunity.

Goldcorp was a gold mining company headquartered in Toronto with mining operations in Red Lake, Ontario. Gold deposits were running out, and geologists had no new ideas. Rob McEwen, the company's CEO, attended a conference at MIT in 1999. He heard the story of how Linus Torvalds had used the Internet to develop the code for the Linux operating system. Thousands of anonymous programmers contributed to the development of Linux. The story inspired McEwen to consider a similar broadening of knowledge to the task of finding gold deposits. He returned to his company and released to the Internet all its geologic data from 1948 through 1999. He invited all geologists to help the company find new deposits.

The actual project was the Goldcorp Challenge, which took place in March 2000. Prizes of more than a half-million dollars were offered for the best estimates of the location of gold deposits. More than 1,000 individuals tackled 400 megabytes of data. They came from every conceivable background and discipline. Submissions were made by, among others, geologists, mathematicians, consultants, graduate students, and military officers. Applied math, advanced physics, artificial intelligence, chaos theory, and other techniques were used to analyze the data.

The results were astounding. Entries identified 110 potential large deposits, half of them never previously identified. Rob McEwen ordered that $10 million be spent following up on the suggestions, drilling in the deepest and most remote areas of the mine. Substantial gold deposits were found in 80 of the sites. The company grew in revenues from $100 million to $9 billion.

Lesson Learned: A danger in all four of Handy's cultures is that people will not share information, a critical requirement of ERM. Goldcorp and other examples suggest that collaboration in cultures can produce high-quality results. Collaboration requires an interaction among knowledge, mutual learning, creative decision making, and solutions to problems. The process can repeat itself indefinitely. If an organization does not have a collaboration culture, it might face a high level of subculture risk.

Cultural Control and Effectiveness

To reduce risk, ERM should pay attention to both control and effectiveness in various cultures. *Control* is the effort to ensure that a specific outcome is achieved. It may be direct, as when an individual manages a task and all critical activities and decision points. Alternatively, it may be indirect, as when a manager establishes devices and techniques to monitor progress toward goals and reviews critical activities and decision points. We have already seen that direct and indirect control have applications in enterprise risk management. The chief risk officer or other leader of a central risk function is not likely to have direct management control over risks. Rather, the chief risk officer exerts control through the indirect process of influencing risk owners.

Similarly, risk is reduced when subcultures are working in alignment with the business model. Which culture is the most effective culture for achieving short-term goals? Which culture values speed? Which one values accuracy? Which one works only if the unit coordinates effectively with other units? Which one works only when technicians work on their own projects? Which one must develop linkages with other entities to produce results?

FELONS IN OUR MIDST?

A felony is a serious crime, with examples including aggravated assault, arson, embezzlement, robbery, murder, and kidnapping. A felon is a person who commits a felony. Organizations do not intentionally hire many such people. Or do they?

ERM encourages scanning subcultures as it expands the search for enterprise risk. It is instructive to consider the lessons from "The Real Enron Risk", an article by Nancy Parsons in the August 2002 issue of Risk Management magazine. Ms. Parsons contrasts the energy trader who assumes risk to earn profits with an incarcerated felon who has assumed risk outside the legal system. She finds several similarities between energy traders and incarcerated felons: As a start, she identifies an energy trader seeking to outpace competition by quickly capturing lucrative deals within the complex hedge markets for petroleum, gas, coal, and other energy commodities. She compares him to an incarcerated felon, who, prior to confinement, assumed risk outside the boundaries of the legal system while dealing with the need to outpace the authorities.

She identifies the following common traits:

- **Philosophy.** Both behave as though they deserve more than others. They believe they are entitled to take property away from others and keep it for themselves.
- **Goal.** They want to win and see nothing wrong doing so at the expense of others.
- **Organized Chaos.** Compared to others, life is an adventure lived on the edge of society.
- **Breaking of Rules.** They do not identify with cultural norms. The rules simply do not apply to them.

- **Relationships.** They are seen as being deceitful and reckless. This limits meaningful or affectionate interactions with others.
- **Interactions.** They are seen as insensitive and impulsive and tend not to deal effectively with others.

Energy traders and incarcerated felons also have common differences including the following:

- **Charm.** Traders tend to exude charm and even appear to be gracious. Felons are occasionally charming but are more likely to be harsh and even abrupt.
- **Manipulating Skills.** Traders seem to have a natural born ability to convince others to trust them. Felons do not.
- **Success.** A high percentage of traders have historically been successful. Few are punished by the system. The reverse is true for felons.
- **Intelligence.** Traders tend to be bright, sharp, and quick. Felons are often clever but not particularly noteworthy for their skills at assessing the relationship between risk and return.

Lesson Learned: ERM suggests that cultural risk is a product both of the existing culture and key personnel added or removed from it. As an example, assume a company is experiencing problems as a result of aging products and declining financial results. The board of directors is considering hiring a new CEO who fits the profile of an energy trader. Should the company hire such an individual? The answer should trade off the need for a turn around with the impact of an energy trader profile.

RECOGNIZING THE SUBCULTURE

To align a culture with a business model, we need to understand what makes it tick. A checklist of issues is provided in the appendix to this chapter.

Conclusion

To understand subculture risk, one must begin with the risk identifiers in each of the four subcultures described by Charles Handy.

Signals can be quite visible as to whether a company has a bureaucratic, team, spider's web, or individual culture. The checklist of factors in the appendix can be applied directly to a specific unit to identify subculture risk.

Enterprise risk management leaves us with a final thought. After reading about subculture risk, we might be inclined to ask two questions. First, which culture is most common? Second, which is preferred by most individuals? The answers are widely accepted: Most cultures are bureaucratic, but most people prefer a team culture.

CHARACTERISTICS TO USE IN IDENTIFYING SUBCULTURES

This appendix contains tips on how to identify what culture is dominant in a company.

- **Leadership.** Leadership patterns vary by culture as follows:
  - Bureaucracy — Many leaders; diffused power.
  - Spider's Web — One leader, who is given undying allegiance.
  - Team — Manager as coach.
  - Individual — Leader hard to find.

- **Personal Identification.** People identify themselves as follows:
  - Bureaucracy — I work at ACI incorporated.
  - Team — I work in the marketing area.
  - Spider's Web — I work for Mr. Jones.
  - Individual — I am an accountant.

- **Creating Change.** The company creates change as follows:
  - Bureaucracy   Change the rules.
  - Team   Persuade.
  - Spider's Web   Change the people.
  - Individual   Gain respect.

- **What Is Valued.** Individuals place a high value on the following:
  - Bureaucracy   Order and predictability.
  - Team   Variety of tasks.
  - Spider's Web   Closeness to the spider.
  - Individual   Personal freedom.

- **Exercising Control.** Managers exercise control as follows:
  - Bureaucracy   Enforcing the rules.
  - Team   Comparisons with past performance.
  - Spider's Web   Giving power to loyal individuals.
  - Individual   Hiring professional administrators.

- **Learning.** Gaining new knowledge in each culture occurs by:
  - Bureaucracy   Attending formal training programs.
  - Team   Developing new skills anywhere.
  - Spider's Web   Trial and error.
  - Individual   Total immersion.

- **Effectiveness.** Cultures achieve goals as follows:
  - Bureaucracy   Succeeds only if it develops linkages with other entities to produce results.
  - Team   Is probably the most effective culture for the modern organization.
  - Spider's Web   Is effective only if the unit coordinates with other units.
  - Individual   Works if individuals meet the needs of other parties.

❧ **Decisions.** The decisions made in each culture are usually as follows:

- ➤ Bureaucracy   Worst decisions.
- ➤ Team   Best decisions.
- ➤ Spider's Web   Fastest decisions.
- ➤ Individual   Slowest decisions.

Subculture Risk and High School Case

The following analysis borrows from an op-ed column written for the *New York Times* (April 30, 2006) by David Brooks, who compares organizational culture, and hence cultural risk, with a stereotypical high school. The language, some of it controversial, belongs to Mr. Brooks.

Scanning the organization for internal risks requires a broad perspective. A knowledge of psychology and sociology is likely to be more useful than training and experience in risk mitigation. To illustrate this belief, we will use the American high school class structure. According to Brooks, individuals assimilate the rules of the culture in which they live starting at birth, but it is during the high school years that they form most of their values. In the typical high school, we see individuals who fit and give rise to certain stereotypes. We cover each in turn.

Jocks

This is a classic stereotype of a male age 14 to 18 (and carrying on further into age 25 or so) who engages in active team sports. In high school, this individual develops selfish and aggressive behavior that comes from physical strength. The stereotype portrays a jock with characteristics later seen in organizations:

- ➤ **Intelligence.** They are not too bright, but neither are they dumb. To be a successful athlete, one must be smart enough to master playing the game.

- ➤ **Education.** Although the individual stays in school, often through four years of college, the goal is not to become enlightened by new concepts. The knowledge base is fully formed by the age of 13. No new learning takes place.

◆ **Appearance.** They have high self-esteem from exercise and fitness activities. Even if not handsome, they consider themselves to be good looking and have all the confidence that goes with such looks.

◆ **Interpersonal Relationships.** They are socially successful and admired by others, but the success is shallow. They are not respected for integrity, compassion, or depth of feeling. If they stop playing sports, either on the field or in their careers, they become invisible.

◆ **Attitude.** In spite of social success, jocks have an attitude. They do not have compassion for others or empathy for ''losers.'' In many cases, their behavior turns to outright bullying.

Athletes

We should not confuse jocks with athletes. According to Brooks, an athlete in high school and college is an individual who engages in sports as part of a broad success pattern. Typical characteristics are:

◆ **Intelligence.** Bright enough to do more than play the game. Realizes the social benefits that come from not behaving like a jock.

◆ **Education.** They may or may not be good students but continue to learn.

◆ **Appearance.** They are physically fit and confident.

◆ **Interpersonal Relationships.** Excellent on all levels except when dealing with individuals who are jealous, cynical, or unhappy.

◆ **Attitude.** They have a positive outlook that goes beyond sports.

Nerds and Techies

''Nerd'' is a derogatory term for someone who pursues an intellectual or obscure activity with a single-minded focus. In high school, most nerds are the techies who display an obsessive interest in computers and other technologies. Characteristics of nerds are:

◆ **Intelligence.** They tend to be bright in the narrow area of their passion. They think they are bright overall.

◆ **Education.** They learn by total immersion. They spend most of their learning and social time improving specific knowledge and skills.

◆ **Appearance.** Tend not to care what they wear or how they are perceived. They do not care if others like them.

◆ **Interpersonal Relationships.** Have few friends or other relationships. If they have friends, the relationship tends to be limited to the specific area of mutual, intense interest.

◆ **Attitude.** Often excluded from social activities and are not accepted as friends; can have attitude problems when dealing with others. In some cases, they just want to be left alone. In other cases, a negative attitude can show itself in many ways, from social ineptness to outright anger.

Popular People

A popular person is on the highest rung on the high school social ladder. Given most adolescents' need for acceptance, popularity becomes almost a drug on which to get high. Typical characteristics of popular people are:

◆ **Intelligence.** May be smart or not. If smart, the individual will play down his or her intelligence. If not smart, the individual will display social skills that create the appearance of intelligence.

◆ **Education.** May or may not be learning new concepts but is constantly working on improving skills with people.

◆ **Appearance.** A popular person is a good-looking person. If a female, she is pretty; if a male, he is handsome.

◆ **Interpersonal Relationships.** Relationships are the passion of the popular person, just as sports is the passion of the jock and technology is the passion of the nerd. A popular person works on popularity as a full-time job.

◆ **Attitude.** Have a great attitude and are well-liked and admired. Why not?

Thugs

Just as the popular person is at the top of the social scale, the thug is at the bottom. Brooks says this individual takes advantage of others through intimidation and force, either verbal or physical. Girls can fit the mold by excluding individuals from a social circle. Boys pick fights and otherwise bully weaker students. Characteristics of this group are:

- **Intelligence.** If bright, they do not use their intelligence visibly and fail to understand the long-term consequences of dysfunctional behavior.

- **Education.** May mature over time or through a life-changing experience. If the negative response to his or her behavior is sufficiently strong, may change behavior. If not, some thugs become dishonest and petty in their adult lives. Some go to jail. Some bring bad behavior into the workplace.

- **Appearance.** Convey a tough image in all dealings with fellow students, teachers, and authority figures. This can continue into adulthood with colleagues and bosses.

- **Attitude.** Thugs have bad attitudes. Most people avoid thugs if possible in high school. After high school, people avoid them when possible at work.

A Morality Play?

Brooks would argue that cultural risk deals with organizational conflicts that start in adolescence, a period when people are trapped with jocks, athletes, nerds, popular persons, and thugs. We can add richness to the story by recognizing that high school teaches us that our lives are shaped by two main characters:

- **One's Adolescent Self.** Whatever stereotype fits one most closely in high school, every individual wants to be the hero of a morality play. We want what we need, whether love, admiration, or power. Each person seeks to meet his or her unmet needs or to continue to experience the joy of the need that was met in high school.

- **One's Adolescent Opposite.** This is the enemy of the hero. For a popular person, the opposite may be a thug. For a jock, it may be the nerd.

Understanding High School Values

Cultural risk in organizations continues the morality play begun in high school. If we identify the risk owner's adolescent self and adolescent opposite, we can predict the attitudes and behaviors that help or impede the achievement of goals. Maybe we can improve a subculture if we recognize the jocks, athletes, nerds, techies, and popular people when they are mixed together. As examples of problems that can arise, Brooks identifies the natural conflict between high school students who work hard at class assignments and homework and jocks, athletes, and popular persons, who do not. All the prestige goes to the second group, not to the hardest workers. Cool people do not acknowledge nerds and techies. Students with high grades may be mocked or isolated.

These pressures are at the root of many aspects of subculture risk as adolescent behavior continues into organizations. We see it all the time. The accounting department does not like the marketing group. Nobody likes the accounting department. Former nerds and techies experience pleasure-inducing dopamine surges in their brains as they savor scandals and misfortunes that harm their formerly popular and currently successful adolescent enemies. Many people experienced satisfaction at the jailing of former Enron executives. Others were joyful at the widely perceived failure of the administration of George W. Bush, seen as a former "frat boy" from Yale.

In adulthood and in organizations, the once-upon-a-time prom kings and queens bring their own agendas to the table. According to Brooks, they tend to have "coldly gracious spouses and effortlessly slender children." Still, it is not enough. Former popular students dislike successful nerds and techies.

Brooks suggests that cultural risk can be managed by meeting the needs of all the former high school students—matching jocks with geeks. Jocks know that geeks should never manage anything. Geeks learn they must speak slowly so that the jocks will understand them. Matching geeks with popular kids will get things done. One gets the job done; the other has the interpersonal skills to gain support from others.

Lesson Learned: The Brooks model seems useful but should be used with care. Not everyone will agree with Brooks when the theory is applied to reality. For each U.S. president since 1976, Brooks might argue for the following descriptions. Some seem controversial. Do you agree with them? Whether you agree or not, does it tell who you were in high school?

- Bill Clinton: A popular geek, well-balanced, interesting, and neurotic
- Jimmy Carter: Interesting, maybe neurotic
- Ronald Reagan: Well-balanced and dull
- George H. W. Bush: Well-balanced, a little interesting
- George W. Bush: Well-balanced and dull
- Barack Obama: Cool, calm, collected, and inspiring

CHAPTER 14

LEADERSHIP RISK

RISK QUOTE: *I've missed over 9,000 shots in my career. I've lost almost 300 games. Twenty-six times I've been trusted to take the game-winning shot . . . and missed. I've failed over and over and over again in my life. And that is why I succeed.*
—MICHAEL JORDAN, STAR BASKETBALL PLAYER

RISK QUOTE: *I feel that luck is preparation meeting opportunity.*
—OPRAH WINFREY, BUSINESSWOMAN
AND TV PERSONALITY

A critical risk involves the leadership of the entity and leaders of key units and initiatives. Rarely discussed in conversations about enterprise risk management, the failure of leadership can be linked directly to unexpected losses and missed opportunities. In this chapter, we examine leadership as a component in an ERM program.

Behavioral Risk

Behavior refers to the actions or reactions of an organism, usually in relation to its environment. Behavior can be conscious or unconscious. A person can know that a behavior is happening or can react automatically to a stimulus without conscious thought. The behavior can also be visible or hidden; it can be observable, or it can be shielded from view. Behavior can be voluntary or involuntary; a person can control the behavior, or it can be driven by uncontrollable emotions or events. Finally, it can be appropriate or inappropriate, meeting norms of the culture or violating those norms.

Behavioral risk arises in a setting with specific characteristics. Bad behavior can take place anywhere, but it is not behavioral risk if it does not occur in an organized system with goals. To represent leadership risk, individuals must display inappropriate behavior that violates the norms of the entity. The misbehavior must have a negative impact, causing either a loss or a missed opportunity.

ERM recognizes that management is not the same as leadership. *Management*, which comes from the Italian for "handle a horse," which derives from the Latin word for hand, is a process for getting things done through people. It directs deployment and manipulation of resources, whether human, financial, material, intellectual, or intangible. *Leadership*, on the other hand, is doing the right thing at the right time to get people to perform in a timely fashion. An exposure arises when an organization has weaknesses in the roles played by those who are expected to manage and those who are expected to lead. ERM addresses exposures that arise from those weaknesses.

In an ERM framework, we recognize that organizations have specific expectations. A manager is expected to stabilize an organization. A manager gets power from his or her position in the organizational hierarchy. A leader, on the other hand, is expected to energize an organization. Deriving power from his or her ability to influence others, a leader has the potential to exert broad influence.

Although organizations often think that management and leadership involve the same risks, ERM recognizes some key differences:

- ❧ **Goal Orientation.** Leaders have a more expansive view of the world than managers. They look beyond short-term goals or requirements. Managers tend to focus on the tasks at hand.

❧ **Vision.** A leader's vision is much larger than the vision of a manager. The leader grasps the relationship between the organization and the larger world in terms of opportunities and changing circumstances.

❧ **Values.** Leaders and managers have different value systems. Managers respect people, relationships, structure, and policies. Leaders respect intangibles and understand the emotional and unconscious elements in the interaction between themselves and others.

ERM scans internally to ensure that managers are located in areas where stability is needed and that leaders are situated in areas where change is needed. Some issues related to the deployment of managers and leaders can arise:

❧ **Multiple Constituencies.** Will a good manager or a good leader be more effective in dealing with multiple constituencies? It depends upon the culture. In a traditional hierarchy, a good manager can use the authority of his or her position to keep organizational units focused. In a team culture, a good leader is more likely to be effective dealing with conflicting requirements of others.

❧ **Speed and Complexity.** Will an effective manager or an effective leader be more able to handle complex and rapidly changing situations? Evidence indicates that effective leadership works better than effective management in crises or otherwise fast-changing environments.

❧ **Communication Skills.** Is a good manager or a good leader better at sharing ideas and strategies? Evidence shows that verbal communication is the key to distinguishing good leaders. Leaders talk more than managers, measured simply by the number of words spoken. Can a manager be effective without a high level of verbal interaction? Many studies support the belief that leadership is not appreciated in a management role in the absence of verbal communication.

Strategic and Situational Leadership

Two concepts are particularly important when assessing leadership weaknesses and strengths: strategic leadership and situational leadership. *Strategic leadership* is defined as an effort to properly manage people, resources, and behavior in order to solve problems and make correct decisions. The process starts with goal identification. What does the organization need to do to sustain competitive advantage? It includes strategy. How will the organization pursue the goal? It evaluates skills. Does the organization have the leadership skills to choose the right strategy and implement it?

Situational leadership, as formulated by Blanchard and Hersey in the 1960s, argues that leaders should match actions to the situation. Different behaviors are needed in different situations to achieve strategic goals. Situational leadership does not refer to a process. Rather, it deals with a specific action. First, there must be a need for action. We are dealing with an individual in relation to a situation at a moment in time. Second, the entity must be seeking an adjustment to existing practice, looking for the individual to consider behavioral choices in light of new realities. Finally, the individual must take an action. Success is judged in terms of the goal of "doing the right thing at the right time."

Situational Leadership Styles

ERM is concerned with strengths and weaknesses in different subcultures and the impact of behavior resulting from four situational leadership styles. They are:

- **Directing.** The leader defines the roles and tasks of followers and supervises them closely. The leader makes the final decisions.

- **Coaching.** The leader defines roles and tasks but seeks inputs from followers. The leader makes the final decision after consultation with the team.

❧ **Supporting.** The leader shares goals and delegates many decisions on the approach to achieving the goals. Followers exercise the most control over the situation in consultation with the leader.

BILL GATES' INTERNET LEADERSHIP

In the early 1990s, Microsoft was developing a technology to compete with the Internet. One day, Bill Gates reversed the effort, brought the Microsoft leaders and software developers into a room, and directed that they stop the project and start working on projects to build the Internet. Is this an example of strategic or situational leadership? The answer is both.

◆ **Strategic Leadership.** Bill Gates launched a project to build Microsoft Network, to compete with the Internet. When he realized that the project was not making the progress he expected, he sought a new strategy. The success of Internet Explorer is an example of strategic leadership.

◆ **Situational Leadership.** Once he knew that Microsoft had to change direction, he wasted no time switching to a winning long-term strategy. The speed and decisive behavior he exhibited are an example of situational leadership.

❧ **Delegating.** The leader is concerned only with outcomes and the achieving of objectives. Followers make decisions on strategies and courses of action that lead to the achievement of goals.

Development Level

ERM recognizes the importance of developmental level in situational leadership. *Development level* refers to the competence and commitment of individuals who follow a leader. Risk is reduced when the leadership behavior recognizes that level of competence and commitment of others. If a person is not competent to perform a task that requires certain skills, the task should not be assigned to that person. If an individual is not committed to success, this is a red flag that endangers the achievement of a goal. In the framework of competence and commitment, leadership must adjust to be effective.

We can identify multiple situational development levels for units and individuals. Some examples are as follows:

- **Low Competence, High Commitment.** Lacks specific skills required to achieve a goal but is eager to learn and take direction.
- **Some Competence, Low Commitment.** Cannot do the job without help and is uncomfortable with the situation.
- **High Competence, Variable Commitment.** Fully capable, but lacks confidence or motivation to do the task.
- **High Competence, High Commitment.** Comfortable with the task and has the ability to do it well.

JÜRGEN SCHREMPP—COMPETENCE AND COMMITMENT

Jürgen Schrempp was the CEO of Daimler Benz when the company merged with Chrysler to become Daimler-Chrysler in 1998. He can serve as an example of strategic and situational leadership. He also shows us the danger of low competence and low commitment.

Schrempp headed the aerospace division of Daimler-Benz prior to becoming the CEO of Daimler-Benz in 1995. He led the acquisition of Fokker, a Dutch aircraft manufacturer, in 1993, at a time when Fokker was having serious problems. He was not able to fix Fokker. After receiving subsidies of billions of Deutsche marks, Fokker filed for bankruptcy. In 1998, Schrempp led Daimler-Benz to acquire Chrysler for $37 billion. In 2007, Daimler sold 80 percent of Chrysler to Cerberus, a private equity firm, for $7 billion. Both Fokker and Chrysler appear to be failures of strategic leadership.

At the time of the merger with Chrysler, in 1998, Schrempp described the union as "a merger of equals, a merger of growth, and a merger of unprecedented strength." In the next years, situational leadership was desperately needed. Daimler and Chrysler had markedly different compensation structures, management styles, and values. In the major Chrysler market segments, manufacturers had chronic overcapacity, buyers had many choices, and people were concerned about the environmental damage done by the internal combustion engine. Moreover, Chrysler was an inefficient manufacturer compared to Toyota and others.

In late 2000, Jürgen Schrempp was quoted in a German newspaper with a statement that he always intended Chrysler to be a subsidiary of DaimlerChrysler. Part of his statement read, "The Merger of Equals statement was necessary in order to earn the support of Chrysler's workers and the American public, but it was never reality."

The "merger" with Chrysler, with its low competence and even lower commitment, was a failure of strategic leadership. The 2000 statement that he lied in 1998, at the time of the merger, was Mr. Schrempp's failure of situational leadership.

Leadership Decision

A final ERM view of leadership involves the nature of decision making in the entity. To fully understand subculture and leadership risk, we need to recognize how people solve problems and make decisions. Approaches to decision making can be based on one of five factors:

1. **Facts.** This is the use of empirical data, observable phenomenon, or other supporting information to verify a decision with logic and evidence.

2. **Beliefs.** This involves a combination of a search for facts and subjective interpretations by problem solvers or decision makers.

3. **Feelings.** Even if people start with facts or beliefs, they have feelings that intensify or diminish the value and accuracy of those facts and beliefs.

4. **Opinions.** In many cases, an individual's value system overtakes facts and beliefs. The person makes a judgment, perhaps accompanied by intense feelings, and brings it to the decision-making process. It is common for individuals to attempt to mask opinions as facts and beliefs.

5. **Assumptions.** Assumptions are beliefs held without reflection. People take things for granted, even when no observable or

intuitive factors support a belief. Sometimes, assumptions are correct and reasonable. Other times, they are not.

How Leaders Decide

We know that leadership risk is reduced if leaders get the correct mix of facts, beliefs, feelings, opinions, and assumptions. They can use these guidelines:

- **Beliefs.** Leaders, like everyone else, make risk mitigation decisions and solve problems on the basis of what they believe. It is that simple.
- **Facts.** Leaders use facts to shape beliefs. Contrary to many views, facts are not true in themselves. Nor are they something that can be "proved." Rather, they are supported by evidence. For strategic leadership, we need to gather evidence to support a decision or mitigate a risk. For situational leadership, we use evidence from earlier experience to shape our belief in a valid direction in the current situation.
- **Feelings.** Leaders know that feelings intensify discussions on risk. They should be conscious of their own feelings that might lead them in the wrong direction. They should also consider the feelings of others that might take a risk mitigation strategy in the wrong direction.
- **Assumptions.** Everybody assumes things, but the source of the assumption may be unknown to the individual. Leaders should continually assess their own assumptions.
- **Opinions.** Leaders know that opinions, based on unknown sources and possibly biased, do not count for much when mitigating risk or pursuing risk opportunities.

TOYOTA—STRATEGIC AND SITUATIONAL LEADERSHIP

Sayaka Kobayashi studied in the United States and then joined Toyota Motor North America in 1997. In 2003, she was transferred to the corporate planning department in New York. In the spring of 2005, Hideaki

Otaka, the CEO of Toyota N.A., transferred the 41-year-old woman to his office as his personal assistant.

In May 2006, Sayaka filed a lawsuit alleging sexual harassment and identified the following incidents:

September 2005. On a business trip, Hideaki summons Sayaka to his hotel room at night and gropes her.

October 2005. Hideaki sends her a greeting card and necklace.

November 2005. Hideaki takes her to lunch, to a museum, and for a walk in Central Park and attempts another groping. Sayaka reports the incidents to human resources. Nothing happens.

December 2005. A Toyota executive advises Sayaka to meet alone with Hideaki to discuss the situation. She agrees. During the meeting, Hideaki says that both he and she have behavioral problems. He criticizes her for not thanking him for roses he sent on her birthday. Ten days after the meeting, Hideaki promotes Sayaka. She remains part of the CEO office.

January 2005. Toyota's general counsel advises Sayaka to consider her options, including resigning. Hideaki learns that Sayaka was married on December 30. He tells her that he would not have bothered her if he had known she was getting married.

Lesson Learned: The behavior alleged is inappropriate in both Japanese and U.S. cultures. That is not the real risk issue. As cultural expectations change, failure to have policies that meet legal requirements is a failure of strategic leadership risk. Toyota's failure to respond to the complaint was a failure of situational leadership.

Conclusion

ERM can identify many dimensions of leadership risk and their impact on risk strategies. In an ERM framework, leadership trumps management. Here is a quick example. Figure 14-1 shows an organization chart with the position of Unit A filled and Unit B vacant. Where does the manager go to fill the unit B vacancy? Almost always, the first place to look is to the heads of subunits 6 through 9. Managers climb a hierarchy. They look below them to fill positions. Where does a leader facing the same question turn?

FIGURE 14-1. LEADERSHIP AND AN ORGANIZATION CHART.

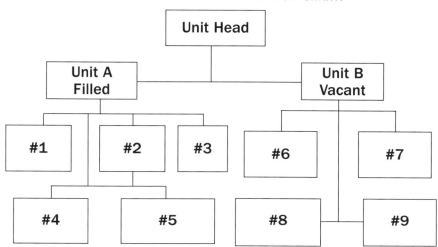

The leader defines the qualities needed in the head of Unit B. Then, the leader goes wherever necessary to find someone with those qualities. The vacancy could be filled with someone from subunits 6 through 9, subunits 1 through 5, or elsewhere.

Now we have leadership that can help an organization match its appetite for risk with the level of risk it accepts. Good management is beneficial in many ways. Good leadership is critical for dealing with enterprise risk.

IKEA—Best Practices in Leadership Risk

IKEA—Best Practices in Leadership Risk

IKEA is a Swedish company that sells home furnishing products around the world. In 2009, it had over 300,000 stores in 36 countries. In terms of high performance management, it is one of the world's most successful companies. It offers a picture of managing leadership risk that was a best practice for global companies.

Leadership at IKEA was not an action, decision making process, or alignment of strategies with goals. Effectively, it was a ''state of mind.'' Many companies assess the quality of leadership in terms of financial success, such as increasing shareholder value. They pursue excellent management for that specific purpose. IKEA pursued something else. Leadership at the company meant contemporary design, low prices, wacky promotions, and customer enthusiasm. Fail to have these in your store, and you were not a leader. Conversely, if you had them, they quickly led to financial success. Even in the 2008 global economic crisis, people still shopped at IKEA stores.

The management of leadership risk at IKEA was directly linked to a recognition of how leaders achieve high performance. In the case of a retail furniture company, leadership is all about the external world responding to the entity, and more specific to the experience. IKEA's ''state of mind'' is an image of lifestyle for customers around the world. Walk into an IKEA store, and your brain tells you things like:

◆ We have arrived.

◆ We recognize the importance of affordable contemporary design.

◆ We have good taste.

◆ We pursue a strong value to price relationship in our purchases.

Perhaps the most interesting aspect of the state of mind deals with the word ''we.'' Who is ''we?'' If you answer quickly, you will say Ikea. If you reflect upon it for a moment, ''we'' is the customer, and perhaps his or her friends, family, and peers. Once ''we'' is the customer, it becomes, by extension, Ikea itself..

Managing leadership risk at Ikea is blended into a high performance strategy as an employer. It has several components:

◆ **Autonomy.** It starts right here. Employees made the decisions and had authority. Performance expectations meant customer service.

◆ **Hierarchy.** Ikea did not have much going on here. The rigid bureaucracy found in so many companies when they reach a certain size did not impede the autonomy to create a state of mind.

◆ **Culture.** Ikea strove to be family friendly. Parents and siblings may fight but not at Ikea. Everybody could find things that were fun.

◆ **Value.** Finally, Ikea recognized that an important belief of shoppers is that they are getting value for their money. Ok. Yes, the store had low prices but that was only half of the value picture. The state of mind combined frugality and style. The merchandise was not "cheap." It was practical, stylish, and also reasonably priced.

Leadership at IKEA takes advantage of beliefs, facts, emotions, and assumptions, but not of the leaders themselves. Rather, of the customers. People believed in a good experience and had evidence of good shopping. They assumed the shopping would be fun, and this created a positive emotional state of mind. An example occurred when IKEA opened a new store. In 2005, the company offered $4,000 in gift certificates and a hundred smaller prizes to the first 101 people in line at the opening of its Atlanta store. Roger Penguino, a 24-year old employee of Apple Computer, arrived seven days before the opening and pitched a tent. Two thousand people were in line when the doors finally opened.

A state of mind. It gets better in the same year with a new IKEA store in London. The store opened at nine in the morning in Atlanta, but at midnight in London. Atlanta's 2,000 people in line were dwarfed by 6,000 at the door in London. No one was injured in the crush in Atlanta while London had 26 injuries, including six that required hospitalization. The Atlanta store stayed open for twelve hours while the London store ran out of goods and closed in 30 minutes.

IKEA operated around the world and clearly showed it had enterprise risk management efforts in place. It pursued the upside of risk and aligned risk owners with the business model. Moreover, it scanned the horizon for changes in circumstances and new opportunities. Its courtship with India in 2007-2009 is a good illustration. It decided that the Indian market would be attractive, and it pursued entry. A thorough scan of the market slowed down the effort. IKEA recognized that India lacked basic infrastructure, had an unstable and corrupt supply chain, did not create modern regulations for foreign direct investment, and had not reformed troublesome tax and import duty structures. The company noted soaring land prices and had questions about whether the right state of mind could be created for customer and employees. In early 2009, IKEA decided to postpone or maybe even cancel its plans to enter the market in India. A thorough assessment in an ERM context.

Lesson Learned: The IKEA focus on creating a customer state of mind has produced strong financial results. The private company did not file an annual report to the public, but probably had $20 billion in sales in 2008, and upwards of $2 billion in profit as it continued growth by opening new stores. With its ups and down—more of the former than the latter—IKEA was a corporate model for the upside of managing leadership risk.

CHAPTER 15

LIFE CYCLE RISK

RISK QUOTE: *It's gonna be a long hard drag, but we'll make it.*
—JANIS JOPLIN, SINGER AND SONG WRITER

RISK QUOTE: *The superior man makes the difficulty to be overcome his first interest; success only comes later.*
—CONFUCIUS, CHINESE PHILOSOPHER

Another risk not assigned to a single risk owner is life cycle risk—the reality that business units and lines of business start up, grow to maturity, and, in many cases, enter a period of stagnation or decline. The challenge for a central risk function is first to understand life cycle risk and then to identify the stage of the life cycle for different units.

Most large companies have units at different stages in the organizational life cycle. The four stages of the life cycle are these:

- 1. **Startup.** The birth of a unit. It occurs when a company invests money in a new operation, assigns managers and workers to build the unit, and designs a product or service to bring it to market. The unit focuses on a business model.

- 2. **Growth.** The period of rapid expansion when the unit has brought products or services to market and now seeks strong growth of revenues and expansion of the workforce.

- 3. **Peak.** After a period of growth, the unit reaches maturity. If successful, the unit sells its products or services at prices and volumes that produce strong profits. It experiences slower growth.

❧ 4. **Decline.** At some point, the business model may no longer match the market. This can lead to declines in profits and market share. If the unit fails to implement a renewal strategy, the organization may shut down the unit.

Life Cycle Risks

Life cycle risk refers to a failure to manage exposures or seize opportunities during any of the stages. The risk depends to some degree on the stage of the unit in its life cycle. Examples include these:

❧ **Startup Unit.** The exposure is the possibility that the product will never be ready or that the market cannot be accessed or developed.

❧ **Growth Unit.** The exposure occurs if growth stalls before the unit reaches a stable level of sales.

❧ **Peak Unit.** This exposure deals with the possibility that the entity is producing and selling mature products but will not be able to sustain its success.

❧ **Declining Unit.** This unit is losing money or soon will be losing money. Managers have ideas for changing course but may not be successful reversing the trend.

Sharing Life Cycle Risk Information

An important value added by a central risk function is the ability to identify the life cycle stage of units and to share information with risk owners. For example, in any large corporation, the entity has its goal, but so does each unit. Are unit goals aligned with the business model?

ERM recognizes that risks may be difficult to identify in different stages of the life cycle. Startups normally do not want to reveal development problems. Growth units tend to be optimistic about success even as they encounter obstacles. Peak units focus on the upside, not on exposures or missed opportunities. Declining units may deliberately hide bad news.

LIFE CYCLE STAGES GOALS

The central risk function can share the reality that different stages have different goals, no matter what the entity goal:

Declining Unit	*The goal is survival. The unit is trying to hang on and to find new products and markets to avoid closure.*
Peak Unit	*The unit aims to increase revenues, make more profit, and maximize success.*
Growth Unit	*The goal is to increase unit sales. The unit needs more units to be stable, to speed up the recovery of development costs, and to start earning a profit.*
Startup	*Enter the market and prepare for a bright future.*

Life Cycle Stage Focus

Organizations have a tactical focus that varies by life cycle stage. It covers such issues as these: What is the entity's primary goal? What does everyone discuss at planning meetings? What dominates the budget discussions? The central risk function can identify the life cycle stage of a unit and explain the focus to a risk owner. This can often help move a unit closer to the organizational goals.

Planning Horizons

A planning horizon is the length of time that management believes will be required for a successful operation. Planning horizons vary at different life cycle stages:

- ❦ **Short Term.** Normally a few months to a year, this planning horizon focuses on near-term profits. Planning is often driven by bonus plans for corporate executives.

LIFE CYCLE TACTICAL FOCUS

Declining Unit	*Focus is lower costs. The unit is losing money. Sales are declining. New products are not successful.*
Peak Unit	*Focus is on maximizing profits. The unit knows its customers and meets their needs. The motto is "Milk the markets."*
Growth Unit	*Focus is on sales volume. Units need volume.*
Startup	*Focus is on product design. The company needs a finished product.*

❧ **Medium Term.** Generally a period from one to three or five years. The emphasis is on reliable products, services, and markets. Planners want to ensure consistency of operations beyond the current year.

❧ **Long Term.** A period in excess of three years to seven years or beyond. Planners evaluate capital investments, changing technology, and other factors to help achieve long-term stability and permanency of operations.

A central risk function can help risk owners understand that they must coordinate risk mitigation with the planning horizon of a unit. If immediate action is needed for a unit looking far into the future, a risk strategy is in danger.

LIFE CYCLE STAGES PLANNING HORIZON

Declining Unit	*Short term: Survive another year.*
Peak Unit	*Medium term: Keep success going for a while.*
Growth Unit	*Medium to long term: Build markets.*
Startup	*Long term: Complete products and find markets.*

Growth as a Risk Factor

Growth may be defined as an increase in revenues, profits, cash flow, or assets. The most common goal of a corporation is to grow revenues or profits. Growth of assets can reflect inefficiency, as when an organization adds equipment and then does not need it when sales lag. Organizational growth is a risk factor. Growing units tend to have greater opportunities accompanied by higher risk levels. ERM should recognize risks associated with growth goals.

As organizations pursue growth, a central risk function can help risk owners understand that life cycle stages affect the kind of growth that is sought. This information may be helpful in moving units to growth strategies aligned with the business model.

LIFE CYCLE STAGES AND DEFINITIONS OF GROWTH

Declining Unit	*Reduction in losses or expenses*
Peak Unit	*Increase in dollar sales (profits and cash flow follow)*
Growth Unit	*Increase in unit sales (pursuing break-even)*
Startup	*Increase in project deadlines completed*

Risks with Change

Managing change refers to the way an entity adjusts a goal, process, activity, or venture by substituting a new strategy for an existing behavior or course of action. ERM programs recognize that change poses risks for organizational units and individuals. The central risk function can identify the likely resistance to change and help risk owners deal with units in different life cycle stages.

LIFE CYCLE STAGES AND RESISTANCE TO CHANGE

Units in various stages will resist ERM because they fear what may be revealed. Example:

Declining Unit	*May show risks that result in decision to close unit*
Peak Unit	*May divert unit from profit goals*
Growth Unit	*May show that product will not reach viable sales level*
Startup	*May show development cost overruns or missed deadlines*

Problems Implementing ERM

Different challenges arise as entities implement ERM in each stage of the life cycle. They include these:

- **Priorities.** Managers will seek to fit ERM into a priority list of projects that are under way. ERM will take time away from other activities. How important is the program in comparison to day-to-day activities?

- **Goals.** Managers have goals handed down from senior managers. They are expected to achieve them. Do managers perceive that an ERM program increases the likelihood that they will reach the goals?

- **Workloads.** Managers are busy. Often, they face a day-to-day frenzy in a pursuit of greater productivity. With heavier workloads and expectations for efficiency, do managers have the time to devote to the project?

- **Money.** The costs of an ERM program are often chargeable to different budgets. They might involve expenses without yielding visible revenues to offset them. Do people want to finance ERM?

A major difficulty with implementing an ERM program is to deal with problems such as the following:

- **Coordination.** Units may be unprepared for coordinating risks with other units. The whole idea may not be consistent with the processes and procedures that have been in place for a considerable period of time.

- **Planning and Linkages.** Units lack strategies and mechanisms for managing risks in a framework beyond their boundaries. Interaction with many units may be infrequent. In some cases, a unit may be competing with another unit for favor, resources, or attention. In other cases, hostility between units may exist.

- **View of ERM.** A unit may see ERM as a threat to organizational stability and individual goals. Everyone knows the current relationships and expectations but worry about what the new system will mean.

Funding for ERM

An organization finances its ongoing activities from cash provided by operations. As they move through the stages of the life cycle, units have different cash flow pictures:

- **Startup and Growth Stage.** Cash flows are negative for units in the startup and growth stages. Startups need funding to bring a product to market. Growth units need funds to finance expansions to reach break-even.
- **Declining Stage.** Cash flows are either negative or soon to be negative. Declining units need money, or think they need money, to cover losses and to finance efforts to turn around the unit.
- **Peak Unit.** Cash flows are positive, often quite positive.

Given this situation, where do the units get the money to finance the future? It must come from the peak unit, where the overage is the only source of internal funding. Assume now that the future project is ERM. If an organization has many declining, growth, and startup units, funding for ERM may have a low priority in budget discussions.

Priority for ERM

The next issue involves the priority given to the implementation of ERM. How important is ERM to units in each stage of the life cycle? The answer is that ERM is not important. Instead, it threatens each unit:

- **Startup and Growth Units.** ERM is seen as a distraction. Managers have a job to do and wish to get on with it.

LIFE CYCLE RISK—DEAD HORSE BEHAVIOR

One of the most difficult subculture decisions involves declining units. At what point do you pull the plug? Dakota tribal wisdom says that when you discover you are riding a dead horse, the best strategy is to dismount. Modern corporations have not always been as wise as their native American brothers. We can identify other strategies for handling life cycle risk:

◆ Buy a stronger whip (increase negative incentives).

◆ Change riders (fire people).

◆ Say things like "This is the way we always have ridden this horse" ("Everything is okay.").

◆ Arrange to visit other sites to see how they ride dead horses (seek external support).

◆ Create a committee to study dead horses in today's business environment (slow down the process).

◆ Change the specifications for what constitutes "dead" (lower expectations).

◆ Hire contractors to ride the dead horse and charge double (see if someone else can do job).

◆ Harness several dead horses together for increased speed (bury unit in other units).

◆ Provide additional funding to increase the horse's performance (Seek a financial rescue).

◆ Award the rider a huge bonus for reducing the horse's operating costs (change criteria for evaluation).

    ❧ **Peak Unit.** ERM is not perceived as being needed. Managers believe all is going well and question what ERM can do for them.

    ❧ **Declining Unit.** Managers perceive ERM as a threat. It may uncover the hopelessness of the situation. They do not need that.

Politics of ERM

The politics of an organization can be a major factor in an ERM implementation. The declining unit can be a particular problem, even as it may need ERM the most. The unit may be past its peak, but it still has a number of senior and powerful executives. The number of vice presidencies in a unit tends to rise with time and may be slow to drop when the unit matures and then declines. As the declining unit is most likely to resist ERM, it also has considerable senior executive clout. Resistance may be fierce.

Another political issue arises with cultural risk. Facts, beliefs, feelings, opinions, or assumptions will become factors in efforts to slow down an ERM implementation. The startup and growth units often believe they are the future of the organization and will use beliefs. The peak unit may point to the evidence showing their current success and thus use facts. The declining unit may use beliefs intensified by feelings. The message: We were once great (feelings) or we can be great again (beliefs).

To counter resistance to the implementation of an ERM system, the organization needs to overcome negative feelings, opinions, and assumptions with different messages. To the startup and growth units, the message can be that ERM offers benefits that increase the chance of success in the future. To the peak unit, the message can be that ERM can keep the unit on top. To the declining unit, it can help to point out that ERM might solve some of its problems.

Conclusion

Life cycle exposures pose a variety of risks to an organization. Any ERM effort should recognize the stage of the life cycle of each operating unit and include a strategy for dealing with varying goals, needs, and concerns. An independent central risk function can bring considerable light to the darkness of behavior often found in situations where real intentions are hidden.

GM and Toyota Life Cycle Risk Case

Note: This case study is based on a article that appeared in *The Wall Street Journal* on May 24, 2006.

Toyota and General Motors offer a view of life cycle risk in their manufacturing plants in San Antonio and Arlington, Texas. In 2006, GM had
a 50-year-plus aging plant in Arlington, Texas. Toyota opened a new
plant in San Antonio. A comparison of the two plants shows the following:

	GM	Toyota
Annual Vehicles	200,000	200,000
Work Space (sq. ft. million)	3.75	2.2
Property, Acres	249	2,000
Workers	2,800	1,600
Hourly Wages	$28	$22
Hourly Total Labor	$35	$28
Labor Cost per Vehicle	$1,800	$800

Toyota was in an earlier life cycle stage, opening as it did a
new facility. This gave Toyota's operation considerable advantages.
Smaller and lighter machinery took up less space than similar but
older equipment in the GM plant. Toyota had less complex machinery that was easier to use, and was less likely to break down.
Toyota's new automated machinery required fewer laborers to operate, maintain, and repair.

Lesson Learned: Prior to 2006, General Motors failed to update and modernize its operations. Thus, it trapped itself in an
uncompetitive life cycle position as the disadvantages it faced in
Texas were repeated at other GM plants. General Motors protected
declining operations rather than create new business processes to
meet changing conditions in automobile markets. These behaviors, which were found at Ford and Chrysler as well, were visible
in 2006 and earlier. They came to a head in late 2008 when GM
and Chrysler were forced to ask Congress for a bailout. By then, it
may have been too late for ERM.

CHAPTER 16

HORIZON RISK

RISK QUOTE: *It doesn't matter if a cat is black or white, so long as it catches mice.*

—DENG XIAOPING, CHINESE REVOLUTIONARY, POLITICIAN, AND REFORMER

RISK QUOTE: *Greed, for lack of a better word, is good. Greed is right, greed works. Greed clarifies, cuts through, and captures the essence of the evolutionary spirit.*

—GORDON GEKKO, IN *WALL STREET* (1987)

The final risk category that crosses organizational boundaries, horizon risk, is, all too often, ignored. Horizon risk is an external exposure that arises when the organization is not actively scanning its external environment for developments and changing trends that could affect business and operations. With a global knowledge economy and increasingly complex structures for conducting business, scanning the horizon has become an increasingly important role of a central risk function.

In an ERM framework, we should investigate the mechanisms that are used to ensure an effective program of scanning outside the entity, identifying latent exposures, and communicating them to interested managers. The scanning should focus on risk factors that could threaten the alignment of goals and strategies. Three broad goals of the scanning process are:

1. **Vision Risk.** Do we have a compelling business model that is consistent with changes that are occurring outside our control or current risk mitigation strategies?

2. **Resources Risk.** Have we linked and will we continue to be linked proactively so that resources expended will not be wasted as a result of changing external conditions?

3. **Market Risk.** When we assess capabilities and likely actions of customers and competitors, are we considering new developments and trends that could destroy our business?

The ERM model gives the central risk function a role in the development and vetting of corporate strategies: to identify risk and share its findings. Any such role is compromised if the unit is not scanning the horizon. It is essential to try to see horizon risk before competitors and others recognize the danger and to share findings so that risk owners can adjust and respond. With respect to profits and cash flow, this means identifying opportunities as the upside of risk and, once again, sharing them. In the sharing process, it is important to show how distant external developments might affect corporate strategies.

EXERCISE

A central risk function has scanned the horizon and has seen the following.

Moral and Ethical Values: Declining.

Interactions Among Political Leaders: Increasingly hostile.

International Relations: Government is overconfident and somewhat arrogant, so that even foreign relationships are accompanied by failures.

Fiscal Responsibility: Central government has no constraints on borrowing and spending.

Questions: What is the year? What is the entity?

Answer: We can choose between the Roman Empire after 300 A.D. and the United States after 2000 A.D.

Scanning the horizon, a central risk function might success-fully identify megachanges in the business environment. In retro-spect, we can see massive changes in human, social, and economic development that affect organizations. Can we see them while they are still in their early stages? Would we have seen them in any of three critical time periods in our history? In the agricultural age up to the early nineteenth century, wealth came from the owner-ship of land. In the industrial age, from the early nineteenth cen-tury to 1980 or so, wealth was based on ownership of capital. Since 1980, wealth has been based upon the ownership of and the ability to use knowledge. It is more important than ever to scan for new knowledge and to adjust to changing conditions.

To illustrate the scanning process, let us consider two areas where changing conditions have a global impact. China and India are large countries. They have many smart people. They are chang-ing the face of business. What will we find if we look closely?

Scanning China

For most scanning purposes, we go to 1978, when China opened to the West. It also began a transition from a centrally planned to a socialist market economy. Change was driven by a rigid and cen-trally controlled government that engaged in a mandatory dis-placement of citizens as it leveled residences and businesses. Reforms moved the economy from a sluggish and inefficient Soviet-style of planning to a market-oriented system. The strong central government role produced amazing economic growth.

In many ways, however, the results were mixed. By 2009, gross domestic product had quadrupled from the level in 1978, making China the second-largest economy in the world after the United States. Still, economic progress has been slow outside urban cen-ters. The government has struggled to create enough jobs for citi-zens who migrate from the countryside to the cities. As the government subsidized inefficient state-owned enterprises, it was unable to reduce corruption and economic crimes.

The Chinese legal system did not make as much progress as the economic system. The system is a complex structure of customs and statutes, with extensive criminal law and inadequate civil law. China claims that it is improving civil, criminal, administrative, and commercial law. The conflicting administrative requirements afford few protections against fraud and intellectual property violations and complicate dispute resolution.

The banking system also struggles. As recently as 2004, more than 30 percent of bank loans were not performing. Government bailouts to cover defaults on loans from state-run banks reached $45 billion by 2004. In 2007, China implemented financial reforms, including new accounting standards and a new bankruptcy law.

China struggled with health programs and environmental reform. The World Trade Organization reported that 7 of the 10 most polluted cities in the world are in China. Their report covered air and water pollution and industrial dumping. With 20 percent of the world's population, China accounts for 30 percent of tobacco consumption. Greenhouse gases and sulfur dioxide particulates from coal produce acid rain. Water shortages exist, often in conjunction with pollution from untreated waste. Deforestation has reduced agricultural land by 20 percent since 1949. China has no serious government regulation of oil and coal consumption. Nor does it restrict automobile production or imports. The government is building new highways and refineries that will increase pollution.

In addition to other risks, China is prone to natural disasters. In 1998, the flooding of the Yangtze River caused 4,000 deaths and the dislocation of millions of people. This is not surprising, as 85 percent of the forest cover in the Yangtze basin has been cleared. On a list of the 100 most deadly disasters of the twentieth century, 23 occurred in China.

China is also facing difficulties with its population. For many years, its one-child policy has limited a husband and wife to raising a single child. Even so, the population continues to grow. In 2008, China's 1.4 billion people made up 20 percent of the world population. The large population complicates efforts to find solutions for the country's economic, social, and environment challenges.

MCGREGOR ON CHINA

James McGregor is a journalist and former chairman of the American Chamber of Commerce in China. He claims that the Chinese will ask you for anything because you may just be stupid enough to agree to it. One consequence of this kind of behavior is that the legal, regulatory, and economic system is geared to gain maximum advantage, even unfair advantage, from foreign interests. McGregor believes that the Chinese understand the outside world much better than the outside world understands China. If this is true, Chinese governments at all levels will be strong fighters for Chinese interests and present potential obstacles for foreign interests. A characteristic of Chinese companies is that they choose expatriate managers for operations outside China on the basis of their deep interest in China and keep them in place for extended periods. The Chinese do not agree with the revolving door in the executive ranks that is favored by Western and Japanese companies. With a deep interest in China, foreign managers will take actions that can be enforced by the Chinese. This is consistent with the view that disputes are to be resolved by discussing mutual benefits rather than resorting to the courts.

McGregor concludes that, at its core, Chinese society is all about self-interest. It is strong on competition and weak on cooperation. He recommends that companies consider framing their strategies to show how their business is good for China and that they not discuss what is wrong with the Chinese government. Chinese do not respond well to criticism of the Chinese system. Regulators and courts take such criticisms into account negatively and hold them against foreign companies. With respect to intellectual property and legal enforcement of patent and copyright claims, U.S. companies can forget about legal recourse. They should assume that their designs, products, and ideas will be copied and distributed without their knowledge or consent.

Factor such behavior into your plans. When sharing technology, isolate components so that your Chinese partner does not have the whole picture.

Lesson Learned: China is not a single legal and regulatory system. It is a collection of local jurisdictions, each with its own practices, traditions, and methods of protectionism and dispute resolution.

CHINA CARDBOARD

A French company built a factory to produce televisions in China. A Chinese company agreed to a three-year contract to supply cardboard as packing material. A month before the start of the contract period, the Chinese company said it could not supply the cardboard. It had a more profitable contract to sell the cardboard in Australia.

The French company signed a new three-year agreement to obtain the cardboard at a higher price from a Korean company. Six months later, the Chinese company said it would start delivery under the contract in one week. The French company balked, and the matter was referred to the office of the governor of the province. The governor upheld the contract and demanded that the French company accept and pay for the Chinese cardboard.

The company considered its options. It could close the plant, call the French embassy, cancel the Korean contract, hire armed guards to block delivery of the cardboard, pray to Buddhist gods, or pray to French gods. None of these strategies worked well. The French company accepted and paid for the cardboard and, at significant cost, negotiated its way out of the Korean contract.

The French company had no legal recourse in China. Contracts are interpreted within a framework of mutual benefit. It is acceptable to adjust business agreements when conditions change. A contract may be voided when compliance becomes difficult or too costly or the initial purpose is frustrated by subsequent events. Chinese law allows the voiding of contracts that harm China. A loss of jobs is harmful. The best way to resolve conflicts with Chinese business partners, customers, or suppliers is not through the legal system but rather by mustering patience and respect, more patience and respect, and still more patience and respect.

PATMONT MOTOR WERKS

In 2004, Patmont filed a lawsuit against several Chinese companies, accusing them of improper practices as they flooded the U.S. market with motor scooters. In 2008, a Chinese court ruled that Patmont was supposed to have served the defendants. Since it had failed to do so, the case was dismissed. Patmont actually had served the companies. In every case, it received a reply that the company was no longer at the address. No forwarding address was provided.

The goal of the Patmont lawsuit was partly to win the right to sell motor scooters in China. The company was not competitive because China levied a 150 percent tariff on scooters. The suit sought to ban the imports to the United States until China opened its own market to U.S. exports of scooters. This is not likely to happen easily as China needs to create jobs for millions of individuals moving into urban areas. Job creation is the second most important regulatory priority in China. (The first is political stability.)

VISIT TO TOY FACTORY

A *New York Times* reporter visited the RC2 Industrial Park in the city of Donguan, the largest toy manufacturing center in the world. An interpreter and a photographer accompanied him. The group signed in with company security, was admitted to the facility, and was greeted by Mr. Zhong, the plant manager. The group toured the facility and took pictures. During the tour, Mr. Zhong confronted the reporter and scolded him for entering the grounds and taking pictures. The group was led to a small luxury villa on the grounds. At the villa, Mr. Zhong offered an interview and an additional tour. Then, Mr. Zhong changed his mind and issued an ultimatum. The reporter was told to hand over the pictures. If he did not, Mr. Zhong would call the police. The reporter refused and told Mr. Zhong to call the police.

When the police did not arrive after one hour, the group started to leave. It was stopped by 16 security guards and 4 factory supervisors. The gates were locked. Trucks were rerouted. Large crowds gathered to watch, both inside and outside the gates.

The translator called the police. After another hour, the police arrived and listened to both sides but did nothing. More police arrived. When nothing happened, the translator called a government official. The government official told the translator to call another government official, who said to call another government official, who said to call another government official, who said to call another government official, who said to call another government official, who said (and so on and so on).

After a few more hours, a government official arrived. He was friendly but said he did not have the power to release the group. He recommended negotiation. For five hours, he shuttled between rooms in the villa trying to negotiate a settlement. The scene included shouting matches and demands that the reporter turn over the pictures.

Mr. Zhong demanded a confession that the group had trespassed. He settled for a statement explaining why the group had visited the factory and that stating that no one had asked permission to take pictures. The group was then released. The next day, the group had to make a report at the local police station. At the police station, they noted the presence of the factory bosses, who were in an adjoining room laughing and dining with the police.

Scanning India

Like China, India is large and important in global business. With a population of 1.1 billion people and a land area of 3 million square kilometers, the country is big, with a growing economy. Like that of China, the culture of India is old, unique, and diverse. Every state has carved out its own niche within a vast country with a wide variety of geographical features and climates. India is the home to some of the world's most ancient civilizations and religions.

India is becoming an attractive place to invest in service industries such as call centers and the outsourcing of services. It also has a rapidly growing industrial sector. Foreign direct investment in 2008 was more than $20 billion.

Corruption is a way of life in India. A World Economic Forum survey ranked India forty-fifth out of 49 countries for the honesty of its officials and forty-fourth of 49 in the effectiveness of its laws for protecting shareholders. The Bribe Payers Index of 30 top exporting countries, which ranks countries from least to most corrupt, includes Mexico, Saudi Arabia, Turkey, and China among the countries it studies. It was India, however, that ranked last in a survey of 11,000 businesspeople in 125 countries. In 2007, a survey identified an inefficient bureaucracy, corrupt government officials, restrictive labor regulations, and an inadequate infrastructure as obstacles to doing business in India.

DISMISSING EMPLOYEES IN INDIA

There are considerable costs for dismissing employees in India, including monetary severance, notification, and penalties. Labor inspectors who visit sites have considerable discretionary powers. They often demand bribes from companies they supervise, and most companies bring gifts and money to meetings with labor inspectors.

TRANSPORTING GOODS IN INDIA

India produces valuable goods for the global economy. Manufacturing companies are able to transport goods in a timely fashion to port and embarkation cities and to ship the goods for export. To do this, they pay bribes to obtain permits and erase traffic violations and include bribes as part of their operating costs. As a result of the corruption and multiple payoffs, it takes 18 days to export a standardized shipment of goods.

BRIBES IN INDIA

Transparency International estimates that citizens pay $5 billion a year in bribes to government officials in India. The money is given to poorly paid civil servants to obtain approvals, to the police for special favors and protection, and to judges and court officials for favorable outcomes of lawsuits. Bribes go to government bureaucrats to win approvals in a system of dated and conflicting laws and to tax authorities for obvious reasons. One example shows the extent of the problem. Various licenses and permits are required for construction projects, including registration, allotment of land, land use permits, environmental site approval, and approval for construction activity. A lack of transparent and consistent regulation leaves public officials with wide discretionary powers. To win their support, applicants are expected to offer gifts. Another example occurs with taxation. Tax Administration officials enforce myriad tax rules and regulations for businesses and decide which rules to enforce on inspection visits. The result is frequent, arbitrary, and excessive inspections, which create thinly disguised excuses to demand bribes. Companies pay off tax officials to avoid disruptions in production schedules and wasted staff time.

The overall picture is that widespread corruption exists in every section and at every level of Indian society.

INDIAN LEGAL ISSUES

The judicial system statistics tell part of the story of regulation in India. Some statistics:

Payment Disputes. Years to settlement: 4

Bankruptcy. Years to liquidate a company: 11

Legal Backlog. Cases pending in court: 29 million

Although multinational investment is strengthening the economy, entrenched practices are likely to slow down India's economic rise. A simple statistic on the difficulty of reform: 40 percent of the country's gross domestic product consists of unreported and untaxed earnings, so-called black money.

As a democracy that enjoys significant citizen participation in elections, why does India have so many corrupt legislators and elected officials? The answer lies in splintered political parties, bad laws that trump the efforts of honest officials, and local conditions that ignore national laws. Global Integrity rates India as being weak in government accountability and very weak in judicial accountability and civil service regulations. When disputes arise, the parties choose between staying out of court and bribing judges.

Transparency International ranked 180 countries on specific criteria related to doing business. India was virtually last in enforcing contracts and ranked low in ease of doing business, ease of starting and closing a business, and ease of obtaining licenses. Overall, India ranks in the bottom quartile of developing nations in ease of doing business.

Indian democracy and the economic system are rapidly turning into a system by the elite, for the elite, and of the elite. The system fails to provide equal education or maintain quality education in rural areas. Kerala is the only state that keeps poor children in school. Few schools have computers, and the educational system has a high dropout rate among girls.

A bright spot in the Indian economy can be found at the Mumbai Stock Exchange. Regulators are taking a hard line in their efforts to control the country's stock market and to avoid market disruptions. This trend is likely to continue.

What do you get for your bribe in government hospitals in India?

Admittance.

Medication.

Consultation with a doctor.

Diagnostic services.

What do you get for your bribe in electrical utilities?

Resolution of billing issues.

Start of electrical service.

Repairs for failures of electrical service.

Conclusion

We have scanned China and India. Before doing so, we thought we knew something about each country, its culture, and the way it does business. Did our scan change any attitudes or beliefs? For most people, the answer is yes. If we have not searched for horizon risk recently, we may not know what is happening in areas that can affect our organization. Our level of knowledge is even lower for Africa, South America, the Middle East, and Southeast Asia than it is for China and India. Organizations need a proactive scanning function to anticipate changing conditions, and thus risks and opportunities, that are on the horizon.

PART FOUR

ERM STORIES

PART FOUR takes us to stories that enrich the risk management process. We begin with risk categories and how they should align with the business (Chapter 17). This is a process of customization. We recognize business disruption and its consequences, which can be far reaching (Chapter 18). We look at the Sarbanes-Oxley Act as a component within an ERM structure (Chapter 19) and then tell three risk management stories about candy bars and mugs, exotic jams, and Toyota (Chapter 20). Chapter 21 takes us in the direction of risk mitigation when no central leadership function exists, while Chapter 22 takes us through the Cerberus acquisition of Chrysler.

Part Four concludes with a look at the past, the present, and the future. Chapter 23 looks at the recent history of risk management, Chapter 24 surveys ERM's evolution since 2004, and Chapter 25 looks to the future of ERM.

CHAPTER 17

ALIGNING RISK CATEGORIES WITH THE BUSINESS MODEL

RISK QUOTE: *Everyone is a star and deserves a chance to shine.*
—MARILYN MONROE, MOVIE STAR

RISK QUOTE: *If you talk to a man in a language he understands, that goes to his head. If you talk to him in his language, that goes to his heart.*
—NELSON MANDELA, SOUTH AFRICAN STATESMAN

Risk identification is often the hardest part of any risk management effort. One aspect of risk identification involves coordination across the enterprise. If those seeking out risks do not consider relationships, they may miss major risks completely. Another aspect is responsibility; a central risk function is required to identify risk and share its findings with risk owners.

Nonaligned Risk Categories

A number of organizations have developed risk categories. These are some examples:

- **Marsh, Aon, *CFO* Magazine, and Economist Intelligence Unit.** In 2001 and 2002, they identified four categories of risk: *hazard*, affecting property, people, and tangible assets; *operational*, affecting production and marketing; *financial*, affecting availability of resources; and *strategic*, affecting mission and goals.

- **KPMG.** In 2001, KPMG identified seven categories of risk: *strategic*, affecting business objectives; *operational*, affecting strategic processes; *reputation*, related to brand and image; *regulatory/contractual*, related to compliance and agreements; *financial*, affecting availability of resources; *information*, affecting timing and accuracy; and *new risks*, reflecting changing conditions.

- **Discover eHoldings.** This company identified four broad categories of risk: *external factors*, or risks outside the control of the entity; *business operations*, or how the organization provides goods or services; *relationships,* related to stakeholders' interaction with the enterprise; and *marketplace,* where customers and competitors shape the environment.

- **Tillinghast.** In 2000, this company declined to develop categories, arguing that risk cannot be directly managed. Rather, it identified "risk factors"—the causes of risk that can be managed. Examples are *culture,* reflecting the values, beliefs, and behaviors inside the organization itself; *capital,* dealing with the adequacy of funding for operations; *business processes,* covering techniques to pursue objectives; and *capacity for change,* examining the ability to respond to new developments and make adjustments.

Aligned Risk Categories

In our framework, problems arise with all of these risk categories because they are not aligned with the business model. Nor are they easily assigned to a single risk owner. For a profit-making company, an aligned structure might have the following risk categories:

- **Production:** The creation of the goods and/or services sold or distributed by the organization.

- **Marketing:** Efforts to reach customers or clients or to identify or develop markets for products or services.

- **Finance:** The management of cash flows from operations and investment of capital and creation of an appropriate return on invested assets.

- **Technology:** Activities related to changing technologies and their impact on the organization's ability to compete effectively in the marketplace.

- **Administration:** Processes for efficiency, performance, and structure.

- **Business Units:** Operations that manage their own functional risks.

- **Key Initiatives:** Projects that are so important that they are handled individually.

Then, we fill in the details of subcategories.

PRODUCTION RISK SUBCATEGORIES

The Chief Production Officer directly manages the creation of quality goods or services with subcategories like these:

- **Design Risk:** Efforts to develop the right product or service for a market.

- **Supply Risk:** Working with suppliers and component vendors to purchase and secure components or inputs for inventories or permission to distribute goods or services.

- **Process Risk:** Overseeing manufacturing, engineering, or other processes to efficiently create products or services.

- **Efficiency Risk:** Efforts to control costs and improve processes.

MARKETING RISK SUBCATEGORIES

The Chief Marketing Officer directly manages how the company enters markets, finds customers or clients, and prices and sells goods or services. Subcategories of risk include:

- **Needs Risk:** Understanding what potential customers will buy on the basis of their real or perceived desires to purchase.

- **Distribution Risk:** Activities involved in moving a product or service from creation through a channel to a final customer or client.

- **Volume Risk:** The reality that a company must sell sufficient units to justify the original investment of capital and to provide an adequate return for risk undertaken.

- **Pricing Risk:** Obtaining an adequate price to cover variable and fixed costs, including financing charges, and to provide a return on invested capital.

FINANCE RISK SUBCATEGORIES

The Chief Finance Officer directly manages financial decisions and controls such as:

- **Capital Budgeting Risk:** Managing the need to obtain an adequate return on the value of invested assets.

- **Valuation Risk:** The need to protect or increase the value of a company. This is particularly visible for publicly traded corporations but applies to all enterprises.

- **Capital Structure Risk:** Deals with sources of funding and includes decisions on risk to be accepted from debt and to selling or buying back a company's common stock.

- **Credit Risk:** The need to obtain the value expected from business transactions. A company sells on credit and then must collect the money from clients. Credit risk includes loans made to other parties and gains or losses from currency or hedging transactions.

- **Portfolio Risk:** Refers to managing liquid and illiquid assets and earning a return on them. Includes investments in bonds, stock of other companies, real estate, and other assets held so that risks in some assets can offset the risks in other assets.

- **Financial Reporting Risk:** Involves an effort to put in place detailed procedures and controls to produce accurate financial statements while complying with generally accepted accounting principles and guidelines of regulators and stock exchanges.

- **Compliance Risk:** Manages exposures when an organization lacks internal controls or effective internal audit processes and risks finding itself in trouble with government agencies or other regulatory bodies.

TECHNOLOGY RISK SUBCATEGORIES

The Chief Technology Officer directly manages technology exposures:

- **Business Support Risk:** Exposures when an organization uses technology in its production and marketing.
- **Information Systems Risk:** Exposures when key managers, suppliers, or customers do not receive responsive information on products, markets, and finances.
- **Communications Risk:** Deals with linkages among operating units, vendors, customers and others if information is not exchanged accurately and on a timely basis.
- **Records Management Risk:** Exposures that endanger the ability to maintain complete, accurate, and timely records that make up modern information and accounting systems.

ADMINISTRATION RISK SUBCATEGORIES

A chief administrative officer manages risks in the ordinary course of operations:

- **Efficiency Risk:** Efforts to organize work in cost-effective processes that achieve goals.
- **Performance Risk:** Efforts to ensure the achievement of leadership, management, and behavioral objectives.
- **Structure Risk:** Pursuit of optimal hierarchical, partnering, and other relationships.

Business Unit and Key Initiative Categories

In addition to the functional risk areas, business units and key initiatives must fit into the ERM structure. They pose their own risks:

❧ **Business Unit:** The CEO of a region or autonomous subsidiary is responsible for risks that might overlap production, marketing, finance, technology, and administration categories of the central entity and add factors unique to the region or line of the business of the operating unit.

❧ **Key Initiative:** Initiatives must be visible at the right level of the hierarchy. When the business model pursues a single activity identified as an important risk, a high-level individual may be assigned as the risk owner.

Conclusion

ERM identifies risk as part of its coordination of exposures that endanger stability and survival. The trick is to ensure that the process incorporates risks not easily seen on the radar screen of the entity. We can expect to have greater success implementing an ERM program when the organizational structure can identify the specific risks in its current hierarchical structure, rather than identifying broad categories of risk that do not easily lend themselves to risk owners and accountability.

CHAPTER 18

AVOIDING BUSINESS DISRUPTION

RISK QUOTE: *We made too many wrong mistakes.*

—YOGI BERRA, BASEBALL PLAYER

RISK QUOTE: *Not to have control over the senses is like sailing in a rudderless ship, bound to break to pieces on coming in contact with the very first rock.*

—MAHATMA GANDHI, INDIAN POLITICAL

AND SPIRITUAL LEADER

S upply chains are one of the most important tools for pursuing the upside of risk and avoiding disruption as the downside of risk. We will use some examples of supply chain issues to identify risks in the production and distribution of goods and services. I extend my thanks to Yossi Sheffi, from whose book *The Resilient Enterprise* (Cambridge, Mass.: The MIT Press, 2005) I have drawn ideas and examples.

Dell Computer

In 2005, Dell employed a build-to-order business model by which customers, on the company Web site, www.dell.com, could design just the computer they wanted. Called Dynamic Value Chain Management (DVCM), this system was designed to minimize idle cash, receivables, and inventories. It was arguably the most efficient distribution system in the world, a just-in-time process supporting direct sales at the Web site. Parts arrived, and were assembled, tested, and shipped. Inventory equaled four days of sales.

The upside of the supply chain at Dell derived from strong management. Quick Internet purchases built good relations and long-term alliances with customers and suppliers. The model allowed sales prior to stocking inventory, increasing the speed of payment and reducing inventories. It allowed low cash, receivables, and inventory balances while allowing business-to-business (B2B) and business-to-consumer (B2C) sales.

Dell was operating a world-class supply system where speed, reduced costs, and quick response created pull rather than push marketing. The company achieved superior price for performance as its supplier, manufacturing, and distribution systems lowered costs. Customers could buy exactly, and only, what they needed. Four-day inventory turnover allowed quick updates of technology.

Dell's use of Intel's Pentium processors from 2000 to 2005 was supported by a supply chain that spanned three continents. Toshiba Ceramics grew silicon and sliced it into wafers in Japan. An Intel semiconductor lab in Oregon etched the wafers. Intel packaged the wafers in Malaysia. Dell's factory in Ireland inserted the wafer package into the computer.

Lesson Learned: In light of Dell's use of different locations to perform a variety of tasks, what is the ERM lesson for Intel and Dell? Simply stated, it was redundancy, redundancy, redundancy. Maybe that is why Dell had manufacturing operations in the United States, China, Ireland, Brazil, Poland, Malaysia, and India.

BORDER DISRUPTION AT FORD MOTOR COMPANY

Ford Motor Company experienced a 13 percent drop in production during the fourth quarter of 2001. Something quite unexpected caused the decline. Trucks carrying components for automobiles and trucks were stopped at the Mexican and Canadian borders in the weeks following the 9/11 attack on the World Trade Center and the Pentagon. Components could not reach manufacturing sites. Soon, the system slowed or shut down.

Figure 18-1 shows the insertion of redundancy into supply chain management. Using a high-tech platform, authorized users enter the system and view risk mitigation for multiple suppliers, key manufacturing components, the status of the crisis management team, and other threats and opportunities.

New ERM Paradigm

The traditional management practice is to develop a strategy (the plan), provide resources (the budget), approve the plan and budget at various hierarchical levels, give individuals goals and incentives for meeting the plan goals, and execute the plan. Does the model contain a risk management component? In most cases, the answer is no. Business disruption gives us a growing recognition that ERM is reaching maturity, not in the sense of getting old but rather of getting it right. Supply chain disruption is a perfect example of the need for speed and redundancy. ERM encourages us to scan, identify, share, and get moving. If ERM encourages quick responses, it will do us a great service indeed.

FIGURE 18-1. REDUNDANCY IN THE SUPPLY CHAIN.

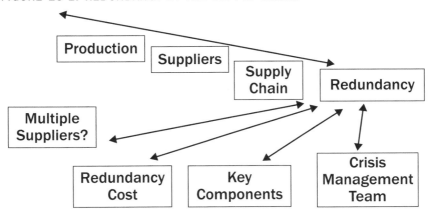

BRING IN THE MARINES

Risk management was different in the 1950s, when organizations operated largely in a domestic economy. The world changed slowly, and
economists had time to build predictive models. In the 1990s, a faster-
moving global economy brought down trade barriers and technology
changed business. Now, organizations have to be in constant motion.

ERM looks to the U.S. Marines, who "move, shoot, and communicate." This is anathema to many senior executives. How can you move
before you know where you are going? What do you shoot at? What is
the plan? Are resources being used as approved? These are not questions when an amphibious force attacks a dug-in enemy in coastal hills.
What is the plan? Nobody cares once the landing door drops. Shoot at
the bad guys. Move out of harm's way. Communicate about what is happening. Make decisions as the landscape and competitive positions
change.

This approach characterized the world's response to the 2008 financial crisis. Whatever else might happen, the world could not sit and wait
until a plan was finalized. We needed to stop the foreclosures on houses,
provide liquidity to the banking system, and protect jobs. A failure to
move guaranteed a collapse of the global financial system.

Lesson Learned: Uncertainties are real, but that is not the point. The
world is in flux. Organizations can create a central risk function to scan
emerging markets, technology, logistics, and the global conundrum and
then share the findings with key executives. Then, the organization must
respond quickly to changing circumstances. This is the future of enterprise risk management.

CHAPTER 19

ERM AND SARBANES-OXLEY

RISK QUOTE: *I never think of the future. It comes soon enough.*

—ALBERT EINSTEIN, PHYSICIST

RISK QUOTE: *The lion and the calf shall lie down together but the calf won't get much sleep.*

—WOODY ALLEN, WRITER/ACTOR/DIRECTOR/PRODUCER

The Sarbanes-Oxley Act of 2002 (SARBOX) established new standards for corporate governance, internal control assessment, and financial disclosure. It required new controls for managing and reporting risk. The Act is a driver for ERM but is not the same as ERM. It is a subset, and a relatively small subset at that. In this chapter, we cover basic tenets of the Act but do not put it into an ERM structure.

The goal of the Act is "to protect investors by improving the accuracy and reliability of corporate disclosures." The board of directors is responsible for achieving this goal by developing new risk management processes for compliance and setting new standards for risk management in governance.

Not all boards have to comply with the requirements of Sarbanes-Oxley. The Act regulates U.S. companies that issue securities to the public under the U.S. Securities Act of 1933 and non-

U.S. companies that do business in the United States. Having said this, Sarbanes-Oxley produced governance changes in private, nonprofit, charitable, and public sector entities. Many boards feel compelled by fiduciary responsibility to comply with provisions of the Act.

With respect to the board of directors and its responsibilities, Sarbanes-Oxley requires boards to develop new processes and standards. One change involves the company's external auditor, who must report directly to the audit committee of the board. In appointing, compensating, and overseeing the work of the auditor, the CEO and CFO have no roles at all. The audit committee of the board resolves disagreements between management and the auditor regarding financial reporting and the audit.

The Act specifies requirements for audit committee membership: Only members of the board may serve on the audit committee, and each member must be independent of the company itself. That is, the individual must not accept consulting, advisory, or other compensatory fees from the company, except for compensation received for services as a member of the board or board committee. Further, the audit committee member can have no other affiliation with the issuer or any of its subsidiaries.

The Act imposes requirements for corporate whistleblowers. It requires the audit committee to establish procedures for receiving, retaining, and treating complaints regarding accounting, internal controls, and auditing matters. The committee must ensure that employees can make confidential, anonymous submission of their concerns regarding questionable accounting or auditing practices.

In another provision, the Act requires that there be a "financial expert" on the audit committee. The expert must understand GAAP accounting, including estimates, accruals, reserves, financial statements, and audit committee functions. The individual must be experienced at dealing with internal controls and preparing or auditing financial statements.

Sarbanes-Oxley imposes requirements in two other areas. The first is internal audit, a management-oriented discipline that evaluates the effectiveness of operating activities. This includes accounting practices, financial reporting, risk management, compliance with directives and policies, and governance and management processes. The second is internal control, the process designed to provide a reasonable assurance of achieving the effectiveness and efficiency of operations, reliable financial reporting, and compliance with regulations, laws, directives, and policies.

Under Sarbanes-Oxley, the CEO and the CFO are responsible for internal controls. They must certify that they have established and maintained internal controls designed to ensure that material information is made known to them by others in the organization. Moreover, they must evaluate the effectiveness of internal controls 90 days prior to certification. They must certify that they disclosed any significant deficiencies or material weaknesses in internal controls and disclose fraud, whether material or not, involving management or other employees who have a significant role in internal controls. The disclosures must be made to the auditors and to the audit committee of the board. Finally, if a company makes significant changes in internal controls subsequent to the date of the CEO's and CFO's evaluation, the report must include corrective actions with regard to significant deficiencies and material weaknesses.

Conclusion on Sarbanes-Oxley

What can we conclude about Sarbanes-Oxley, accompanied as it was by actions of the Securities and Exchange Commission, the Basel II Capital Accord, and other regulatory actions? Many observers believe that companies now spend a great deal of money on internal controls and other processes that add only a negligible value to governance, risk management, and accurate reporting of financial results. The 2008 disaster at AIG and the collapse of a variety of banks and financial institutions shows the weakness of risk management and compliance. The reality is that we had it backwards. Organizations do not need compliance to manage misbehavior. They need ERM to enforce risk management. Compliance should follow effortlessly.

WHISTLEBLOWER PROVISIONS

A focal point for ERM is the whistleblower provisions of the Sarbanes-Oxley Act. On the surface, the idea to provide a channel by which people with information about improprieties can forward complaints and anonymous submissions are quite logical. As we dig down, a problem arises. The real issue is not whether the company has to protect whistleblowers. Rather, we know that the need for a whistleblower is also a failure of governance and risk management. If an organization has an effective central risk function, the whistleblower is an added control but should not be necessary. Everybody should be empowered to report wrongdoing and unethical or illegal behavior.

Lesson Learned: Do not count on whistleblowers. Create a culture where people are accountable for proper behavior as they pursue financial and other incentives. An ERM program can reward integrity and teamwork while not tolerating misbehavior. Encourage ethical behavior with performance expectations, and establish incentives that reward ethical managers.

ERM will not be successful if a company thinks that managing it is a job for a risk manager or an executive who oversees Sarbanes-Oxley compliance. ERM drives compliance. Compliance does not drive risk management.

CHAPTER 20

COFFEE MUG, CANDY, EXOTIC JAMS, AND TOYOTA

RISK QUOTE: *We may encounter many defeats but we must not be defeated.*

—MAYA ANGELOU, POET

RISK QUOTE: *Every really new idea looks crazy at first.*

—ALFRED NORTH WHITEHEAD, ENGLISH PHILOSOPHER

I n spite of the failures or near-failures of Enron, Lehman Brothers, AIG, Citibank, and others, we recognize the need for ERM. The problem is its difficulty in gaining traction in the corporate world, partly because of its complexity and partly because often it has not been implemented effectively. Companies talk about ERM and flirt with it, but their implementation of it often makes it seem like they are going through the motions rather than really coordinating risk management.

We acknowledge that ERM has a modicum of complexity, but

This chapter is based on a presentation at the sixth annual Conference of the Federation of Asian, Pacific, and African Risk Management Organizations in September 2006 in Singapore.

we can simplify its implementation. A few questions may help. Do people prefer a coffee mug or a bar of chocolate? How do we purchase strawberry or grape jam? Do we want our automobiles to break down on the highway?

Coffee Mug and Candy Story

Researchers conducted an experiment at an executive training seminar. They gave half of the attendees a coffee mug and the other half a bar of Swiss chocolate, two items with approximately the same monetary value. After distributing the items without giving attendees a choice of what they received, the researchers offered participants the opportunity to exchange their gift for the other item. If other things were equal, we might expect about half the people to make an exchange. The actual number that opted for the exchange was 10 percent.

This is the status quo trap. Once committed to an idea, a direction, or an object, most people are reluctant to change their minds. Psychologists have considerable evidence that people view their beliefs and possessions as being more valuable than new beliefs or other objects. What does this mean for ERM? If a company is achieving stable sales and earning an acceptable profit, why should it consider a completely new approach to managing risk? Well done is well enough. Absent a good story, not much will happen.

Exotic Jams Story

The next story deals with research on how people make choices. Researchers conducted an experiment on two consecutive Saturdays in San Francisco. An upscale grocery store allowed them to set up displays of Wilkin & Sons exotic jams. On the first Saturday, shoppers passed a tasting booth with a display of 24 different gourmet jams. On the second Saturday, the booth contained only six jams. Observers calculated the number of people who stopped and tasted jam at the booth and the number of those who purchased jam. The results for each booth were:

	24 Choices	6 Choices
Percent Who Stopped	60%	40%
Percent Who Bought	3%	30%

When offered many choices, people were interested in and sampled jams, but they did not buy. They were more likely to buy when there were fewer choices. What does this mean for an ERM implementation? Like the jam tasters, managers may sample ERM, but if they have too many choices, this can kill the sale. It may be as simple as a concern about the number of chances to make a mistake. If given too many risks, managers may be reluctant to participate because they worry about what can go wrong and the possibility that they will be held accountable for bad results.

Toyota Story

The third story involves risk in the purchase of an automobile. When shopping for cars, buyers bring specific perceptions and goals to the showroom. One goal is to find the highest quality car available in the buyer's price range. A measure of quality is the number of recalls made by automobile manufacturers after discovery of a defect in a model.

A recall should occur as soon as possible after a defect is revealed. A high number of recalls reflects that many defects have been found, an indication of low quality to the buyer. Or is it? In 2005, the percentage of recalls for all DaimlerChrysler, General Motors, and Toyota cars on the road ranged from 2.5 percent to 10.1 percent. Chrysler recalled 2.5 percent of its cars, Toyota 10.1 percent. In June 2006, Toyota recalled 1 million vehicles worldwide. In 2005, it recalled 10 percent of all Toyotas sold that year in the United States.

After the large number of recalls, the 2006 annual J. D. Power & Associates' initial-quality survey ranked Toyota number one in quality. This leads us to conclude that the product recall is not the risk exposure, nor is it the perception of low quality. The real risk may be the failure to recall. Toyota detected and fixed problems before customers noticed them. The owners had fewer breakdowns on the road and therefore had no bad feelings toward the manufacturer. That is how to manage risk across the enterprise: Find and fix problems before they have a negative impact.

Truth in advertising requires us to report that Toyota had quality problems in 2007, when *Consumer Reports* found some models to be below average. Toyota responded by recalling almost 500,000 cars.

Conclusion

There are many stories, in this book and elsewhere, that can be used to overcome resistance to ERM. We need to recognize that it is natural for people to resist the changes ERM signifies. We can use the stories—homegrown ones in the organization itself are desirable—to reduce the complexity of comprehensive risk identification and sharing. If the stories simplify ERM, they increase the chance that we can use ERM to produce action, rather than curiosity.

CHAPTER 21

ERM AND SWARM THEORY

RISK QUOTE. *Half the lies they tell about me aren't true.*

—YOGI BERRA, BASEBALL PLAYER

RISK QUOTE. *Money was never a big motivation for me, except as a way to keep score. The real excitement is playing the game.*

—DONALD TRUMP, BUSINESSMAN

The value of enterprise risk management rises dramatically when a central risk function supplements the risk owners' efforts to identify risk and opportunities. If an organization finds hidden sources of risk ideas, it can respond early to threats and move to take advantage of opportunities. The idea of scanning the horizon was enhanced by a July 2007 *National Geographic* article titled "The Genius of Swarms." Two concepts stood out. First, a *swarm* is a large body of individual organisms that move together in the pursuit of a goal. Second, *swarm theory* describes efforts to understand the success of swarms.

The article started with the information that 12,000 species of ants currently live on the planet in colonies that date back 140 million years. As a behavioral trait, ants organize highways along the shortest path to the nearest food source, build elaborate nests, and stage massive raids on other creatures. Such successful behavior seems to show that ants are clever engineers, architects, and warriors. According to the entomologists—entomology is a branch of zoology that studies insects—who wrote the article, nothing could be further from the truth. As these scientists point out, "When it comes to deciding what to do next, most ants do not have a clue."

An ant colony can contain millions of individuals, divided into workers (commonly sterile females), drones (fertile males), and queens (fertile females), none of which have any vision for the colony. Instead, leadership arises from the collective action of the colony, or *swarm intelligence*. Simple creatures follow simple rules. Each party acts on local information. No one has the big picture.

How do ants find food? They communicate by touch and smell. Early-morning patrollers seek food outside the nest. If many come back quickly, it means they have found food. Next, foragers go out. If many come back, it means that much food was found. Everybody then goes out, following a chemical path called a food trail pheromone.

Bees also display swarm intelligence. When selecting a new hive, scouts go out. An individual bee returns and dances with enthusiasm for a specific site. More go out to search for a site. When a site attracts even as few as 15 bees, it becomes the choice. Entomologists believe the site chosen is usually the best among competing sites for the new hive.

A real-life example of swarm theory in risk identification is found in Chapter 10, which deals with Airbus and the Power8 program that addresses the risk of developing the A380 jumbo jet. The risk analyst omitted the exposure that would occur if the giant plane could not land or was perceived as too big to land at a sufficient number of airports. When teams of Saint Peter's College MBA candidates were assigned to study the A380 as an ERM risk identification project, two of the teams discovered that many airports were unable to handle the aircraft. They added airport risk to Airbus's exposures. Almost immediately, the other teams swarmed by adding the risk to their own list.

Another example is the story we related in Chapter 2 about the Valentine's Day disruption of operations at New York's John F.

Kennedy Airport and the struggles of JetBlue airlines to deal with the aftermath. It is unfortunate that JetBlue did not have a central risk function sharing exposures. Surely, some little "ant" would have identified the negative effects of a disruption at JFK. We might even have expected a disruption pheromone that would lead right up to the CEO. A public relations disaster could have been avoided.

We cannot claim that ERM discovered swarm theory, but James Surowiecki spotted a version of it. He believed that assessments made independently by diverse individuals would provide more accurate forecasts and more successful outcomes than decisions and central guidance emanating from experts. This assessment was presented in his 2004 book *The Wisdom of Crowds*. Effectively, he offers a risk management application of swarm theory.

It also appears that companies have discovered swarm theory. The above cited *National Geographic* article describes the effort of Air Liquide to find the best routes for its delivery trucks to follow. It tracked the routes taken by individual drivers and inserted the data into a computer model along with plant scheduling, weather information, market pricing, and truck routing. The software "pheromone" resulted in huge savings. Other companies throughout Europe use the process to develop delivery and telecommunications networks.

It is time for ERM to incorporate swarm theory into its efforts to improve risk identification. Companies will likely identify and mitigate many exposures if they incorporate the collective wisdom of the "colonies and hives" that are scattered throughout an organization.

CHAPTER 22

CERBERUS AND CHRYSLER

RISK QUOTE. *We shall not flag or fail. . . . We shall fight on the beaches, we shall fight on the landing grounds, we shall fight in the fields and in the streets, we shall fight in the hills; we shall never surrender.*

—WINSTON CHURCHILL, BRITISH STATESMAN

RISK QUOTE. *I don't want to achieve immortality through my work. . . . I want to achieve it through not dying.*

—WOODY ALLEN, WRITER/ACTOR/DIRECTOR/PRODUCER

The story of Bob Nardelli from Home Depot, begun in Chapter 3, continues with his acceptance of the CEO position at Chrysler. After Cerberus acquired the company, the board and senior executives knew that something bold would be needed to turn around Chrysler. Cerberus hired Mr. Nardelli in August 2007.

We do not know how Cerberus evaluated the turnaround of Chrysler. An ERM approach could have been used. The board simply had to ask, "What are our 7 to 10 most critical risks?" In many boardrooms, and perhaps at Cerberus, the question would produce an uncomfortable silence, followed by a vigorous and maybe even

The author thanks John Farrell, National ERM Lead Partner, KPMG, for contributions to this discussion.

rancorous discussion. Then board members would realize that it takes considerable work to understand risk across an enterprise.

The first task confronting Mr. Nardelli was to identify risks and to develop agreement on critical risks. In September 2007, five teams of MBA candidates at Saint Peter's College took on this task for Cerberus. Teams learned that Cerberus acquired Chrysler after DaimlerChrysler could not fix its problems and also understood the serious nature of the situation. They drew this conclusion largely because Cerberus brought in Mr. Nardelli. Now the task for each team was to identify a short list of critical risks. Figure 22-1 shows the results.

FIGURE 22-1. TEAMS' LISTS OF CRITICAL RISKS FACING CHRYSLER.

Team #1	Team #2	Team #3
Production Overseas	Mr. Nardelli	Mr. Nardelli
Housing & Gas	Reorganization	Legacy Health/Pension
Prices	Product	Financial
Mr. Nardelli	Innovation	Change in Technology
Wages & Benefits	Production	Production Efficiency
Foreign Competition	Supply Chain	Competition & Marketing
Hybrid/Fuel Efficiency	Financial	Recruitment & Training
Recalls	Reputation	

Team #4	Team #5
Production	Product
Mr. Nardelli	Technology
Technology	Financial
Loss of Talent	Legacy Health/Pension
Resources	Competition
Product Line	

Several observations based on these lists can be drawn:

❧ **Leadership Risk.** Four of the five teams identified Mr. Nardelli as a critical risk. Will his management style work better in the crisis environment of Chrysler than in the noncrisis situation at Home Depot? Would Mr. Nardelli be pleased to see the list?

❧ **General Risk vs. Specific Risk.** Should the risks identified be broad or narrow? If we identify the wrong risk, the mitigation strategy we settle on will not matter. What can Chrysler do about housing and gas prices, its own reputation, or competition when it faces pressing issues from production efficiency, legacy pension and benefit costs, or supply chain exposures?

❧ **Short-Term Risk vs. Long-Term Risk.** Where do we start? The company will not survive in the long term if it does not address deeply embedded risks. It will not survive in the short term if it runs out of money.

Absence of Cultural Risk

One interesting observation is the absence of cultural risk on any of the five lists. It does not seem reasonable to limit the leadership exposure to the style and skills of the new CEO. Aside from governance risks and strategies a CEO might develop to address them, will the culture allow the execution needed to turn around the ailing company? This was a massive problem for Daimler-Benz in its merger with Chrysler. It should be a red flag after the Cerberus purchase.

As this is being written, it looks as though Chrysler may not make it. We cannot tell whether Chrysler will focus on the right exposures and develop the strategies to succeed. Chrysler may have run out of time as the unexpected 2008 financial crisis steals the opportunity for it to turn around. It is unfortunate. Mr. Nardelli succeeded at GE and struggled at Home Depot. Cerberus rolled the dice and was bold in selecting him to do what he does best— get results. The company faced a crisis, and Mr. Nardelli is a crisis-style manager. Cerberus and Chrysler could have been a classic study in enterprise risk, but the opportunity was taken away from us. This may be the last risk management story to focus on Robert Nardelli.

CHAPTER 23

RISK MANAGEMENT AND THE HISTORY OF ERM

RISK QUOTE: *It is easy to fly into a passion. Anybody can do that, but to be angry with the right person to the right extent and at the right time and in the right way? That is not easy.*

—ARISTOTLE, ANCIENT GREEK PHILOSOPHER

RISK QUOTE: *You gain strength, courage, and confidence by every experience in which you really stop to look fear in the face. You are able to say to yourself, "I lived through this horror. I can take the next thing that comes along."*

—ELEANOR ROOSEVELT

E RM is the most recent development in the evolution of risk management. Like all modern ideas, it builds upon a foundation that started in the industrial age and moved into the knowledge age. We pause at this point to identify risk management concepts and events that contributed to our ability to scan the horizon, identify risks broadly, and use technology to share exposures with risk owners.

Risk Management Supersedes Insurance

From the late 1800s, organizations recognized the importance of insurance. Still, it was not until the 1960s that Hartford Steam Boiler Inspection and Insurance Company taught us a new lesson. In the company name, "Inspection" comes before "insurance." When the company started in business, boilers exploded with disturbing frequency. This caused devastation to people and property. Hartford Steam Boiler therefore refused to write an insurance policy if the owner of a boiler did not pay Hartford to conduct regular inspections. The world quickly learned a risk management lesson. When boilers are inspected and maintained, they rarely explode. Over the next 80 years, the lesson was expanded to many other areas of business. A milestone occurred in the 1960s after Massey-Ferguson appointed Douglas Barlow as the first risk manager. Risk management now trumped insurance. Recognizing the new reality, the American Society of Insurance Management changed its name to the Risk and Insurance Management Society (RIMS) in 1975.

Formation of Captives to Retain Risks

A captive insurance company effectively retains a portion of hazard risks for a parent company, a group of parent companies, or a group of associated companies that do not want to transfer certain exposures to arm's-length insurance companies. Since the founding of the first captive, in Bermuda, in the 1960s, organizations have gained a more sophisticated understanding of insurable risk. A captive allows the retention of high-frequency, low-severity exposures such as vehicle accidents and employee injuries. Efficiencies are achieved when an organization controls the processing of claims, using its own captive rather than dealing with an unrelated insurer. Captives also can be a critical risk management tool when traditional insurance markets lack the capacity or coverages needed by organizations.

Risk Management Addresses Liability

By the 1980s, risk managers faced the rising cost of liability lawsuits. They knew that legal liability arose in the normal course of business, even as they saw the U.S. tort system exploding with new lawsuits. New legal theories and court judgments produced implied warranties, express disclaimers, and strict liability. Courts awarded punitive damages to compensate injured parties for real and perceived pain and suffering. At the pinnacle of freewheeling lawsuits, courts awarded judgments for psychic injuries and even hypothetical damages. The number of class-action and medical malpractice lawsuits grew exponentially. Action was needed. New risk management practices were developed to create safer products and services, as well as new behaviors in the workplace and business arena.

Decline of Historical Data

When Hurricane Andrew struck Florida, in 1992, risk managers and insurance companies were forecasting losses on the basis of historical and actuarial data that were viewed as being quite accurate. Risk analysts knew that past strong hurricanes caused the loss of 10 to 20 percent of the roofs of homes in stricken areas. This did not happen with Andrew, however. Historical data were based on the use of masonry walls and tile roofs. A 1980s boom in Florida produced different forms of construction and substandard workmanship. After Andrew, every single roof in many subdivisions was gone. Insurers were reminded that actuarial data have to be examined carefully, assumptions must be tested, and underwriting must be augmented by qualitative assessments of what is changing on the risk landscape.

Performance Risk Augments Hazard Risk

As the 1980s ended, corporate boards wanted to reward CEOs for improving the performance of a company's common stock. Bonuses were tied to rises in the market price of the stock. When the Dow went from 3,500 in the early 1990s to 11,000 after 2000, the rising tide lifted all boats, and CEO compensation produced spectacular rewards for mediocre performance. The weakness of companies under stress after 2000 caused risk managers and boards to realize that business and operating risks exceeded the level of danger posed by most hazard risks. Their interest turned to ERM.

ERM and Internet Risk

Between 2000 and 2008, a broad spectrum of new English words arose to identify exposures from electronic communications. They include *hackers*, *scams*, *spam*, *viruses*, *phishing*, *pharming*, *illegal downloading*, *identity theft*, *spyware*, and *cyberterrorism*, which joined old terms such as *credit card fraud* and *industrial espionage* as focuses of risk management.

War Risk

The terrorist attacks of September 11, 2001, exposed the insurance industry and others to the possibility of catastrophic loss caused by human action. Individuals and small groups could expose a nation to massive losses previously associated with wars. A dirty bomb in New York City could cause $800 billion or more in insured losses. Insurance reserves were half that amount. This new realization reached maturity with the financial crisis of 2008. More than ever, risk observers knew the importance of an effective program to prepare for and respond to critical exposures.

Outlaw Environments

Global sourcing and distribution caused an expansion of operations into remote areas of the world, even as the Internet and terrorism were perceived as major risk exposures. Companies discovered that corruption permeates governments and the legal and banking systems. Counterfeit products and brands, violations of patents and copyrights, and theft of intellectual property became rampant. Many companies lacked effective risk mitigation strategies or remedies to fight back. This is a current challenge facing ERM.

Environmental Risks

Temperatures and ocean levels seem to be rising in the early years of the twenty-first century even as natural resources are declining. The increased mobility of billions of people on a small planet may lead to pandemics, interrelationships of economies and politics, and other complex exposures. Governments may be unable to mobilize resources until after a crisis occurs. Even then, as Hurricane Katrina showed in 2005, the response to an environmental disruption may be too little, too late.

Conclusion

It is hard to escape the conclusion that, with the exception of global nuclear destruction imposed by two superpowers, the risk of which has perhaps receded, the world has become more and more risky. Enterprise risk management is the latest development in efforts to identify and deal with critical risks. We will see if ERM holds the answers to mitigate our largest exposures.

CHAPTER 24

EVOLVING ERM SINCE 2004

RISK QUOTE: *Champions aren't made in the gyms. Champions are made from something they have deep inside them—a desire, a dream, and a vision.*

—MUHAMMAD ALI, BOXER

RISK QUOTE: *It is impossible for a man to be cheated by anyone but himself.*

—RALPH WALDO EMERSON, POET AND ESSAYIST

When I arrived at Saint Peter's College in 2004, I asked permission to put the words "specializing in enterprise risk management" on my business cards. I received that permission. Since then, every time I hand someone a card, he or she says something like "Oh, I've heard of enterprise risk management. Exactly what is it?"

That would be a fine reaction to a new idea that needs more traction. It is, however, something of a sad commentary on the status of ERM, which has been around for 12 or so years. Since 2002, risk managers, internal auditors, actuaries, the Committee of Sponsoring Organizations (COSO), and others have promoted ERM in their organizations and professional associations. A 2008 Google search of "enterprise risk management" produced 3,670,000 hits. At the same time, Amazon was selling books and articles on ERM, including the definitive *COSO Enterprise Risk Management—Integrated Framework*, a 230-page comprehensive description of ERM supported by professional associations of accountants and auditors. In 2004-2006, the Risk and Insurance Management Society (RIMS) formed an ERM online discussion group, established an ERM Center of Excellence, and offered a risk maturity tool for evaluating ERM programs.

One of the Amazon articles, from the April 2004 issue of *Risk & Insurance* magazine, is titled "ERM: All Talk, Little Action. While we have had some improvement in the situation since 2004, we need to rethink how we present ERM so that it can evolve in organizations and to consider the problems and questions that impede ERM implementation.

Problem #1. Definitions

Everybody has his or her own definition of ERM. We have already covered a number of them. Fair enough, but where do we go from there? No matter what the definition, ERM sounds like a lot of work. Will ERM produce results different from those achieved with existing risk management processes?

Problem #2. Risk Categories

Brokers and others use different risk categories as they promote ERM. We have already seen approaches to categorization championed by Marsh, Aon, and others. All offer insights into ERM while leaving a practical problem. In terms of accountability, responsibility, and process, most companies are not structured against the risk categories. Organizations do not have an operational risk manager, an external factors risk manager, a capacity-for-change risk manager, and so on. The solution is to align risk management with the business model. Unfortunately, this does not appear to be widely accepted in the literature of ERM.

Problem #3. Failure to Tell a Good Story

Another problem is that the real value of an ERM approach is lost in the weeds when we focus heavily on processes, internal controls, and details. Board members, senior executives, and even middle managers do not see the real benefit of ERM. Instead, they are presented with a cumbersome model that offers an expensive way to manage risks they are already managing. Many business people pay lip service to Sarbanes-Oxley, Basel II, and ERM. In their hearts, they believe the processes required by all three were designed by bureaucrats, professors, or regulators who do not really understand risk.

Solutions to Speed the Implementation of ERM

Now that we have identified the problems and objections facing ERM, we must seek solutions to these problems are. We can solve the definition problem quite easily. Let us simply say that ERM is an effort to coordinate the management of the risks that face an organization, skipping more complex definitions and pointing out that they add little value to the discussion.

The solution to risk categories has already been proposed. We can match risk categories to the business model that provides the strategy of a company as it pursues success. It includes (1) the value to be created by the entity; (2) the architecture of the firm; (3) the network of partners for creating, marketing, and delivering value; and (4) the capital, assets, and other resources needed to generate sustainable profits. The business model contains both the downside of risk and risk opportunities. Corporations can use their existing model in ERM and align it with C-suite functional areas, major business units, and key initiatives.

The third solution is to tell the story. Most stories are complex, building upon traditional risk management. Invariably, the story states the benefits of coordinating all risk across an enterprise. Then, it encourages a process with five to seven steps. This approach can work nicely for traditional risk, and it does. It falls short in the broader perspective of ERM. We need a different story. We need to tell about a new risk structure that works with the existing business model. The story should identify the current structures where goals are pursued and risk is being managed. Additionally, it should show the benefit of adding a centralized risk management function to augment existing business goals and risk management efforts.

The first part of the story argues that an organization really does not have ERM if it does not have a centralized function to identify external and cultural risks. We can reinforce this message with example after example of subpar performance by organizations that failed to recognize critical exposures, including these notable industries:

- **Automobile Manufacturers.** They failed to see the future impact of defined-benefit pension plans and lifetime health care for retirees, as well as the importance of modernization of their manufacturing facilities.
- **Airlines.** They failed to make adjustments to be competitive in the wake of low-cost carriers and rising oil prices.
- **Financial Institutions.** The financial crisis of 2008 was driven by commercial banks, investment banks, and insurance companies that thought they had no serious exposures in their portfolios.

We can hardly blame the CEOs of car companies, airlines, and banks for the failure to identify internal and external risks. Their watch is often as little as three to five years. Who needs to look for trouble? Instead, we could ask the board of directors to insist upon a centralized risk identification structure as part of an ERM program.

Conclusion

We conclude the discussion on evolving an ERM program with the following recommendations:

- **ERM Definition.** Do not spend too much time on defining ERM.
- **Risk Categories.** Align risk categories with the business model, recognizing functional areas, major operating units, and key initiatives.

- **Central Risk Function.** Install such a function, led by a senior executive. Make it a proactive entity that scans the external environment and internal culture seeking changing conditions, emerging trends, market developments, advances in technology, and competitive business practices. Encourage it to collect information on strategies, subcultures, leadership, life cycles, and developments on the horizon. When risks or opportunities are found, share them and their potential impact.

- **A Good Story.** Tell a good story. Help key managers and stakeholders understand how ERM increases the likelihood of identifying emerging exposures and opportunities that threaten or ensure long-term sustainability.

CHAPTER 25

RISK MANAGEMENT AND THE FUTURE OF ERM

RISK QUOTE: *Keep away from people who try to belittle your ambitions. Small people always do that, but the really great make you feel that you, too, can become great.*

—MARK TWAIN, HUMORIST AND WRITER

RISK QUOTE: *I haven't failed, I've found 10,000 ways that don't work.*

—THOMAS EDISON, INVENTOR

We have taken a journey that began in 1998 when organizations began to realize they were not respecting risk interaction in their financing and operations. Corrections included the concept of a chief risk officer. Accounting firms and consultants discussed strategic risk management, holistic risk management, and, of course, enterprise risk management. The last of these seems to have stuck. Progress was slow, but two approaches to ERM have developed:

1. **Hazard ERM.** Traditional risk managers focused on insurance, loss control, and risk retention, reduction, transfer, and avoidance. ERM sought to bring various silos together and help them understand relationships among their exposures.

243

2. **Finance ERM.** Individuals who managed investments, rates of
   return, working capital, and the adequacy of capital focused on
   the interaction among financial assets, reported earnings, and
   cash flows. Efforts were supported by computer models that
   used quantitative tools to manage money and forecast future
   results.

In 2008, we are seeing a different picture of ERM. It focuses
on neither hazard nor financial risk. Rather, it is built around a
central risk function that constantly scans for changes that affect
the entity. What are the horizon risks that need to be brought to
the attention of risk owners? What is happening in the organization itself with regard to strategies, leadership, subcultures, and
life cycles? Scanning can find obstacles to achieving the upside of
risk as it uncovers negative conditions. After scanning, it is important to share the findings so that risk owners can make adjustments.

ERM can work in organizations of all sizes. The megacorpora-
tion can use it in a structured hierarchical system with risk owners and subrisk owners. A single business unit in such an entity
can use it as part of the parent system or even in isolation. A
smaller organization can seek an understanding of the challenges
it faces as it seeks to grow and prosper.

This is the closing message of ERM. Managing risk is not
about hundreds or thousands of unorganized exposures. It is about
getting value from an effort to understand the impact of risks and
interrelationships of risk and opportunity. With new technology
and the impact of the 2008 financial crisis, we can expect a renewed interest in getting it right with enterprise risk management.

The Horizon in 2009

Until September 15, 2008, I directed most of my ERM research to
a few specific situations that were publicly known: Boeing, Airbus,
Home Depot, the problems at Chrysler, the failure of risk management at JetBlue, the exposure from the massive dollar reserves
being held by the Chinese government, and the future of fossil
fuel. The problems at AIG, Lehman Brothers, Fannie Mae, and

Freddie Mac seemingly came out of nowhere. The financial crisis and shortages of fossil fuel revealed that there are bigger and maybe largely unsolvable problems on the horizon. A central risk function cannot predict the future, but, as an example, it can alert management and the board to the warning signs of credit default swaps and the likelihood that the world will want to consume 100 million barrels of oil a day by 2013 and that there is little likelihood that such a quantity will be available. ERM encourages organizations to face the emerging risk trends and to take action to protect themselves.

As part of scanning the horizon in 2009, let us examine two issues from a perspective in January 2009. We will apply an ERM evaluation to auto companies that were seeking aid from the United States government. The second issue will discuss risk forecasting when we consider the concept of "normal" times.

First Issue: 2009 ERM Auto Crisis

In late 2008, General Motors, Ford, and Chrysler asked the federal government to help them survive a liquidity crisis resulting from the global financial meltdown. The following ERM analysis covers the situation in January 2009.

RISK IDENTIFICATION

The starting point for an ERM analysis is risk identification. The companies had the following exposures:

- **Diminished Sales.** The U.S. auto market changed over time. In 2008, GM and Toyota each held 20 percent of it. This compares to the 1980s when GM alone had half of the auto market.
- **High Worker Costs.** The auto companies had bloated staffing. The salaried employees exceeded the needs of a lean organization, probably 25 percent more than needed. The cost of hourly workers exceeded national norms and the wage levels paid by foreign manufacturers who opened U.S. factories.
- **Legacy Exposure.** The companies were paying nonworking individuals as a result of agreements with the United Auto

Workers. The companies also had agreements to provide pro-hibitively-costly retirement and health care benefits.

- **Excess of Dealers.** With too many dealers, auto companies have unnecessary costs. In 2008, GM and Toyota, with the same level of U.S. market sales, had vastly different dealer networks. GM had 7,000 dealers compared to Toyota's 1,500.

- **Contractual Agreements.** Union contracts required a "Jobs Bank" program with 90 percent full wages and benefits to for-mer employees. Financing arrangements required supporting revenue bonds for municipalities that borrowed to build facili-ties that were no longer needed.

- **Management and Leadership.** The three companies lacked the ability or the courage to make obvious changes to improve their cultures and competitive position.

RISK STRATEGIES

An ERM analysis in January 2009 would recognize strategies to deal with the identified exposures:

- **Diminished Sales.** Become smaller. Some brands, such as Chevrolet, Buick, Cadillac, Ford, Chrysler minivan, and Jeep, had strong customer loyalty. The cars were made to global quality standards. One strategy is to focus on strong sellers and augment them with hybrids. A related sales strategy would be to reduce U.S. manufacturing plants. The big three had 35 fac-tories, but only needed about 20. With fewer plants, sales would become balanced with cars and trucks that were in demand.

- **High Worker Costs.** These needed to be reduced to competitive levels with foreign manufacturers in the U.S. Salaried positions needed to be reduced along with the hourly labor costs.

- **Legacy Exposure.** Something needed to be done here, perhaps along with the government as a partner to reduce abuses and economic disruption during a transition.

- **Dealers.** Steps needed to be taken to reduce the number of dealers. It would be sad for local communities, but the dealer-ships would close anyway if nothing were done.

- **Contractual Agreements.** They needed to be voided as it was unlikely that the most oppressive burdens could be lifted by direct negotiation.

- **Management and Leadership.** The companies had long-term weaknesses. The new CEOs at Ford and Chrysler may be the right choices. GM's CEO did not have a track record of cultural change. Aside from who does it, all three companies needed to change the managerial cultures.

RISK MITIGATION OPTIONS

The companies, in partnership with the U.S. government, had specific options:

- **Diminished Sales.** Reduce production, eliminate brands, and close inefficient plants. As UAW and municipality contracts made it prohibitive to close plants, this option points in the direction of a Chapter 11 bankruptcy.

- **High Worker Costs.** Reduce the workforce. It would not be easy for hourly workers. A union employee reflected the union position in a quote: "I think we've given enough." This becomes another support for Chapter 11.

- **Legacy Exposure.** Reduce them as the companies had no chance for success if they continued. The costs are contractual. The other parties will not agree to reductions. Chapter 11 bankruptcy is the only choice.

- **Dealers.** State laws made it prohibitively costly to close dealerships. Another indicator of the need for bankruptcy.

- **Contractual Agreements.** Bankruptcy changes the negotiating environment.

- **Management and Leadership.** The auto makers needed stronger boards of directors and executive leadership. This could occur with or without bankruptcy.

ALTERNATIVE VIEWS

A good ERM analysis scans the horizon and internal structure for opposing views. Some were:

- **Option of Bankruptcy.** It was not an option according to Rick Wagoner, former CEO of GM. He may be right. The term *option* implies other choices. If there are none, bankruptcy is not an option. It is an eventuality. Time will tell or already has told.

- **Number of Dealers.** Michael Jackson, CEO of AutoNation, the largest U.S. retailer of cars, said the big three improved quality, reduced labor costs, and rationalized production. Did he believe this meant they needed so many local dealers?

- **Labor Costs.** The union view is not encouraging as it leads to no solution.

- **Likelihood of Change.** GM's Wagoner was on record that he would not resign.

- **Effect of a Bankruptcy.** One marketing research said 80 percent of car buyers would not purchase a car from a bankrupt company. Another said 51 percent would not buy a car from GM in any case.

THE OUTCOME

In January 2009, an ERM analysis pointed to a Chapter 11 bankruptcy. We recognized that such a move would have negative effects, but they would be offset by the possibility of fixing high costs, legacy costs, an excessive number of dealerships, and burdensome contractual commitments. A bailout without conditions offered short-term continued operations. It appeared the companies were not choosing between bankruptcy and a bailout. The choice was between bankruptcy alone—an eventuality, not an option—and a bailout contingent upon filing Chapter 11. It will be interesting to read this story after all decisions have been made.

"Normal" Value at Risk

Our second story takes us to the period between 1990 and 2008. Professional investors were using quantitative tools to measure risk, with value at risk (VaR) being the most common model. VaR is a tool built with specific characteristics and limitations. It assumes a "normal" market and makes short-term projections in that market. It measures risk in a portfolio of investments, and offsets the risk and opportunities in each investment compared to all other investments in the portfolio.

As an example, let us consider the *real* (BRL), the currency of Brazil. A company has borrowed $30 million BRLs at a time when it has 40 million BRLs as receivables from Brazilian sales. In "normal" times, 90 percent of the receivables are collected. If the exchange rate between the BRL and the dollar fluctuates 20 percent, the value at risk is 1.2 million BRLs as follows:

- Debt   30m BRL
- Receivables 40m BRL x 90%   36m BRL
- Exposure   6m BRL
- Fluctuation   20%
- Value at Risk   1.2m BRL

Is this the real exposure in an ERM framework? We start with a "normal" market that is based on five guidelines:

1. Industry or Country Norms. Are there wide variations?
2. Similar Firms. Who is similar?
3. Historical Trends. Will the future be the same as the past?
4. Future Expectations. Can we be sure we know what will happen?
5. Common Sense. This is a catch-all. What does it mean?

Then we consider common sense. What does common sense tell us about "normal?" This is not a difficult question to answer in an ERM context. Simply stated, it is no longer "normal" to be "normal."

Taleb on Normalcy

We have already met the leading voice on normalcy in risk management. He is Nassim Taleb, author of *Fooled by Randomness* and *The Black Swan*. He gave a November 2008 lecture at Columbia University where he announced that he was a distinguished professor of Risk Engineering at NYU. He said he will give seven lectures per semester on certain topics. What topics? Taleb would lecture on "non-Mickey Mouse probability and general misperceptions about risk." He also said he verified something prior to accepting the position. What did he verify? Taleb confirmed that there was NOT A SINGLE economist in his building on the NYU campus.

Taleb argues the lesson from value at risk models is that you can get pretty good within a 95 percent confidence range for short-term projections. You can accept multiple risks. You can study them and give them a mathematical dimension. You can stay within parameters 95 percent of the time. You can improve your performance 95 percent of the time. Therein lies Taleb's challenge to VaR analysis. Ninety-five percent fails to understand risk. It is the other 5 percent that contains both disaster and opportunity.

Having said this, Taleb bases much of his understanding of risk on his experience as a trader of financial securities. He claims that he outperformed the market when he was a financial securities trader, but it was rare. He made a killing each time as a result of three events. The first was the 20 percent crash in the stock market in 1987. The second was the 1999 bust of the dot-com bubble. The third was the 2008 global financial crisis. Other traders treated each time period as being "normal" and managed 95 percent. He did not.

Taleb's position is reinforced by the story of Long-Term Capital Management (LCTM), a successful hedge fund that made extensive use of quantification trading models. LTCM used VaR models that included the possibility of a regional financial crisis. Unfortunately, the model did not consider two financial crises at the same. When both Asia and Russia collapsed, so did LTCM. The models worked 95 to 99 percent of the time. The last one percent was fatal.

What was the lesson learned by financial risk managers as a result of the collapse of Long-Term Capital Management? The evidence is not good. It appears they concluded LTCM was a one-in-a-million event that would never happen again. As a result, they expanded the use of quantitative models, forming a membership association. The Professional Risk Managers' International Association (PRMIA) had 50,000 members in 184 countries in 2008. PRMIA offered a program of certification on risk management.

ERM does not totally denigrate value at risk. It simply recognizes that VaR is focused on increasing return while understanding the risk of 95 percent of events. Assume a company used VaR to forecast a maximum loss for the next month as 15 percent. If it actually had a loss of 18 percent, the outcome is within the scope of VaR. Although it reflects somewhat greater variability than predicted by the model, most factors were probably considered during the period of the event. Now assume the company actually made a profit of 11 percent during the month and went bankrupt during the third week of the month. This outcome is not within the scope of VaR. Even if the VaR model was working with internal and foreseeable factors in "normal" times, a liquidity crisis can destroy the entire model in a matter of moments.

Another example of VaR involves a company that borrowed $100 million to finance a long-term project. It used two securities. It sold an 8 percent corporate bond to raise $60 million. The bond matures in 10 years. It sold a 5 percent, $40 million short-term security with no fixed maturity but with a provision that either party could bring it to maturity with 72 hours notice. In a financial cost analysis, the short-term security offers financing at a lower cost than the longer-term bond. If VaR treats the future as offering a "normal" time, the short-term security does not appear risky because it can be refinanced if redemption is demanded. If we recognize liquidity risk as a possibility, the short-term security is quite risky in times that are not "normal." The 72-hour on-demand redemption could bankrupt the company.

David Viniar, CFO of Goldman Sachs, saw VaR as "a useful tool." He said, "The more liquid the asset, the better the tool. The more history, the better the tool." He is right that more history of the past is instructive if the future is the same as the past. What happens when the future deviates from the past? How do we answer the risk question: "Who will provide funding during a market collapse or liquidity crisis?"

On May 5, 2008, the stock of American International Group

was priced at $40 a share. With a 95 percent chance of accuracy, a VaR model could have forecast the likely price, high price, and low price on December 31, 2008. If that happened, who really cares about the model used to forecast the price? No model was close the 2008 closing price of $1.69 a share.

Conclusion

Knowing that scenarios for change are taking place in the world and in organizations can help management and the board to be proactive. We can develop strategies to help us meet the challenges posed by the exploding economies of Asia, Africa, and South America, environmental concerns about energy from coal, rising populations, U.S. government deficits, China's need for jobs and economic benefits for one-fifth of the world's population, and the inability of the U.S. political process to solve real problems. These and other important issues should be the concern of ERM. They encourage us be proactive in a risky world where every exposure offers a vulnerability to loss and an opportunity to gain advantage. ERM is not about internal controls and compliance. It is about risk identification and flexible strategies to deal with a reality on the horizon. One ERM lesson is that the only constant in modern organizations is change. Another lesson is that no system of risk management is complete if it does not include the possibility of "abnormal" times.

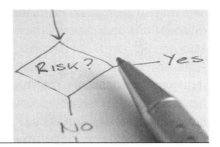

PART **FIVE**

THE PEOPLE OF RISK MANAGEMENT

WE HAVE NOW laid the foundation for a complete ERM program, having defined the steps that go into creating such a program: Understand risk and seize opportunity using modern tools; align risk management with the business model; identify risk owners and hold them accountable; create a central risk function; identify and share risks and opportunities using new technology.

Part Five concludes our presentation of ERM. We meet people who manage risk (Chapter 26). How do they structure functions? Who is in the game, or at least nearby waiting to enter the arena? The narrowest view is that of the modern risk manager, working largely in the hazard risk area but expanding his or her role into operations and strategies. As you will see, successful risk managers are highly skilled individuals who perform a massively important function: retaining, avoiding, reducing, and transfering insurable risks.

Next, in Chapter 27, we look at strategic players. Under the titles of chief risk officer and chief strategy officer, strategic players take on a role that we evaluate from the perspective of authority, responsibility, accountability, and power. We give particular attention to the interaction of a strategic player and organizational flows and senior executives.

Then, in Chapter 28, we meet real-life, highly talented risk managers and others who are spokespeople for ERM. They share their philosophies and ideas about the nature of risk and tell some of their stories.

Part Five concludes with an examination of the concept of a central risk management committee (Chapter 29). Do organizations need such a body? What role can it play? What should it do? What can it do? The discussion is followed by a case study that helps us to think about who should be the leader of such a committee.

CHAPTER 26

MODERN RISK MANAGERS

RISK QUOTE: *In the case of sawmills, it is not a question of if it will burn but when it will burn.*

—LANCE EWING, PROMINENT RISK MANAGER

RISK QUOTE: *A jury consists of 12 people who determine which client has the better lawyer.*

—ROBERT FROST, POET

R isk managers are leading advocates of ERM. As a result, a number of organizations have surveyed them to learn who they are and how they perceive their responsibilities. In this chapter, we examine and interpret the findings of recent surveys. Marsh was particularly active, working with the Risk and Insurance Management Society (RIMS), from 2004 to 2008 and completing these surveys of ERM professionals:

- **2004:** Survey of successful risk managers
- **2005:** Characteristics and practices of organizations implementing ERM
- **2006:** Changes occurring in risk management
- **2007:** Examination of how companies were turning risk into opportunity

❧ **2008:** Broadening the scope of risk management with current practices in ERM

Two other surveys help us understand how risk managers turn risk into opportunity. They are:

1. **Aon Risk Consultants:** Aon surveyed 376 respondents in a study titled *Risk Management and Risk Financing Benchmark Survey, 2004.*

2. **RIMS/Mercer:** RIMS and Mercer surveyed 582 organizations and produced a report titled *2004 Risk Management Compensation Survey.*

Risk Manager Roles

Clearly, the modern risk manager role starts with the culture of the organization. Some entities want the risk manager to have a narrow role as essentially a buyer of insurance, a processor of legal and other insurable claims, and an advocate for safety. Others see the risk manager in a wider role, often with the title of "Enterprise Risk Manager" or even "Chief Risk Officer." In 2004, Marsh/RIMS collaborated to survey risk management practices of 30 top-performing risk managers in North America. The survey found that successful risk managers took on three distinct roles:

1. **Strategic Player.** In this role, the risk manager works with the CEO and the board to design risk management programs.

2. **Competent Risk Manager.** In this role the manager seeks to reduce hazard risks either through the use of loss control techniques such as safety improvement or by transfer of risk, primarily through the mechanism of insurance. This individual also advises managers on risk mitigation strategies.

3. **Risk Specialist.** In this role, the risk manager performs a technical risk management function such as purchasing insurance, managing insurance claims, or supervising employee safety and physical security.

After respondents completed a lengthy written questionnaire and hours of interviewing, Marsh determined that a strategic player is likely to have certain characteristics: The successful strategic player has significant responsibilities for activities that have a major impact on bottom line, brings broad experience in production, marketing, finance, or other areas outside insurable risk and traditional risk management, and has the confidence of the CEO and board. Further, the risk manager has personal chemistry with the chief marketing, finance, and other top-level executives.

Marsh learned that a competent risk manager is important to an organization and is recognized for bringing a high level of skills to the job. The individual is likely to have significant insurance and risk management experience, a departure from the profile of the strategic player. The organization expects the person to have strong skills in risk identification, assessment, and mitigation. The risk manager can expect, and will get, support and encouragement from managers in other units including production, finance, human resources, and legal.

The third category of risk specialist has responsibilities that are narrower in scope but are also important. These individuals assume their positions after years of experience in the world of insurable risk, generally having worked as insurance agents or brokers, underwriters, or claims processors of insurance claims. Many competent risk managers start out as risk specialists who have technical skills in areas such as analysis, loss forecasting, and claims management. With such prior experience, specialists have knowledge of best practices and are judged on their analytical skills and their ability to prepare detailed risk management reports.

Mercer/RIMS used a different categorization of risk managers in a 2004 Compensation Survey in which it identified three levels:

1. **RM-A Level.** This is the highest risk management position in the organization, with responsibility for risk transfer and mitigation. Like the competent risk manager in the Marsh survey, the individual is not described as a strategic player nor is there any indication that A-level risk managers work in ERM.

2. **RM-B Level.** The person in this position is an important decision maker but does not have ultimate authority for major risk management decisions. The B-level risk manager appears to qualify as a competent risk manager if he or she has the final authority on settling claims or purchasing insurance or otherwise makes important risk management decisions.

3. **RM-C Level.** This person recommends or advises on risk management activities and strategies, but higher-level executives make most decisions. A C-level risk manager usually goes into depth in a narrow area including collecting and interpreting data on losses, ensuring efficient processing of claims, and preparing reports on loss control successes and weaknesses.

Many people use the title "risk manager." The Marsh and Mercer surveys show that the title's meaning varies from organization to organization.

Marsh 2007 Update

Marsh updated its risk management survey each year from 2003 to 2008, with 391 risk managers and 77 C-suite executives interviewed in 2007. It was a survey of diverse organizations, with half the organizations having revenues below $1 billion and service companies making up 55 percent, manufacturing 35 percent, and retail 10 percent of respondents. The survey probed three broad risk management categories. Traditional risk management was the most restricted, consisting of risk identification, loss control, claims analysis, and insurance. Progressive risk management reflected an expanded role that included alternative risk financing, business continuity, total cost of risk, and risk education and communication. Strategic risk management was the broadest, involving ERM, indexing of risk, and use of technology.

In the 2007 survey, Marsh changed the playing field in the direction of ERM. The survey addressed turning risk into opportunity—the upside of risk. Topics addressed that were, in Marsh's estimation, essential parts of risk strategies including managing people risk, strengthening vendor and customer relations, minimizing business interruption, accepting risk to increase profit, diversifying operations, leveraging regulatory compliance, and leveraging technology. The 2007 survey was a big step forward for ERM.

Marsh 2008 Update

In 2008, Marsh continued to move toward ERM with a survey of 394 RIMS members and 60 members of Financial Executives International. One question dealt with changes since the 2007 survey. One-third of the 2008 respondents described their approach to risk management as being strategic, whereas only 15 percent had responded that way in 2007. The traditional description was the choice of only 18 percent, down from 34 percent in 2007. Even more interesting was the aspiration of the respondents. Fifty-two percent of respondents in traditional companies and 73 percent of those in progressive companies stated that they sought to be strategic in their risk management activities.

The companies were at different stages in the implementation of ERM. Seven percent agreed that they had fully implemented ERM, 60 percent were planning for it or had partially implemented it, and one-third had no such plans. Of the companies with ERM, 92 percent planned to maintain or increase ERM expenditures in 2008 over 2007 levels. Ninety-six percent of the companies with ERM were satisfied with the results. The survey showed that companies where ERM was fully implemented and where the company had at least two years' ERM experience expressed the greatest satisfaction.

An interesting aspect of the survey was a question presented to companies with no plans to implement ERM. They question was why they had no such plans. Risk managers and C-suite executives had different answers. Risk managers said that other areas had greater priority, that risk was managed at the operational level, and that senior management did not see a need for ERM. C-suite executives cited a lack of personnel resources and lack of demonstrated value.

The world of the risk manager becomes clearer as a result of three questions in the 2008 survey. Sixty-one percent of the risk managers agreed that senior management understood the top exposures in terms of measured risks and immeasurable uncertainties. Fifty-six percent agreed that senior management understood the company's risk profile and the mitigation strategies being used to manage major risks. Forty-two percent agreed that senior management knew how much it was willing to lose from all sources of risk over a selected time horizon to achieve its overall, long-term financial objectives. Then came the rub. Although all three statements are important in risk management, only 34 percent of risk managers overall gave management a positive answer to all three of them. The breakdown was 23 percent in traditional companies, 38 percent in progressive companies, and 45 percent in strategic companies.

The surveys on risk management environments show that there is a wide variety of risk management activities and viewpoints and that progress is being made in understanding ERM.

Profiles of Risk Managers

Given the variety of levels, duties, and organizational expectations attached to risk managers, we would expect to find that risk managers have diverse backgrounds. Indeed, this is one finding of the surveys. Let us examine risk managers' education, work experience, level in the hierarchy, and compensation.

In terms of educational credentials, the Mercer survey showed that half of risk managers were college graduates, almost half had graduate degrees, and fewer than 2 percent had limited or no college. Focusing solely on the A-level risk managers with graduate degrees, the Mercer survey showed that two-thirds had an MBA, one-sixth had a master of science degree, and 10 percent had a law degree.

Shifting to work experience, the Marsh 2004 survey showed that risk managers had varying experience prior to becoming a risk manager. Sixty percent had backgrounds with insurance carriers, brokers, or service providers, whereas 18 percent came from consulting, government, legal, or financial backgrounds. Twenty-five percent had prior in-house risk management experience.

The reporting line for the risk managers also tells a story. According to the Mercer 2004 survey, more than half of risk managers reported to individuals in the finance area. Fourteen percent reported to the CEO, 9 percent reported to the chief counsel, and 22 percent reported to individuals holding a variety of titles.

Another view comes from examining the mobility, or lack thereof, of risk management professionals. The Marsh 2004 survey showed that 70 percent of the successful risk managers had at least 20 years' experience in risk management. One-fourth had more than 30 years' experience. Only 7 percent had less than 10 years' experience. The same picture emerges from the length of time they held their current positions. Two-thirds had more than 10 years in the job, whereas only 4 percent had 5 years or less. Risk managers stay risk managers once they enter the field and usually do not change jobs once they are successful. They encourage brokers and other vendors to build long-term relationships, which their longevity seems to encourage.

Organizational Risk Management Function

Separate from the profile, we can obtain employers' views of the risk manager role. One indicator is the number of employees in risk management departments. The Mercer 2004 survey showed that almost half of the departments had fewer than three employees, and three-fourths had fewer than 10. Risk management departments are small, partly because many services such as claims processing are outsourced to third parties.

In a different survey, *National Underwriter* magazine ("Risk Managers Pack Punch Despite Modestly-Sized Staffs," by Sam Friedman, April 18, 2005) identified the size of risk management departments by company revenues. Companies with revenues up to $500 million a year had fewer than five risk management employees, whereas companies with revenues above $2 billion averaged 10 such employees.

Still another view of the risk manager can be derived from their compensation. The *National Underwriter* 2007 survey identified the median (50th percentile) total cash compensation of risk managers in companies by level of revenues. Risk managers in companies with more than $15 billion in revenues had a median compensation of $333,000. For companies with revenues between $1 billion and $15 billion, the range was $190,000 to $282,000. For companies with revenues below $500 million, the median compensation was $110,000.

Areas of Attention

What do risk managers actually do on the job? The 2004 Marsh survey identified four primary risk areas: Hazard or insurable risk, affecting property, people, and tangible assets; operational risk, dealing with production and marketing; financial risk, covering availability of resources; and strategic risk, involving the organizational mission and goals. The survey asked risk managers to identify the importance of each risk area and the percentage of time that they spent working on each area. Seventy-eight percent reported that insurable risk was the most important, saying that they spent half their time on that area. Only 7 percent identified operational risk as most important, even though it took up 21 percent of their time. Only 4 percent reported that strategic risk was most important, but they spent 17 percent of their time on that area. These are rather interesting findings. That which is most important does not always get the most time.

An Aon 2004 survey offers greater depth. It asked risk managers to identify the greatest risks their companies faced. Seven insurable risks make the top 10 list of critical risks, with business interruption, employee accidents, and general liability ranked one, two, and three. The three noninsurance risks were a failure to change or adapt (ranked fourth), loss of reputation (ranked sixth), and employee recruitment and retention (ranked tenth).

Conclusion

Modern risk management means different things across the range of organizations, and profiles of risk manager reflect this diversity. The profiles show that risk managers need advanced education, that the importance of risk management differs in different entities, and that there is a movement, albeit slow, away from insurable risk in the direction of strategic risk. This leads us to the conclusion that the supervisors of risk managers may be gaining a broader understanding of ERM and its importance to modern organizations.

CHAPTER 27

CHIEF RISK AND STRATEGY OFFICERS

RISK QUOTE: *Capitalism tries for a delicate balance: It attempts to work things out so that everyone gets just enough stuff to keep them from getting violent and trying to take other people's stuff.*
—GEORGE CARLIN, COMEDIAN

RISK QUOTE: *Without passion you don't have energy. Without energy you have nothing.*
—DONALD TRUMP, BUSINESSMAN

A s already discussed, ERM proponents should pay attention to the fundamental difference between risks that are managed and those that are influenced. This difference encourages a central risk function to provide value to risk owners who want a broad understanding of risk and opportunity. At the same time, risk owners do not want to be annoyed or distracted by ERM, so real value should be delivered without busy work or intrusion. A high-tech platform for assessing the visual risk cluster can help. An issue that quickly becomes relevant is the two roles played by the head of the central risk function. Is the individual a chief risk officer, a chief strategy officer, or both? Let us explore the issue.

Chief Risk Officer

The chief risk officer (CRO) title first appeared in a 1988 Peat Marwick study on global capital markets. The first CRO was James Lam of GE Capital, in 1993. Since then, the position of CRO has had diverse meanings, and there is little agreement on the responsibilities that go with it. Banks, insurance companies, and other financial institutions were early adopters in the 1990s. The title was usually given to someone with responsibilities for balancing exposures across financial investments and holdings, complying with regulatory and statutory requirements, and providing security and internal controls on flow of data and access to information.

After 2001, the title made slow progress in nonfinancial organizations, but a renewed interest in ERM may speed up its acceptance in publicly traded corporations. A 2004 report by Forrester Research forecast that 75 percent of utilities and energy companies planned to have a CRO in place over the subsequent few years. A 2005 survey by the Economist Intelligence Unit showed that 45 percent of 137 companies had a CRO, and another 24 percent planned to create the position by 2007. In early 2009, it does not appear that progress has been as rapid as predicted. As I already proposed, the head of a central risk function does not also have to hold a chief risk officer title.

As we watch to see whether a CRO title grows in popularity, we can observe that the title has two meanings and sets of responsibilities. It can refer to a financial CRO or to a nonfinancial CRO. A financial CRO manages financial and internal control functions, such as portfolio risk, compliance, credit and commodity risk, and the security of information technology, data, and systems. The individual is trained in finance, actuarial science, and auditing or accounting and has major experience as a financial or investment analyst, treasurer, or controller. The reporting line leads directly to the CFO. Alternatively, the title can reflect the additional duty of a senior finance executive, such as a treasurer or controller.

The nonfinancial CRO role is quite different. This individual helps identify risks and opportunities and shares the knowledge with risk owners. This individual can have any kind of training and experience, including finance, business administration, engineering, or law, and has a significant understanding of the industry, lines of business, and the external environment. This CRO coordinates risk through an indirect process of influence, rather than taking the direct approach of the financial CRO, who solves problems with computers and technology. The nonfinancial CRO builds relationships with risk owners.

One option is to recognize that the financial and nonfinancial roles are so different that the organization needs two individuals to play the two roles.

Chief Strategy Officer (CSO)

As part of a central risk function, an organization might believe it needs a chief strategy officer. Strategic risk is defined as exposures or missed opportunities that threaten the organization's ability to align entity goals with the pathways to pursue those goals. Strategic risk covers a lack of vision, faulty planning, emerging or aggressive competitors, and the inability to respond to changing conditions in the business environment. We need to face a fact. Most C-suite officers are busy people with significant responsibilities. They lack the time, and often the skills, to scan the horizon for strategic risks and opportunities.

The model of a chief strategy officer and nonfinancial chief risk officer recognizes that corporate strategies evolve from focusing on opportunities, not on exposures. The CRO role has much to contribute once a strategy is identified to help ensure that enterprise risk factors are identified and vetted. The development of the strategy itself, with its innovation and creativity aspects, may be a precursor to the CRO role. Figure 27-1 shows a central risk function with separate roles for the CRO and the CSO.

CRO AND CSO AREAS OF FOCUS

In the three-position approach to the central risk function, each individual has a different focus.

1. **Financial CRO.** Looks outside and inside the entity, with primary activities dealing with computers, financial institutions, and the organization's finance department support staff.

FIGURE 27-1. CENTRAL RISK FUNCTION WITH CROS AND CSO.

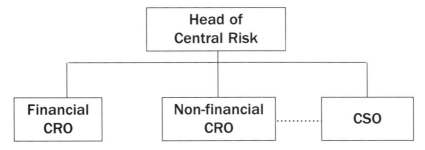

2. **Nonfinancial CRO.** Works inside face-to-face with risk owners, business unit heads, internal audit, and compliance and outside to scan the horizon.

3. **CSO.** Works inside and outside the entity but largely with senior executives and the board.

Critical Risks

What would CROs and CSOs look at in 2009? What skills will be needed to deal with the financial crisis if it continues? What risks are posed by the emergence of India in production and service operations? What is the impact of the typical American production worker's salary of $40 an hour when an equally skilled Mexican working just across the border from El Paso receives $4? Is there anything that China cannot produce to world-class standards at a low production cost? How will we deal with a situation where the need for oil is growing rapidly but the ability to supply it is highly constrained? Is the company prepared for the changing demographics and diversity of the workforce? How will we manage far-flung operations and supply chains? By all indications, a company has plenty of work for CROs and CSOs in a central risk function.

The dual strategic and risk/opportunity roles are powerful tools with which to make solid business decisions. Suppose we spot a risk on the horizon. What is the upside of the risk? What strategies can we develop to deal with it? What risks in leadership, culture, and capabilities will impede our ability to succeed with a strategy? Advocates of combining strategy and risk/opportunity encourage senior executives to participate fully in ERM.

Authority, Responsibility, Accountability, and Power

We expect the head of a central risk function to have solid credentials and wide experience. The individual probably has many years in the industry, prior C-suite responsibilities, an advanced degree, participation in continuing professional education, and a reputation for innovative and creative problem solving. These characteristics are not enough, however. The organization must address the amount of authority, responsibility, accountability, and power that goes with the position.

Authority is the right to give direction to others in an organization. It comes from two sources. The first is the person. An individual can convince others to follow a path or take certain actions. When other units respond to a respected central risk function head, the individual has personal authority. The second source of authority is the position on an organization chart. If an individual's title has a higher box, lower-level individuals have an obligation to take direction from the "boss." This is structural authority.

One thing is particularly important with the concept of authority: It must be accepted by others. The right to influence risk management may be personal or structural. If it is not accepted, the CRO/CSO has no authority.

Although related to authority, *responsibility* is totally different. It refers to a person's assumption of duties and obligations. As an example, a risk manager may be responsible for safety in a refinery. Two factors establish responsibility. First, it derives from a position in the hierarchy. It is delegated by the organization itself. In some cases, individuals take responsibility for their own actions or the actions of others. In either case, the CRO/CSO can achieve results by claiming responsibility for risk. Second, the CRO/CSO must accept responsibility. An oil company may tell a CRO that he or she is responsible for safety programs in refineries. If the CRO assumes that the refinery manager is responsible for safety, the CRO may not accept responsibility.

It is poor management technique to appoint a CRO/CSO without clearly specifying to others the level of authority to get the job done. If risk owners and others refuse to cooperate, the CRO/CSO will lack authority and will be unable to assume responsibility.

Accountability is a third dimension of the CRO/CSO position. It refers to the ability to provide a satisfactory explanation of one's actions or outcomes. It also refers to accepting responsibility for the success or failure of risk mitigation efforts. Accountability involves both measurement and achievement. We measure achievement of risk reduction or business opportunity goals. We evaluate the performance of parties and their achievements. What happened? Why did it happen? Should it have happened?

This can be tricky, as the CRO and CSO are not risk owners in their own right.

Power is the element that links authority, responsibility, and accountability. Power refers to the ability to get things done even when someone else does not agree with the decision. An organization can provide responsible parties with the power to coordinate and mitigate risk. A mismatch occurs when the organization expects the CRO/CSO to make changes that reduce risk. The CRO/CSO may be accountable and responsible, but if an important risk owner disagrees with an assessment, a power play may ensue. Suppose a risk owner disagrees with a recommendation from a CRO. If the risk owner has power and refuses to accept the authority of the CRO, the risk owner will do nothing. In the end, if the CRO proves to be right, the organization will realize that responsibility and accountability were not aligned with authority and power. The risk owner had the responsibility and the power to do something but did not. This is the individual who should be held accountable for a negative outcome.

In terms of accountability, the Deloitte 2008 survey identified the senior executives with primary responsibility for ERM. As shown in Figure 27-2, 34 percent of respondents reported that the CFO was the accountable person. This analysis of accountability is incomplete if we do not consider the reporting line for the chief risk officer. Figure 27-3 shows the reporting lines for the CRO. It is interesting to note that 46 percent of CROs report to the CEO, the board, or a board committee.

FIGURE 27-2. POSITION ACCOUNTABLE FOR ERM (DELOITTE SURVEY).

	Percentage of Respondents
Chief Financial Officer	34%
Chief Risk Officer	25%
Chief Executive Officer	9%
Director of ERM	7%
Internal Audit	7%
Other	18%

FIGURE 27-3. POSITION ACCOUNTABLE FOR CRO (DELOITTE SURVEY).

	Percentage of Respondents
Chief Financial Officer	33%
Chief Executive Officer	27%
Board of Directors	14%
Management Level Risk Committee	7%
Board-Level Risk Committee	5%
Other	14%

The Deloitte 2008 survey also showed the level of board of director involvement in ERM. The audit committee of the board most commonly exercises the ERM fiduciary role. The survey asked, "Does the written charter of the audit committee include the requirement for at least an annual discussion with management regarding its policies and guidelines with respect to risk assessment and risk management?" Fifty-two percent of the respondents answered yes. Fourteen percent said no. A second question was, "Does the audit committee regularly discuss the company's major financial risk exposures and the steps management has taken to monitor and control such exposures?" Fifty-three percent said yes. Thirteen percent said no.

CRO Skills and Behavior

When looking for a CRO, the organization seeks specific characteristics. One is usually a bias for action. Boards try to find someone who is a self-starter and who wants to get things done. Action leads to real risk mitigation. A second characteristic involves ability to time actions appropriately. The CRO seeks to forecast the possibility of a disruption, loss, or missed opportunity and to influence the risk owner to take steps to make corrections. A third characteristic reflects the network role of a CRO. The entity needs an individual who cultivates a wide number of key managers and professionals. This gives the CRO influence as he or she coordinates internal risk with risk owners.

A different view of the CRO develops when we consider task skills. We can expect the CRO/CSO to seek information—basically identifying and assessing exposures. Then comes sharing information with others and interpreting the meaning of the findings. A CRO/CSO also needs analysis skills, the ability to clarify exposures or opportunities and to help others focus on solutions.

Task skills are not enough for a CRO, who must influence risk owners and others to mitigate exposures. A CRO's people skills should include the ability to encourage others to act. If an area is struggling, a CRO can provide support. Another people skill is the ability to recognize and acknowledge effective risk management efforts, including using humor to refocus units in times of tension. With strong people skills, the CRO can open doors so that all interested units and individuals contribute to risk mitigation.

The Deloitte 2008 study identified specific duties assigned to a CRO, including risk analytics and the monitoring of exposure. Figure 27-4 shows the percentage of respondents who had primary and secondary responsibilities in four specific areas.

Preparedness to Manage Risk

The Deloitte survey asked whether the organization is fully prepared to manage risk. It correlated the answer with whether the company also had a single executive in charge of ERM or had a separate ERM function. It asked whether ERM was combined with another function, such as compliance or internal audit. It checked the answers against the length of time the company had an ERM function in place and by whether the company had a fully operational ERM program. Figure 27-5 shows the importance of having a CRO and a separate ERM. Companies with longstanding ERM programs were most likely to be fully prepared to face risk.

FIGURE 27-4. DELOITTE FINDINGS ON CRO/CSO RESPONSIBILITIES.

Responsibility	Primary	Secondary
Analyzing Risk and Reporting	72%	18%
Developing Controls, Policies, and	41%	39%
Monitoring Compliance		
Monitoring Risk Exposures		
Independent Verifying Risk Methodology	40%	32%

FIGURE 27-5. DELOITTE FINDINGS ON PREPAREDNESS TO MANAGE RISK.

	Fully Prepared
Single ERM Executive in Place	64%
No Single ERM Executive	28
Separate ERM Function in Place	69%
No Separate ERM Function	46%
ERM in Place More Than 4 Years	100%
ERM in Place Less Than 1 Year	44%
ERM Fully Operational	82%
ERM in Development	44%

Alternative CRO View

Two observers of risk management, Charles R. Lee and Prakash Shimpi, published their own view of the CRO in their article, "The Chief Risk Officer: What Does It Look Like and How Do You Get There?" (*Risk Management,* September 2005). The authors argue that executives ask two questions about ERM: Should we consider an ERM program? If yes, will we need a new executive position to manage it? The authors believe that, before 2005, many executives recognized ERM as an important management practice that could create and improve shareholder value by encouraging risk-based decision-making and capital allocation. They considered additional questions: What should a CRO do? What should be the background and experience of a CRO? Where does a CRO fit in the organization?

According to the article, the CRO plays three roles:

1. **Process.** The CRO ensures that the organization has processes to comply with rising risk management expectations of shareholders, regulators, and other stakeholders.

2. **Implementation.** The CRO develops a comprehensive framework for mitigating risk across the organization.

3. **Decision Making.** The CRO helps the CEO and the board allocate capital to build shareholder value while recognizing both the positive and negative potential of major risks.

To fulfill these responsibilities, the CRO must create a risk-aware culture. This includes instituting central oversight of risk assessment and risk appetite, promoting ERM among employees, shareholders, regulators and other stakeholders, managing ERM in operational areas, and developing tools to mitigate risk and cover the cost of risk. It also includes partnerships. The CRO works with senior operating managers, others in business units, and staff departments such as finance, legal, and human resources. A key partner is internal audit, where the CRO can gain important information on risks in compliance and internal control. A final component of a risk-aware culture is bringing the CRO into processes of strategic planning. In this role, the authors argue, the CRO should provide a risk assessment for future organizational strategies.

The next section of the article describes the specific competencies of a CRO. With technical skills, he or she must be analytical and bright, have skills as a collector of complex data, possess the ability to understand information from all business areas, and know how to use sophisticated modeling tools to sort out complex relationships. Nontechnical competencies include skills as a leader, project manager, and synthesizer, capability for effective communication using clear and understandable language, active participation as an integrative thinker, and interpersonal skills to facilitate group action.

The success of the CRO does not depend only on the individual. The culture of the organization plays a role. One critical success factor is access: Can the CRO influence the CEO and the board of directors? The organization might also create a central risk management committee chaired by CRO. A culture that encourages a strong working relationship between the CFO and the chief operating officer is also a plus. Having said this, the authors believe that the CRO must be careful to avoid turf battles with the CFO and the COO. They conclude that the CRO role is likely to fail if the CRO tries to carve out major responsibilities. Rather, the CRO is more likely to succeed if the the person in the position plays a cooperative and conciliatory role that helps other C-suite executives. This is consistent with the concept of ERM in which the function of the central risk function is limited to identifying and sharing risks and does not include managing them.The authors finish with an acknowledgement that risk managers have much of the background and even the breadth of experience to be CROs. They see a problem if the risk manager is viewed as a technical expert rather than as a communicator, facilitator, or leader. This, too, is consistent with our approach to ERM.

Conclusion

Our discussion of financial and nonfinancial CROs and a CSO gives us options when forming a central risk function. We cannot expect every organization to follow the same path to risk identification, assessment, and mitigation. With respect to the roles in a central risk function, organizations can customize ERM to fit their individual cultures.

CHAPTER 28

RISK MANAGERS IN PERSON

RISK QUOTE: *You can observe a lot by just watching.*
— YOGI BERRA, BASEBALL PLAYER

RISK QUOTE: *The illiterate of the twenty-first century will not be those who cannot read and write, but those who cannot learn, unlearn, and relearn.*
— ALVIN TOFFLER, FUTURIST

We have now covered risk managers in the abstract and examined their collective views, the risks they manage, and the roles they play. Now we introduce individuals in risk management front and get up close and personal. When we finish reading their stories, we may have a new view of the risk management function.

Paul Buckley, Tyco Risk Manager

In March 2006, Paul Buckley, vice president for risk management at Tyco International (US), Inc., explained his role at Tyco. Paul joined Tyco after 29 years in the Bell system, finishing as risk manager of Lucent Technologies. He received many awards while at AT&T and Lucent, and he was named Risk Manager of the Year in 2000 by *Business Insurance* magazine.

Paul's story begins in 2002. In the wake of Securities and Exchange Commission investigations of accounting improprieties, Tyco's former CEO L. Dennis Kozlowski was indicted and convicted on fraud, conspiracy, and grand larceny charges. Paul joined Tyco in May 2003, after the scandal broke. His view was that it was the right place to be from a risk management perspective. Tyco had a new board—totally new. News reports stated that all 125 headquarters personnel had been replaced. Paul confirmed that many new senior executives had joined the company. He further confirmed that Ed Breen, Tyco's CEO since 2002, was attracting good people to a refreshing environment. These considerations overcame Paul's reservations about leaving the Bell system after so many years.

Paul reported that Ed Breen was joined in top management by Jack Kroll, a board member and a retired chairman and CEO of DuPont. These leaders and everyone else on the board or in top management wanted to do it right. They set a tone from the top, indicating that they would not tolerate even the appearance of compromising behavior. They would ensure accurate financial reporting and create the perception and reality that Tyco was now an open and honest company with total integrity. This sounded like real enterprise risk management.

Paul said the new environment meant big changes for risk management, which had previously been limited to activities such as buying insurance, processing claims, and helping with loss control. Everything changed when Paul arrived, as the company developed a centralized risk management strategy. Coordinated programs drove down costs, implemented a new return-to-work program, and otherwise brought all units together in unified programs. One big change was that the role of risk management shifted from advising others to a functional role with specific tasks and responsibilities.

Paul concluded that risk management had become highly visible at Tyco. As risk manager, he had access to top officers, including Martina Hund-Mejean, senior vice president and treasurer; retired Tyco CFO Dave FitzPatrick; John Davidson, Tyco senior vice president, controller, and chief accounting officer; and Chris Coughlin, chief financial officer. The learning environment was exciting, and the support from his direct line of senior management was exceptional. He stated, "I would not be as good a risk manager had it not been for this experience."

Chris Mandel, USAA Risk Manager

In 2006 Chris Mandel was risk manager at USAA, with enterprise risk management in his title. Chris is a former president of the Risk and Insurance Management Society (RIMS), a former *Business Insurance* magazine Risk Manager of the Year, and an award winner for USAA's ERM program. Chris has been a long-time ERM proponent.

Chris believed that ERM had made substantial progress since 2000. He received daily communications from consultants and brokers about ERM products and services. He observed a linkage between ERM and other key initiatives, including Sarbanes-Oxley compliance, regulatory emerging requirements, and effective internal and external audit functions. He saw evidence that operations, control, and finance professionals were expressing an interest in and concern about managing effectively exposures that are more than the typically insurable risks.

Chris remarked that the position of chief strategy officer with no responsibilities other than scanning the changing risk horizon and bringing back early warning signs while might be ideal but that it is unrealistic in today's stressed industries. He pointed out that a CSO could play a unique and important role integrating risk management with strategic risk. In addition, external environmental scanning is necessary. If an organization considers having a CSO, it is critical that the person work effectively with the risk manager to ensure that they miss no key risks.

Chris also commented on the position of nonfinancial chief risk officer. He supported varied approaches to risk management and believed that the most important element of a good risk strategy is designing it to align with the company and its culture. He recognized that financial risks are the most significant risks in certain institutions. The leaders of risk management in these companies focus on credit and other financial risks to the exclusion of strategic risks. He observed that nonfinancial risks can cause by far the most harm to the success of the entity's mission. Furthermore, a nonfinancial CRO type is appropriate in many cultures to ensure that the most significant risks are appropriately addressed. He also noted that many different models can work. One such model holds subject matter experts in specific risk areas accountable for risks in partnership with a senior risk process leader.

Chris then addressed insurable risk—the stock in trade of today's risk managers. He discussed whether traditional risk managers are properly prepared for the larger role of CRO and whether they have the necessary additional knowledge and skills. He concluded that traditional risk managers may be well-suited to assume broader responsibilities because they have a deep and broad understanding of how key company segments interact. Risk managers who do not know their companies in depth or who have limited relationships with senior and powerful leaders represent a weakness in the organization. He concluded that individuals who have focused on a wide range of risk over their careers might be most successful as enterprise risk managers. They know how to build relationships across key business segments. It also helps if they have a solid understanding of finance and business management.

Chris discussed a concept he presented when he was president of RIMS. He was a leading voice for a broadened view of risk management and even coined the term "World Class Risk Management." He reported that his thinking had changed and that world class had given way to "best in class," which he defined as the result when culture and continuous improvement combine to achieve long-term success. He had not changed his criteria for success but had made adjustments to pursue a higher level of performance. His thinking changed because he has seen the importance of key stakeholder alliances. Both internal and external alliances ensure a broad and deep mandate that can be driven into a company's culture. To achieve that goal, practitioners need to be closely aligned with internal audit, compliance, legal, operations, business continuation, internal control, and the CFO.

He concluded with thoughts on the future of ERM. It is up to risk managers to be leaders, to ensure a place at the table with senior decision makers. Stakeholders must work together because critical risks are too wide ranging for any one person to handle. A critical part of enlisting long-term support of key leaders is that the risk manager develop rigor around the risk process, especially risk value measurement.

John Bayeux, Willis Financial Institutions Practice Leader

John Bayeux has heard that ERM started in financial institutions, as did the title of chief risk officer, but he does not believe that these stories are correct. John thinks he may have heard similar terms when he was risk manager at L. F. Rothschild, a securities firm in New York. The terms might have been used by individuals in a unit responsible for credit and financial risk. He believe ERM and the CRO title came together in the 1990s, driven, to some extent, by the Basel I Accord, which governed the amount of capital a financial institution had to set aside to protect itself against credit and market risks assumed in daily business.

John's view on the current status of the CRO in financial institutions is shaped by the tighter standards imposed by Basel II. In addition to monitoring credit and market risk, banks must assess capital against operational risks. They are increasingly assigning compliance to CROs, even as they assign operational risks to other risk owners. John notes that one of his clients in 2006, a South Carolina bank, had a fully staffed risk department consisting of credit, market, and operational risk managers, all reporting to a CRO. This team determined appropriate levels of risk, methods of mitigating it, the risk impact on regulatory capital, and the potential for transferring risk via insurance or other methods.

John addressed the possibility of creating the position of chief strategy officer. He saw the person as a leader in implementing the vision of senior management and the board. John believed that it would be difficult to convince the CEO of the need for such a stand-alone position. Instead, he suggested that every risk owner, as a normal part of his or her responsibility, "scan the changing risk horizon" to provide financial institutions with early warnings about developing exposures.

John did not accept the idea of creating a nonfinancial chief risk officer. Within the Basel II environment, banks appoint operational risk leaders and insurance risk managers to control risk as a core responsibility. With the growth of employment- and fiduciary-related claims, the proactive insurance risk manager is already working with key senior officers to address these risks. Like most observers prior to the 2008 financial crisis, John believed that the largest financial institutions had complied with the risk capital requirements of regulators and created robust operational risk management environments. They focused on identifying, assessing, and quantifying risk, collecting and utilizing loss event data, and determining risk capital. Still, he noted that banks had to do a lot more to bring all the relevant constituencies together. He was right, and he was as surprised as everyone else in 2008 that the situation got so out of control.

Lance Ewing, Harrah's Risk Manager

Lance Ewing is hardly an unknown individual in risk management. In addition to holding a high-profile position as vice president of risk management of Harrah's Entertainment, Lance was president of the Risk and Insurance Management Society (RIMS) during 2003-2004. He traveled domestically and internationally as a representative of the Society. He was an active advocate of risk management education, serving as an instructor for the National Alliance for Insurance Education and Research, based in Austin, Texas.

Lance is having a successful career as a risk manager. His story shows how an individual can move from being a risk specialist to being a competent risk manager. Part of the story lies in education. He is a perpetual student, holding two master's degrees—one in law and justice and another in occupational safety engineering. He has an Associate in Risk Management (ARM) designation, an International Certified Risk Manager (CRM) designation, an Enterprise Risk Management Professional designation, and was pursuing the Chartered Property Casualty Underwriter (CPCU) designation in 2008. Lance always says, "The world is changing. We have to keep up with it." He does exactly that, staying on top of risk management developments.

Lance Ewing, like many risk managers, started in an insurance company. It is difficult to picture Mr. Ewing—a somewhat flamboyant personality by any measure—in a traditional insurance environment. Once, I was asked to pay tribute to Lance at a ceremony in his honor. I told the audience that "not everyone is annoyed by Lance Ewing. Some people do not mind him at all." The audience recognized the banter as praise for an individual who combines his skills with the enthusiastic personality of a motivational speaker.

His early days in insurance shaped Lance's thinking about his career. He assessed risks for high-hazard industries such as sawmills, logging companies, hospitals, trucking companies, and mobile home manufacturers. As Lance says, "My experience forced me to stay away from insurance technical jargon that merely baffled business owners and corporate CFOs. They were interested in results, not words." Lance learned quickly that his customers did not want insurance. They wanted to bring down losses and the consequent costs. When he found himself working as an engineer with highly protected risks, prevention and loss control became ingrained in his DNA.

After five years in insurance, Lance became risk manager for the Philadelphia school district. During a six-year tenure, he dramatically reduced losses, resulting in significant savings. He applied loss control techniques to 300 schools and facilities, initiating a rooftop-to-boiler-room inspection of every single building. His team documented conditions and made recommendations and corrections. The effort discovered unknown assets, such as fine art, that needed to be secured. The team identified previously unknown exposures, such as storage tanks that lacked overflow shutoff valves. The strategy paid off. By correcting deficiencies, the system reduced its losses. By providing accurate information to carriers, the system reduced its insurance premiums.

In the late 1990s, Lance joined GES Exposition Services as senior director of risk management. The company provides logistical support to hundreds of major conference and exhibitions annually, with forklifts racing around convention centers and hundreds of trucks unloading in a few hours and reloading a few days later. Lance expanded his understanding of the link between insurance and risk management by building an internal consulting team. It advised managers on everything from environmental hazards to contract reviews and even compliance issues. The team conducted training for managers and union workers. The goal was to find ways to say "yes" when risk conditions seemed to say "no."

This approach paid off many times, but particularly in 1999, when a tornado struck the convention center in Salt Lake City during a GES exhibition. Although damage was extensive, it was mitigated by the strong relationships between the risk management department and managers, workers, carriers and brokers. Losses could easily have been much higher.

When GES downsized, Lance joined Park Place Entertainment (later Caesar's Entertainment) after an interesting negotiation. Offered the job of director of risk management, Lance pressed for the title of executive director. He argued for an expanded role for risk management and pledged to bring bottom-line results. He got the title and job in November 2002 and quickly built a risk management department to reduce liability claims. Operating units worked closely with the new team, and the results were immediate, with savings in the millions of dollars in a matter of months. Park Place recognized Lance's success in July 2003—eight months after his start date—when it made him a vice president.

In time, Park Place became Caesar's, and then, in 2005, Harrah's bought Caesar's. Lance kept his VP position at the newly merged company and moved from Las Vegas to Memphis. He was in new territory at Harrah's but had no time to adjust. Four weeks after his arrival, Hurricane Katrina destroyed three of Harrah's major casinos in Mississippi and Louisiana. Thirty days later, Hurricane Rita damaged the company's hotel and casino in Louisiana. It was baptism by fire for all parties, but Harrah's responded quickly and forcefully. The company engaged in crisis management, reaching out to employees, guests, clients, and local Gulf coast communities, and quickly restored some stability. This part of the story is nicely told in detail in the April 2006 edition of *Risk Management* magazine. In a longer-term response, Harrah's sold damaged properties in Gulfport and Lake Charles to provide resources to build a new $1 billion property in Biloxi. Maybe Lance is correct in one of his favorite sayings: "Whatever does not kill you only makes you stronger."

What is the value of the story of Lance Ewing? His is a poignant tale of change from being a risk technician to occupying a position with high-level impact. Lance shows the importance of education, knowledge, energy, and innovation for individuals seeking career opportunities in risk management. For this reason, his is a story worth telling.

Roger Egan, Former CEO of Integro and Former President of Marsh

Roger Egan believes that risk managers need to reevaluate the broker's role in managing risk with its clients. Across the globe, multinational corporations are facing an unparalleled spectrum of interrelated risks, and the need for advice, analysis, and problem solving is greater than at any time in recent history. Brokers must regularly and effectively communicate new and emerging trends and their impact to clients. Additionally, to develop proactive solutions, risk managers must offer clients the collective experiences and successes of the organization, along with a full suite of risk management tools, customized analyses, and state-of-the-art technology. The result is of significant value in developing risk strategies for complex organizations.

Egan believes that a brokerage really adds value by tapping the range skills and experiences of its employees. A diverse range of brokerage specialists can support the risk manager throughout the entirety of the relationship—not simply at the onset or at the placement phase. An integrated approach has distinct advantages because it creates a sharing of information and perspectives that leads to insightful, up-front risk analyses and solutions.

Egan agrees with Lance Ewing that risk managers do not want insurance as much as they want a reduction in losses and consequential costs. The joint focus of brokers and risk manager should be the total cost of risk. This goes to the heart of the advice every broker should provide. Risk transfer, retention, and reduction should work together to recognizing that risk occurs in "multiple buckets" and that the tools to evaluate them are constantly evolving. The tools include advanced analytics that add dimension to exposures. By effectively leveraging technology, brokers can bring clients an ever-increasing range of potential solutions, each customized to the specific situation.

Brokers are in the game, according to Egan. They develop new analytical models every day, addressing risks in various industries and lines of business. They examine benchmarking, including where it works and where it can be misleading. When he was at Integro, his brokers had customized, advanced tools to help risk managers, CFOs, and CEOs understand volatility and other measures of exposures.

Egan has a broad perspective on the role of brokers, recognizing that their job is not to focus solely on insurance coverage. Insurance plays an important role, but total cost of risk is best minimized by combining risk retention—both known and unknown—and risk transfer. Risk managers know this, as they have grown to be increasingly sophisticated professionals.

George Niwa, Panasonic Risk Manager

George Niwa believes that the Matsushita Group had a solid "business basic philosophy" that was well understood by all employees in 2006, when he spoke to an audience in Singapore. The company's mission was to contribute to society through its business activities. Top management announced the establishment of an enterprise-wide risk management system.

Niwa believed in risk management stories. He strongly encouraged risk owners in every unit to provide case studies to help the staff understand possible risk scenarios. Calling ERM "value chain risk management," he expected risk owners to "draw" a risk scenario as part of every annual risk assessment.

Niwa shared a story about the risk of an improper selling price put in place following a cost increase. When he applied this scenario to a value chain flow, it identified possible causes, such as soaring material prices, deteriorating production yields, rising transportation costs, and surging oil prices. These factors rarely exist independently, but it was important to carefully review the level of impact of each factor.

Niwa believed that "There is no business management without risk management." A company should build risk management practices into the organizational culture and apply techniques consistently throughout the enterprise. This means that risk management must go up to the level of top management and gain strong support for its efforts.

Part of Niwa's success was that he had three risk management "champions" in top management—an executive in charge of risk management and legal affairs, the CFO, and the chief strategy officer. This support allowed him to create both global and group risk management, freeing the company from the traditional management style of isolating risks in silos. He noted that the company was working on visualizing risks so that all risk owners can see them clearly.

Susan Meltzer, Aviva Risk Manager

In 2008, Susan Meltzer was the assistant vice president of risk management for Aviva Canada, Inc., in Toronto. Previously, she had performed the risk management function at a number of major corporations, including Sun Life Financial. She is an excellent spokesperson for risk management.

Not every risk manager starts out in a college insurance program studying insurance and risk management. Susan Meltzer is a graduate of Carleton University in Ottawa, where she majored in English. She took a position with an insurance broker and subsequently transferred over to risk management. She observed that it is one thing to get a risk management job; it is another thing to have the skills to manage risk. The keys to success are based upon knowledge, relationships, and sharing of best practices.

Susan was so successful that she became president of the Risk and Insurance Management Society in 1999. In this role and afterward, she got involved with the International Federation of Risk and Insurance Management Associations (IFRIMA). She has spent her career encouraging insurers, brokers, and risk managers to keep current on risk trends by taking a global perspective and forging relationships with peers around the world. In 2006, the Federation of Asian, Pacific, and African Risk Management Organization

(FAPARMO) invited her to Singapore, where she shared several important lessons.

Susan argued for a global perspective on risk, even for organizations that operate in a single region. She encouraged risk managers to engage with risk experts across a broad spectrum and to learn lessons from other parts of the world. She observed that some areas of the world were ahead of others with respect to ERM and identified Europe and Australia as leaders in applying cutting-edge concepts and technology to mitigate risk in a world of terrorism, natural disasters, and pandemics.

Curiously, Susan was not impressed with ERM in the United States, placing that country at the bottom of the list for ERM practices. She was criticizing not U.S. risk managers but rather the U.S. organizations that do not support their risk managers. Compliance is a focus, to be sure, thanks to Sarbanes-Oxley and stiff federal sentences for failure to comply with its provisions. At the same time, compliance is not risk management, which extends beyond internal controls. She noted that the board has a fiduciary duty to join with institutional investors and regulators to demand that organizations achieve risk transparency, risk disclosure, and risk mitigation.

A hidden message in her presentation in Singapore was Meltzer's ability to network with risk professionals. She formed a panel of three prominent risk managers who were advancing the global agenda of ERM. They were Marie-Gemma Dequae, president of the Federation of European Risk Management Associations; Jorge Luzzi, head of the Asociacion Latinoamericana de Riesgos y Seguros; and George Niwa, risk manager for Panasonic in Japan and president of the RIMS chapter in Japan.

Susan believes that risk management does not get interesting until risk managers join the discussion. Without excluding brokers, insurers, auditors, or others from an exchange of information, the risk manager must have a place at the table.

In 2006, Susan Meltzer was arguably the best-known risk manager in the world. It helped that she had ideas and promoted them with energy and enthusiasm. Natural intelligence and a curiosity for problem solving were key ingredients, but her story had an extra component. She knew that bringing people together is the most important aspect of achieving efficiency, safety, and economy. Networking gives risk managers a broad perspective, particularly when they are sharing best practices. She practiced what she preached, primarily through RIMS, where she was highly active, teaching courses, forming panels, and participating in annual conferences and local chapter activities.

Susan showed the risk management community the path to developing the next generation of risk managers. As risk manager at Sun Life, she encouraged and enabled her staff to network with other risk managers. Niver Rubenyan became director of operational risk at Sun Life and said, "Susan is keen on the training and development of her staff. She got me involved in RIMS, supported me when I joined the board of the local chapter, and encouraged me to take up public speaking."

In retrospect, her most important accomplishment may involve her role, in 2007, as chair of IFRIMA, where she worked tirelessly to bring together risk managers from around the world to share their best practices. She knows that risk managers need to cross borders with ideas to deal with technological change, global warming, rapid economic development in developing countries, and complex supply chains.

A career in risk management has the potential for challenge, excitement, and contribution to others. Meltzer, who received the 2001 Don Stuart Award for outstanding achievement in risk management and the 2005 Dorothy and Harry Goodell Award, RIMS' highest honor, reflecting lifetime achievement, has fulfilled that potential.

CHAPTER 29

CENTRAL RISK MANAGEMENT COMMITTEE

RISK QUOTE: *For the want of a nail, the shoe was lost; for the want of a shoe the horse was lost; and for the want of a horse the rider was lost, being overtaken and slain by the enemy, all for the want of care about a horseshoe nail.*

—BENJAMIN FRANKLIN, SCIENTIST, PUBLISHER, AND DIPLOMAT

RISK QUOTE: *If a man does his best, what else is there?*
—GEORGE S. PATTON, U.S. ARMY GENERAL

A central risk management committee (RMC) is a formal body established to provide advice on ERM. It is one tool for involving the board and senior managers in an ERM program. In most formulations, we can identify common characteristics of such a committee. Its purpose is to advise senior management and the board on policies to manage the full range of risks facing the enterprise. This broadens the advising role beyond the head of the central risk function. The committee should meet periodically to discuss risks and to make recommendations. If committee members are using the high-tech knowledge warehouse effectively, they will have some insights to post on the platform but will also have ideas to share at a committee meeting. Such a committee provides risk management leadership that acts proactively to encourage all managers and professionals to participate in identifying and mitigating critical risks.

Forming the Committee

An immediate question is whether an organization needs such a committee. If it has a central risk function and an ERM knowledge warehouse, is it overkill? Maybe yes, maybe no. Senior management can assess the need for such a group by considering the size and complexity of the company. Will a central RMC improve risk management linkages? Are risk management processes highly developed? Are they centralized or decentralized?

If the organization decides it needs such a committee, an entirely new set of issues arises. Top management can expect to hear multiple concerns and objections as a new entity intrudes upon existing territories. The chance for success increases if committee expectations are carefully communicated. What are the committee's goals and responsibilities? How will the committee interact with functional areas, business units, and key initiatives?

A central RMC will be of particular interest to risk owners, who will have questions about the committee's impact on their units, time, and workloads. What exposures and critical risks will be managed with the participation of the committee? What role will the committee play in risk identification, assessment, and mitigation? What questions on risk will be raised by the committee? Who will answer the questions? How will the committee work with risk owners when problems or disagreements arise?

The first steps for a central RMC should be to manage the concerns about the committee itself. It should pursue a limited agenda, perhaps suggesting changes with a few exposures and solving problems as they arise. When its first efforts are successful, the committee can expand into other areas. The committee should be open to feedback.

Multiple Roles for the Committee

One benefit of a central RMC is that it can perform multiple functions, including advising, providing information, assisting, and communicating. In the advising role, it can share views on risk with senior executives and the board. How should the organization coordinate risk management among functional areas, business units, and key initiatives? How can it avoid gaps in communications or processes? What steps will help it reduce the costs of risk mitigation? The committee can also play a role in risk analysis and measurement. It can recommend tools to measure frequency and severity of exposures. It can agree or disagree with risk assessments offered by others. It can identify actions to be considered by risk owners.

In the information role, the committee can provide guidance and suggestions about exposures and opportunities. It can suggest or initiate research, encouraging a central risk function and risk owners to investigate risks and monitor trends, technology, risk transfer, and best practices. It can even play an information role on risk financing as it provides views on costs and benefits of specific risk management efforts.

The central RMC can provide assistance. In risk administration, it can suggest strategies for specific, business unit, or key initiative exposures. It can evaluate resources to support new or existing risk mitigation efforts and improve existing capabilities so that they are more effective. It can comment on crisis management and planning and participate in the formation of plans to manage disasters and business disruption. It can support efforts to restore stability after a loss, damage, or missed opportunity.

The committee can play a communications role, disseminating its views to key managers, professionals, and risk owners. It can support the public relations department with statements and press releases. It can help create a culture of safety and health promotion for employees. In the area of customer and supplier relations, it can encourage reducing exposures with product procurement and sales. It can share best risk management practices with everyone.

Central Risk Management Committee Reporting Line

If a company establishes a central RMC, an immediate question arises about the reporting line. Is the committee accountable to the board, the CEO, the CFO, or another party? Figure 29-1 shows a structure with direct reporting to the board and dotted-line reporting to the CEO.

FIGURE 29-1. CENTRAL RISK COMMITTEE RELATIONSHIPS.

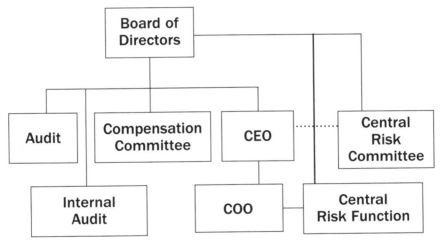

The Deloitte 2008 survey determined that RMCs tended to report to management rather than the board of directors. They also found that most respondents reported that no such committee was in existence in their organization. Figure 29-2 presents information on the prevalence of RMCs as reported to Deloitte.

FIGURE 29-2. DELOITTE 2008 RMC STATUS.

Risk Management Committee Status	Percentage
No Risk Management Committee	60%
Reports to Management	25%
Reports to Both Management and the Board	10%
Reports to the Board	2%
Other	3%

Conclusion

A risk management committee adds another layer of risk management and a possible tool for sharing. It can play an effective role in some situations but may not be needed in others.

Beaumont Central RMC Leader Case

Beaumont, Texas, population 120,000, decided to create a central risk management committee. It sought a chief risk officer to chair the committee and to provide new insights into enterprise risk management. The city asked a recruiter to use the problem-solving, management, and communications styles in Exhibits 1 to 3 as part of the screening process for the final candidates.

Exhibit 1. Problem-solving styles.

These are the most common ways people solve problems:

Analytic	Use logic and consistency. Avoid a mistake. Gather as much information as possible.
	Get something done. Avoid delays. Seek speed in problem solving.
Expressive	Pursue visionary goals. Solution gets people excited about the future.
Amiable	Allow others to provide inputs. Reach consensus if possible.

Exhibit 2. Management styles.

These are the most common ways people approach the task of managing their subordinates:

Hands-Off	Get the job done through independent subordinates. Give people freedom to act.
Task-Oriented	Get the job done by a team led by the manager (playing coach).

Hands-On   Do the job with the team's help if needed.

Team-Oriented Make effective team building the priority. Committing the team to the task is less important.

Exhibit 3. Communication styles.

These are the most common ways people interact with their colleagues:

Two-Way   Excellent rapport with the team. Warm and open. Bonds with others.

Outward   Blunt. Business is business. Respected by team members. Hard but fair.

Intellectual Cold and even remote. Calculating. Respected by team.

Inward   Empathic listener but not really involved. Sensitive, quiet, and supportive.

Candidates

The city has reduced the field of candidates to eight finalists:

Candidate #1. Fred Gonzalez

Current Position   VP of marketing at Sears.

Education   B.A. in History. Six-week Wharton Finance Summer program.

Prior Position   Seven years in charge of production at Seagram's Beverages.

Personal   Amiable. High versatility. Team management style. Two-way communicator.

Achievements   Brought Kathy Lee Gifford to Sears. Turned around losses at three previous business units. Lowered Seagram's production costs by 54% in six years.

Candidate #2. Janet Vicker

Current Position   CEO of European operations, Sun Microsystems.

Education   Executive MBA, University of Phoenix.

Prior Positions	CFO, Charles Schwab. Western Regional Manager, Burger King.
Personal	Analytic. Medium versatility. Hands-off management style. Intellectual communications style.
Achievements	Significant improvements in customer service in all jobs. Motivational speaker for Schwab.

Candidate #3. Mack Anderson

Current Position	Head of Security for Donald Trump.
Education	Law Degree. Graduate of the FBI National Academy.
Prior Position	Chief of Police, San Jose, California.
Personal	Driver. High versatility. Task management style. Outward communications style.
Achievements	Cut fraud in casinos by 35%. Cut crime in inner city by 60%. Purple Heart for being wounded in action in Iraq in 1991.

Candidate #4. William Brannon

Current Position	Commissioner, World Soccer Federation.
Education	Ph.D., INSEAD (a leading French business school).
Prior Positions	Chief operating officer, Six Flags. Vice President, Human Resources, Bank of America.
Personal	Driver. Medium versatility. Task management style. Outward communications style.
Achievements	Doubled sponsorships of World Cup series. Fighter pilot in French air force.

Candidate #5. Kim Yang

| Current Position | Senior Vice President, Customer Relations, Federal Express. |

Education	Ph.D. in Economics.
Prior Position	Vice President, Human Resources, Boeing.
Personal	Expressive. Medium versatility. Task management style. Two-way communications style.
Achievements	Increased customer satisfaction at FedEx. Reduced Boeing labor force by 20% with few problems.

Candidate #6. Phillip DiMarco

Current Position	CEO, American Red Cross.
Education	M.B.A.
Prior Position	Chief compliance officer, Dow Chemical.
Personal	Expressive. High versatility. Hands-off management style. Two-way communications style.
Achievements	Built financial reserves after disastrous earthquake. Won regulatory lawsuit with government agency at Dow.

Candidate #7. Martin Lund

Current Position	COO, Freightways Trucking Company.
Education	B.A., Psychology, University of Texas.
Prior Position	Crisis manager, Shell Oil Company.
Personal	Analytic. Low versatility. Hands-on management style. Outward communications style.
Achievements	Doubled Freightways tonnage in five-year period. Led team to extinguish oil well fires in Kuwait.

Candidate #8. Susan Diaz

Current Position	Deputy Chief of Staff, White House.
Education	M.S. in Mathematics.
Prior Positions	Mayor, Dallas Texas. CEO, Taiwan Steel USA.

Persona	Amiable. High versatility. Task management style. Inward communications style.
Achievements	Improved morale of presidential staff. Increased private investment in Dallas business community.

Question

On the basis of the information provided, which candidate would be most likely to succeed as the leader of a central risk function implementing enterprise risk management? Explain the criteria for your selection.

DENOUEMENT

In French, a *denouement* is the end of a complex sequence of events. To be more dramatic, it is the final outcome of the main dramatic complication in a literary work. So it is that our journey ends. What did we learn? First, risk is best managed in a framework of alignment with the business strategy, accountable risk owners, and a recognition that every risk may be accompanied by a opportunity. A central risk function and a knowledge of ERM are tools to identify and share exposures and opportunities. We learned about new and powerful technology to visualize risk relationships and document mitigation efforts. We looked at often-overlooked exposure with weaknesses in strategies, cultures, and leadership—risks that cross hierarchical divisions. We read stories of success and failures of risk management. We concluded with an introduction to people who manage risk for major organizations.

This is an entirely new paradigm on a concept that is 20 years old. If we move enterprise risk management from the complex and cerebral, we will find that the concept is solid. It produces benefits for organizations. It can help us make sense out of a complex world. If this book helps make ERM more accessible, the journey will have been well worth it.

BIBLIOGRAPHY

Many reference sources are helpful to understanding enterprise risk management. The following are some of the most important, many of which have been consulted during the preparation of this book.

Ariely, Dan. *Predictably Irrational: The Hidden Forces That Shape Our Decisions*. New York: HarperCollins, 2008.

Bacevich, Andrew J. *The Limits of Power: The End of American Exceptionalism*. New York: Henry Holt and Company, 2008.

Flynn, Stephen. *The Edge of Disaster: Rebuilding a Resilient Nation*. New York: Random House, 2007.

Friedman, Thomas L. *Hot, Flat, and Crowded: Why We Need a Green Revolution and How It Can Renew America*. New York: Farrar, Straus and Giroux, 2008.

Gladwell, Malcolm. *The Tipping Point: How Little Things Can Make a Big Difference*. Boston: Little, Brown & Company, 2000.

Kagan, Robert. *The Return of History: And the End of Dreams*. New York: Alfred A. Knopf, 2008.

Khanna, Parag. *The Second World: Empires and Influence in the New Global Order*. New York: Random House, 2008.

Levitt, Steven D., and Stephen J. Dubner. *Freakonomics: A Rogue Economist Explores the Hidden Side of Everything*. New York: HarperCollins, 2005.

Medina, John. *Brain Rules: 12 Principles for Surviving and Thriving at Work, Home, and School*. Seattle: Pear Press, 2008.

Sheffi, Yossi. *The Resilient Enterprise: Overcoming Vulnerability for Competitive Advantage*. Cambridge, Mass.: MIT Press, 2005.

Shiller, Robert J. *Irrational Exuberance*. New York: Doubleday, 2005.

Taleb, Nassim Nicholas. *The Black Swan: The Impact of the Highly Improbable*. New York: Random House, 2007.

Tapscott, Don, and Anthony D. Williams. *Wikonomics: How Mass Collaboration Changes Everything*. New York: Penguin Group, 2006.

Thaler, Richard H., and Cass R. Sunstein. *Nudge: Improving Decisions About Health, Wealth, and Happiness*. New Haven, Conn.: Yale University Press, 2008.

Zakaria, Fareed. *The Post-American World*. New York: W. W. Norton, 2008.

INDEX